First World War Graves and Memorials In Gwent

Volume 1

First World War Graves and Memorials

In Gwent

VOLUME I

by Ray Westlake

Wharncliffe Books

First Published in 2001 by
Wharncliffe Books
an imprint of
Pen and Sword Books Limited,
47 Church Street, Barnsley,
South Yorkshire. S70 2AS

*For up-to-date information on other titles produced under the
Wharncliffe imprint, please telephone or write to:*

> **Wharncliffe Books**
> **FREEPOST**
> **47 Church Street**
> **Barnsley**
> **South Yorkshire S70 2BR**
> **Telephone (24 hours): 01226 - 734555**

ISBN: 1-871647-78-9 cased edition
1-903425-02-6 paperback edition

A CIP catalogue record of this book is available from the
British Library

Cover illustration: *Abertillery Memorial*

Printed by CPI UK

INTRODUCTION

In volume one of this work I offer my first selection from the many war graves and memorials that can be found in the county of Gwent. It is just a selection, however. Subsequent volumes, hopefully, will complete the record. As far as war graves are concerned, this side of the work is pretty straightforward as the Commonwealth War Graves Commission have these well documented in their register for Monmouthshire. War memorials, however, are a different matter. The vast majority of these are hidden away in churches, public buildings, schools etc. Therefore I would be pleased to hear of any that are not mentioned in this volume.

In recording each memorial I have aimed, firstly, to establish its existence and location, then provide an accurate record of any inscription or dedication. In doing this I have recorded a word-for-word account, shown in the text in italics. In the case of names, ranks and regiments, I have generally shown the former exactly as recorded on the memorial. Ranks and regiments, however, I found to be recorded in such a variety of ways, often inaccurate and misleading, that rather than include a lengthy list of abbreviations and explanations as to the regimental titles used, I have maintained a standard pattern for each.

The scope of this book, or geographical area, is based on the old county of Monmouthshire, as it would have stood at the time of the First World War. Formed in 1536 Monmouthshire became Gwent, after local government reorganisations, in 1974.

ACKNOWLEDGEMENTS

This book would not have been possible had it not been for the help and cooperation of the churches visited, and, what must surely add up to several hundred by now, church members whom I have met over recent months. Without exception, all have offered the warmest of welcomes and gone out of their way on every occasion to assist. Space has not allowed me to include a full list of their names, which I hope they understand. I can tell them, however, that this book has given me more pleasure and satisfaction than any other that I have worked on. Much of this statement has been made possible by them. Also essential in any project of this type is the help and encouragement given by one's own family. My thanks to our son Paul, whose mountain bike recognisances played an important part in my tactical plans, and Barbara - wife and 'underpaid' bookseller's assistant. Both, once again, have played essential roles in the day-to-day running of *Ray Westlake Military Books* while the boss has been 'getting around in Gwent.' A short list of those to whom I must give my thanks, however, follows - Headmaster and Staff, Bettws High School; Peter and Jane Blagojevic; John Dixon; Huw Edwards; Angus Evans; Tony Friend; Gwent Constabulary Headquarters; Gwent County Hall; Norman Hurst; Headmaster and Staff, King Henry VIII School, Abergavenny; Cliff Knight; Mr. A. Leighton Bowen; Lorraine Knight (National Inventory Of War Memorials); Warren William Lewis (Friends of the Gwent Record Office); W.G. Lloyd; Jay Mathews; Leslie Morgan (Orb Electrical Steels); Manager and Staff, Newport Post Office; Newport YMCA; Christopher Page, Secretary, Risca Male Choir Headquarters; Manager and Staff, Royal British Legion Club, Rhymney; Headmaster and Staff, St. Andrew's School, Newport; Doctors and Staff, St. Luke's Surgery, Abercarn; Mr. C. Smith (Monmouth School); Susan A. Snell (NatWest Group Archives); Alan Seymour; Gethin and Linda Vaughan; Headmaster and Staff, West Monmouth School; Mike Wilson and Roy Worrall. Also my friends at *Pen & Sword Books* and *Wharncliffe Books* whose confidence in this project is very much appreciated. Finally, I must give thanks to Ordnance Survey for their wonderful maps. How else would a Londoner find his way around the, often just one vehicle width, country lanes of such a beautiful county?

ABERBARGOED

A set of gates in Commercial Street, Aberbargoed represents the town's war memorial. Designed by George Kenshole (architect to the Powell Duffryn Steam Coal Company), and originally forming the entrance to The Workmen's Cottage Hospital, the cast iron gates bear the inscription - *In Glorious Memory Of Those Who Fell In The Great War 1914-18*. A Roll of Honour recording eighty-three names (with ranks) takes the form of metal plaques set into each of three Portland stone columns. The names are arranged as follows:

1st plaque: Lance-Corporal F. Brain, Private H. Baker, Private J. Bateman, Sergeant Major L. Bright, Private H. Bywater, Private W. Bready, Private W. Brown, Private C. Clarke, Sapper A. Collect, Lance-Corporal J. Coles, Captain J. Clarke, Lance-Corporal H. Constance, Sapper J. Cooper, Private J. Cooper, Sergeant W. Dear, Rifleman M. Davies, Private V. Davies, Private W.D. Evans, Private T.J. Ellis, Gunner D.G. Ellis, Private E.G. Fido, Private F. Foster, Private A. Frayling, Private H. Gunter, Private M. Green, Sapper D. Griffiths, Private H. Green, Sergeant P. Garlick.

2nd plaque: Private D. Healy, Private G. Howse, Rifleman S. Hickman, L.S.Gunner F.T. Hall, Lance-Corporal H. Hughes, Sapper F. Harris, Private W.J. Isaac, Private D.L. Jones, Sapper D. Jones, Captain J. Jordan, Sapper W. Jones, Private J. Jones, Private D.H. Jones, Gunner G.I. Jones, Gunner D.J. Jones, Sergeant H.W. Lacey, Sapper A. Mudway, Private D. Macarthy, Private W. Macarthy, Private J.M. Norris, Private E. Price, Private H.J. Perry, Sapper G. Purnell, Corporal A. Rudge, Private D.J. Robbins, Private W. Ralph, Private A. Robinson.

3rd plaque: Private R. Schofield, Private G. Shepherd, Sergeant W. Smith, Private T. Shepherd, Sapper B. Thomas, Corporal L. Tedaldi, Private T.J. Trow, Private J. Turner, Private J. Underwood, Private W. Weaver, Private A. Walker, Private C. Walker, Private Steve Williams, Lance-Corporal J.D. Williams, Private J. Walker, Sapper W. Wills, Private S. Williams, Private I. Wilson, Private H.T. Nutt, Private W. Griffin, Private A. Langley, Private E.J. Hemmings, Private J. Fitzgerald, Private E. Walters, Private A.C. Richards, Driver E.E. Jones, Private T.J. Rees, Trooper W. (surname obliterated).

Plaque showing the obliterated name of Trooper 'W'. Memorial gates, Aberbargoed.

Memorial gates in Commercial Street, Aberbargoed.

One of the two officers listed, Captain J. Clarke, served with the 1st Welsh Field Ambulance, Royal Army Medical Corps. He was a medical practitioner in Aberbargoed and was killed on 9 September, 1915 at Gallipoli (see also St. Sannan's, Bedwellty).

The gates are no longer used by the hospital, now the Aberbargoed and District Hospital, and several additional plaques have been added recording those who fell 1939-1945. Also relevant to the Second World War is a small plaque in memory of Glyndwr Michael, 'The Man Who Never Was'. A native of Aberbargoed, his body, placed into the sea by a British submarine, was used to convey spurious documents (*Operation Mincemeat*) to German intelligence in Spain.

ABERBEEG

Abertillery and District Hospital
The gates to the hospital, opened in September 1922 in Pendarren Road, Aberbeeg, bear the inscription -

> *These Gates Are Presented By The Abertillery Municipal Officers As A Tribute To Their Colleagues Who Served In The Great War 1914-18.*

Christchurch
The church, in Pendarren Road, Aberbeeg, is in possession of a leather-bound book recording the names of those from the parish of Llanhilleth who were killed in both world wars. Within the covers, which bear the inscription - *In Glorious Memory* - there are one hundred and nine names listed for the First World War, each being accompanied by rank, regimental number and regiment. Five of those who died are buried within the churchyard:

Private Brinley, Chaplin of the 2nd Dragoon Guards (Queen's Bays), is buried in

Memorial gates at the entrance to the Abertillery and District Hospital, Aberbeeg.

a private family grave. An inscription notes that he died from wounds received at Arras, France on 22 April, 1917. The headstone also bears the words - *I Have Only Done My Duty As A Man Is Bound To Do*. Brinley Chaplin was twenty-six.

Private Frank Perry served with the 2nd Battalion, Welsh Regiment. He died, aged thirty-one, on 2 October, 1918. Driver H. Wilson of the 10th Company, Royal Engineers, and from Llanhilleth, was thirty-two when he passed away on 30 March, 1916. Also of the Welsh Regiment (9th Battalion) was Private F. Taylor, who, having been wounded in France, returned home, where he died, aged twenty-five, on 10 March, 1919. Thirty-five when he died of pneumonia on 3 December, 1915, was Sergeant George William Willis of the 1st Monmouthshire Regiment.

ABERCARN

Designed by J.H. Highley and unveiled in 1923, the town memorial situated in Market Square, Abercarn, features a female figure holding a wreath of laurels and blowing a trumpet. The words in Welsh - *Gwell Angau Na Chywilydd* (Better Death Than Dishonour) - are set into the stone work of the pedestal, and below this a bronze panel inscribed - *To The Memory Of Our Glorious Dead* - records in three columns fifty-nine names without rank or regiment:

1st column: H. Alcott, J.G. Burnett, T. Bowen, J. Coles, D.B. Dart, W.C. Davies, W.C. Davies, F. Ellaway, T.C. Evans, A. Fleetwood, B. Fletcher, T. Fletcher, W. Ford, R.P. Furber, L. Harley, W. Harper, E.B. Harries, S.G. Hewlitt, F. Hobbs, L. Humphries.

2nd column: D. James, R. James, W.J. Jenkins, A.W.S. Jones, F. Jones, T. Jones, W.F. Jones, A. Lewis, N. Lewis, A.R. Lovell, W. Maidment, T. March, R. Milton, W.R. Morgan, M. Moseley, F.F. Pierce, S. Phillips, W. Price, E. Prince.

3rd column: J. Rawson, A. Richardson, J.H. Saunders, J.H. Selby, W. Simpkins, A.J. Smart, T. Smith, P.J. Stephens, E. Thomas, J. Thomas, J.T. Thomas, W.H. Thomas, B.E. Trayhern, A. Veysey, J. Whitley, F. Wilcox, A. Williams, E.J. Williams, O. Williams, W.G. Williams.

The fallen of the Second World War appear at the back on the memorial.

Abercarn Cemetery
The cemetery, which is located off the B4591 north of Abercarn, contains seven war graves:

Private David W. Bowen Dart served with the 2nd Battalion South Wales Borderers and died on 29 October, 1916.

Acting-Corporal Edward Brett Harris of 'F' Company, Royal Engineers, died on 2 May, 1917.

Private David James was a Territorial of the 1/4th Battalion, Welsh Regiment, and twenty-five when he died on 30 June, 1918.

Telegraphist John Emlyn Davies, Royal Navy, HMS *Victory* was eighteen when he became ill with phthisis and subsequently died on 25 May, 1918.

Private Edgar Orman, Welsh Guards, was gassed in France and eventually died, aged thirty-two, at home on 9 August, 1919.

Private C.G. Wren, Coldstream Guards, died on 7 December, 1919.

Private George H. Smith originally served with the South Wales Borderers, but

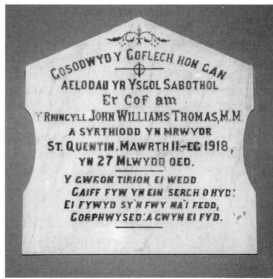

GOSODWYD Y GOFLECH HON GAN
AELODAU YR YSGOL SABOTHOL
Er Cof am
Y Rhingyll JOHN WILLIAMS THOMAS, M.M.
A SYRTHIODD YN MRWYDR
ST. QUENTIN. MAWRTH II-EG 1918,
YN 27 MLWYDD OED.

Y GWRON TIRION EI WEDD
GAIFF FYW YN EIN SERCH O HYD:
EI FYWYD SY'N FWY NA'I FEDD,
GORPHWYSED A GWYN EI FYD.

*Memorial to Corporal John Williams Thomas,
MM, St Luke's Church, Abercarn.*

Abercarn memorial.

Tin-plate workers' memorial, St Luke's Surgery, Abercarn.

transferred to the 45th Royal Fusiliers, who having been formed in April, 1919, later saw service in north Russia. He died at home on 4 August, 1919.

St Luke's Church

Corporal John Williams Thomas served with the 2/7th Battalion, Lancashire Fusiliers and was awarded the Military Medal for gallantry during the Battle of Poelcappelle, 9 October, 1917. He was killed five months later, on 11 March, 1918, near St. Quentin. His memorial, a white marble tablet, can be found in the nave of St. Luke's, on the north side of the chancel arch.

All in Welsh, the inscription reads -

Gosodwyd Y Goflech Hon Gan Aelodau Yr Ysgol Sabothol Er Cof Am Y Rhingyll John Williams Thomas, MM A Syrthiodd Yn Mrwydr St. Quentin, Mawrth 11 Eg 1918, Yn 27 Mlwydd Oed. Y Gwron Tirion Ei Wedd Gaiff Fyw Yn Ein Serch O Hyd: Ei Fywyd Sy'n Fwy Nài Fedd, Gorphwysed: A Gwyn Ei Fyd (This Commemorative Plaque Was Erected By Members Of The Sunday School In Memory Of Sergeant John Williams Thomas MM Who Fell In Battle At St. Quentin, March 11 1918 At The Age Of 27. The Hero Of Gentle Appearance Shall Have A Tender Face And Live In Our Love Peacefully. His Life, Larger Than His Grave. May He Rest In Peace And Be Blessed).

St Luke's Surgery

The memorial commemorating workers from the town's tin-plate works (Thomas Richard & Co. Ltd.) is now situated in the waiting-room of St. Luke's Surgery, Gwyddon Road. The surgery is built on the site of the old Memorial Institute building. In a wood surround, and below the dates - *1914-1918* - a copper tablet bears the inscription -

The Abercarn Tinplators' Memorial Institute In Ever Grateful Remembrance Of Those Whose Names Are Inscribed Heron, Who At The Call Of King And Country, Left All That Was Dear To Them For The Path Of Duty And Self-Sacrifice. Endured Hardships, Faced Dangers And Finally Gave Their Lives That Others Might Live In Freedom.

Twenty-six names follow, arranged in three columns without rank or regiment: T. Bowen, T.C. Callaghan, W. Ellaway, R.P. Furber, E.R. Gillham, W. Harper, A. Highley, E.L. Humphreys, W. Lewis, A. Lewis, M. Moseley, S. Phillips, W. Powell, W.G. Price, J.L. Prosser, J. Rawson, A. Richardson, A.J. Smart, P.J. Stephens, J.W. Thomas, E. Thomas, S. Watkins, J. Whitley, A. Williams, W.G. Williams and F. Wilcox. Below the names the quote - *'See To It Ye Who Come After That They Be Not Forgotten'* - and a plaque bearing five names from the Second World War.

ABERGAVENNY

Located in Frogmore Street, the memorial to the town's Territorial Force battalion, a single soldier resting on his rifle and standing on a pedestal, was unveiled by Lord Treowen on 29 October, 1921. A small metal plaque at the rear of the monument records that it was raised by public subscription within the Battalion area of Abergavenny, Abertillery, Blaina, Cwm, Ebbw Vale, Sirhowy and Tredegar. The front has the dates *1914-1918* above the Regimental Crest, and the inscription - *To The Officers N.C.O.'s And Men Of The 3rd Battalion Monmouthshire Regt. Who Fell In The Great War.*

Below this, added on 8 May 1995, another small plaque commemorates the eightieth anniversary of the 3rd Monmouthshire Regiment's involvement during the fighting at Frezenberg Ridge near Ypres in 1915. Inscribed on either side of the pedestal are the names of places in France and Belgium where the Battalion fought: *Wulverghem - 2nd Battle Of Ypres - Dickebusche* (left side), *Kemmel - Yser Canal - The Somme* (right side). The memorial was sculpted by Gilbert Ledward OBE, RA, whose works includes the Guards Division memorial at Horse Guards Parade in London, and the First World War memorials at Blackpool, Harrogate, Stockport and Stonyhurst College.

Abergavenny New Cemetery
The narrow road leading to the cemetery is off the Merthyr Road (A4143) near Llanfoist and close to the Usk Bridge just outside Abergavenny. There are a number of graves commemorating family members who were killed (and buried) overseas during the First World War. These include Second-Lieutenant James Graham Glendinning, 57th Squadron, Royal Flying Corps, who was killed on 2 December 1917 and buried in Harlebeke Cemetery, Belgium, and Sergeant William Wigley of the 3rd Battalion, Monmouthshire Regiment who fell at Ypres in May, 1915. Several of the Commonwealth War Graves Commission headstones are made from Welsh slate. There are twelve war graves for the First World War:

Lance-Corporal Charles James Booth served with 1/1st Cheshire Field Company, Royal Engineers and lived at 97 North Street, Abergavenny. He was a long serving member of the Territorial Force and held the TF Efficiency Medal. Charles Booth died, aged thirty-nine, on 10 September, 1919.

Corporal Frank Didcote of the 3rd Battalion, Monmouthshire Regiment, was thirty when he died on 5 March, 1919.

Boy Servant A.L. Douglas of HMS *Vivid* lived at 1 South Side, Park Crescent, Abergavenny and died, aged sixteen, on 4 March, 1920.

Corporal H. Gwyther, 6th Battalion, King's Shropshire Light Infantry, resided at 12 Monk Street, Abergavenny and having been wounded in France died at home, aged nineteen, on 1 November, 1918.

Sergeant Ivor John Jackson, Royal Air Force, of 25 Albert Road, Abergavenny was twenty-three when he died of pneumonia on 2 March, 1919.

Captain Brynley Lewis Jones, 3rd Battalion, Monmouthshire Regiment, died of pneumonia on 26 December, 1918. He was thirty-three and a master at the King Henry VIII Grammar School, Abergavenny.

Lieutenant Matthew Morgan, 4th Battalion, South Wales Borderers, lived at 1 Holly Terrace, North Street, Abergavenny and died 8 December, 1918.

Private Roy Dimond Rawlins, 75th Training Reserve Battalion, died, aged eighteen, in Heath Military Hospital on 22 March, 1917.

Gunner George Raymond Roberts of 49 Union Road, Abergavenny served with the 284th Siege Battery, Royal Garrison Artillery and died, aged thirty-five, of pneumonia on 8 February, 1919.

Armament Quartermaster Sergeant Richard Spillane of the Royal Army Ordnance Corps lived with his wife at Park Cottage, Union Road, Abergavenny and

Memorial window, Holy Trinity Church, Abergavenny.

3rd Battalion Monmouthshire Regiment memorial, Abergavenny.

Hereford Road School, Abergavenny, memorial. Now at Bailey Court.

died, aged forty-nine, on 11 January, 1920. A Member of the Order of the British Empire and holder of the Long Service and Good Conduct Medal, AQMS Spillane is buried in a family grave.

Private Victor Osman Walsh served with the 53rd (Graduated) Battalion, South Wales Borderers and resided at 11 Trinity Street, Abergavenny. He was eighteen when he died on 6 October, 1918.

Private Charles Herbert Watkins, 3rd Battalion, Monmouthshire Regiment, died on 22 November, 1915.

Abergavenny Old Cemetery

The cemetery is located on the Hereford Road, Abergavenny and contains four war graves:

Private William C. Abbott, 3rd Battalion, Monmouthshire Regiment, lived at Llanfoist and died from wounds received on the Western Front on 20 April, 1918.

Sapper W. Hearn, Inland Water Transport, Royal Engineers, died on 12 February, 1918.

Private Richard Thomas Mann, 1/3rd Battalion, Monmouthshire Regiment, lived at 34 North Street, Abergavenny. He died on 1 June, 1917.

Private Frederick Walters, 3rd Battalion, Monmouthshire Regiment, died 6 May, 1916.

Bailey Court

At the entrance to Bailey Court in Hereford Road, a slab of white marble inscribed - *To The Glory Of God And In Memory Of The Boys Of This School Who Gave Their Lives In The Great War 1914-1918* - records eighty-four names, without rank or regiment, in three coloumns:

1st column: C.G. Bailey, G.J. Bailey, W.J. Best, W. Boswell, A. Bosworth, A.D. Bowcott, C.O. Bowcott, H.J.G. Bowden, C. Breakwell, W.C.J. Brown, H. Burcher, L.H. Carr, W. Coombey, H. Day, D.S. Davies, G.J. Davies, S.E. Davies, F. Didcote, R. Dodd, A. Gibbons, E.C. Goode, P.D. Griffiths, H. Gwyther, W. Hall, E.E. Hanbury, J.H. Herbert, T. Hooper, F.J. Taylor.

2nd column: W.J.G. Jamieson, A. Jones, G.E.W. Jones, R. Jones, T. Jones, W. Knight, H.E.V. Kynch, N. Lewis, T.A. Lewis, S.T. Light, R.T. Mann, H.R. Marshall, G. Mitchell, M. Morgan, O.J. Morgan, W. Morgan, D.S. Morris, T.G. Nash, A.C. Norgrove, E.C. Norgrove, J.A. Norton, J.A. Pavord, J.W. Phillips, T.H. Pickering, E.F. Pierce, W. Powell, A.E. Price, W. Price.

3rd column: W.H. Pritchard, I. Prosser, W.A. Reed, W.N. Rees, E.J. Reynolds, J. Ridley, H. Roach, G. Roberts, C.L. Savegar, J.E.W. Shaw, L. Simon, S.H. Sketchley, W.E. Smith, W. Southwood, P. Staples, V. Walsh, F. Walters, C. Watkins, C.H. Watkins, J.W. Watkins, C.D. Webb, T.A. Whitehouse, G. Williams, R.V. Winney, E.H. Winter, H. Woodward, A.E. Workman, W.J. Wyatt.

The school referred to is the old Hereford Road Boys' School, the site of which in 1987 was acquired for the purpose of building the Bailey Court retirement complex. For some time the memorial, which was installed within the school in 1927, occupied a new position on an outside boundary wall. But this vulnerable site led to deterioration and soon, notes former Bailey Court resident, Mr A. Leighton Bowen, the monument became badly cracked and broken into a dozen or more pieces. Thanks to Mr. Bowen, and the work of Oxford sculptor, Mr. J. Eastham, the memorial was saved and now, fully renovated, occupies a safer position outside the entrance foyer at Bailey Court.

Abergavenny Baptist Chapel

The Baptist Chapel in Frogmore Street has a brass plaque situated in the vestibule recording twelve names: D.W. Booth, H. Brett, F. Dyer, H. Dyer, S.R. Goulborn, T.C. Griffiths, I.V. Griffiths, W.E. Jones, W. Knight, H. Pilsbury, H.H. Pitt and E.J. Reynolds. Below is the inscription -

To The Glory Of God And The Undying Memory Of Those Connected With This Church Or Sunday School Who Made The Supreme Sacrifice In The Great War 1914-1918. 'Their Name Liveth For Evermore'.

The wording is headed by a laurel wreath tied with a ribbon.

Castle Street Methodist Church

A brass plaque below the pulpit has the inscription -

To The Glory Of God And In Honoured Memory Of The Following Who Made The Supreme Sacrifice In The Great European War 1914-1919.

The three names that follow are those of Private Francis John Balsdon, 11th Welsh Regiment, who died on 27 September, 1918 from wounds received in Salonica; Colour-Sergeant Ivor John Iball, a member of the 3rd Monmouthshire Regiment who fell in France on 1 November, 1917, and Private William Laviers Lee, killed 26 October, 1916 while serving with 9th Royal Welsh Fusiliers.

Holy Trinity Church

The east window of the church in Trinity Terrace includes the dedication - *To The Glory Of God In Memory Of The Men Of The Congregation And Parish Who Fell In The Great War A.D. 1914-1919.* The window, by Jennings of London, was installed in 1920 and shows various Saints along with the Crests of the Royal Artillery, South Wales Borderers, Royal Engineers, Monmouthshire Regiment and Royal Gloucestershire Hussars. The latter had a detachment in Abergavenny.

A brass plaque mounted on wood on the north wall of the church refers to the window -

This Memorial East Window Was Dedicated To The Greater Glory Of God In Perpetual Memory Of The Men Of The Parish And Congregation Who Made The Supreme Sacrifice In The Great War 1914-1919 And In Thanks Giving For Those Who Have Returned. Greater Love Hath No Man Than This That A Man Lay Down His Life For His Friends.

There are one hundred and twenty-eight names, each without rank or regiment, inscribed in three columns:

1st column: Reginald Lawrence Baker, Denis Busher, Harold Day, Alfred A. Fry, Oswald Gardner, Charles Clement Haywood, Granville Mitchell, Matthew Morgan, Charles Straker, William Walbeoffe-Wilson, William Abbott, John Henry Adams, Gladstone George Aspey, Clifford George Bailey, William Joshua Best, William Booth, Herbert James Bowden, James Thomas Bowen, W. Boswell, James Bruton,

Harry Burcher, William C.J. Brown, Gerald Carey, William W. Colerick, John Connolly, William Trevor Cooke, Albert Edwin Corbett, Stanley Aubrey Day, William Heyward Day, Edwin Davies, Trevor Dodd Davies, Arthur Davies, Edward Dimond, Frank Dyer, Harry Dyer, Arthur Evans, Gus Trevor Evans, Alfred Severs Farquhar, Samuel Fellows, William Fitzgerald, Norbert Fitzpatrick, Alfred Gibbons, Percival Dawson Griffiths.

2nd column: Reginald Charles Gibbons, Walter Francis Gough, Lawford Gibson, Ivor Vernon Griffiths, Thomas Charles Griffiths, John Hartley Grouse, Edward Gwenllan, William Hall, John Harrington Herbert, Clarence T.S. Higgs, Albert David Holland, Reuben George Hughes, Ivor John Iball, J.T. Jackson, William James, John James, William John G. Jamieson, Fredrick James Jennings, John James Jones, Thomas J. Jones, Thomas Jones, William Jones, Percy M. Powell Jones, George Jordan, William Knight, Edward Albert Lewis, John Lewis, Samuel Taylor Light, Alfred James Little, Richard Thomas Mann, Henry James Marshall, William James Matthews, Albert R. Morgan, Wilfred Hurst Morgan, William Morgan, Trevor G. Nash, Samuel Neil, Joseph Arthur Norton, William O'Grady, T. Haydn Pickering, Hubert Harry Pitt, William Price.

3rd column: Roy Dimond Rawlings, Bartholemew Regan, John Regan, Charles Richens, John Ridley, Harry Roach, Samuel Rathbone, George Raymond Roberts, George Roberts, Hubert Bourne Sayce, Richard J. Seabourne, William Arthur Seabourne, J.E. William Shaw, James Grant Sherratt, Leich Simon, Sidney Henry Sketchley, William Edward Smith, Herbert John Spilsbury, Henry Stanton, Thomas Stanton, Percy Staples, Fredrick John Taylor, Fredrick Thomas, Victor Osman Walsh, Fredrick Walters, Charles Herbert Watkins, John William Watkins, William John Watts, Charles Daniel Webb, Albert Webb, Ernest Weeks, William Welsh, Albert Ivor White, Alfred Victor Williams, Emile Fredrick Williams, Harry Williams, Moses Williams, William Williams, Edward Henry Winter, William Henry Wigley, Harold Woodward, Arthur Edmund Workman, Richard Spillane.

After the names the words - *Blessed Are The Dead. 'May They Rest In Peace And May Light Perpetual Shine Upon Them'.*

King Henry VIII School

The main body of the memorial located in the Upper School dining-room, is made from red marble and displays at the top, within two flags, the school motto - *'Ut. Pro Sim'* - and below the design of a fleur-de-lys. Above this is the legend - *It Is Only Given To The Few.* The inscription - *All Men Must Die To Die For Their Country* - appears across the top of the memorial, which is flanked by two columns. Then engraved into white marble the following -

To The Glory Of God And In Honoured Memory Of The Masters And Old Boys Of King Henry VIII's Grammar School Abergavenny Who Gave Their Lives In The Great War 1914-1918. 'Their Names Live For Evermore'.

There are thirty-four names recorded: B.L. Jones and W.C. Raymont, who were both masters at the school, C.G. Bailey, E.G.H. Bates, C.O. Bowcott, A.D. Bowcott, W. Briscoe, D.J.B. Busher, G. Carey, L.H. Carr, T. Clark, L.G. Cooper, H. Day, A.E. Edwards, D.J. Games, O. Gardner, J.G. Glendinning, S.R. Goulborn, J.H. Herbert, W. Hall, F.P. Howells, F. Kendrick, V. Kynch, P. Matthews, E. Morgan, F.L. Morgan,

Plaque commemorating three members of the Castle Street Methodist Church, Abergavenny.

King Henry VIII's Grammar School memorial, Abergavenny.

IT IS ONLY GIVEN TO THE TEA...

...ALL...MEN...RES...DIE... ...T·O·DIE·FOR·THEIR·COUNTRY...

TO THE GLORY OF GOD AND ✝ IN HONOURED MEMORY OF
THE MASTERS and OLD BOYS OF KING HENRY VIII'S GRAMMAR SCHOOL
ABERGAVENNY
WHO GAVE THEIR LIVES IN THE GREAT WAR 1914-1918.

B.L.JONES.(MASTER)	L.H.CARR.	J.H.HERBERT.	J.PAYNE.
W.C.RAYMONT(MASTER)	T.CLARK.	W.HALL.	H.H.PITT.
C.G.BAILEY.	L.G.COOPER.	F.P.HOWELLS.	G.E.ROWBERRY.
E.G.H.BATES.	H.DAY.	F.KENDRICK.	A.W.STORRAR.
C.O.BOWCOTT.	A.E.EDWARDS.	V.KYNCH.	L.M.THOMAS.
A.D.BOWCOTT.	D.J.GAMES.	P.MATTHEWS.	F.J.TRUMP.
W.BRISCOE.	O.GARDNER.	E.MORGAN.	H.J.WOODWARD.
D.J.B.BUSHER.	J.G.GLENDINNING.	F.L.MORGAN.	
G.CAREY.	S.R.GOULBORN.	R.PALFREY.	

"THEIR NAMES LIVE FOR EVERMORE."

R. Palfrey, J. Payne, H.H. Pitt, G.E. Rowberry, A.W. Storrar, L.M. Thomas, F.J. Trump and H.J. Woodward.

The two masters, B.L. Jones and W.C. Raymont, both served with Abergavenny's local Territorial Force battalion, the 3rd Monmouthshire Regiment. Captain Brynley Lewis Jones being buried in Abergavenny New Cemetery near Llanfoist, having died at home from pneumonia, while Lieutenant William Clifton Raymont lost his life in Belgium attached to the 5th South Wales Borderers. It was while out of the line on 5 May 1917, that the 5th Battalion were heavily shelled in their billets at Ypres. 'B' Company suffered heavy casualties as a salvo of shells almost completely destroyed the Cavalry Barracks where the men were resting. William Raymont was killed along with forty others killed or wounded that day.

Nevill Hall Hospital

The chapel at Nevill Hall contains a framed and glazed Roll of Honour with the dedication -

Abergavenny And District War Memorial 1914-1918. A Bed Was Endowed By Public Subscription In Memory Of The Abergavenny Men Whose Names Are Recorded Below Who Made The Supreme Sacrifice During The Great War.

There are three hundred and thirty-five names recorded. (See also Abergavenny Town Hall). The hospital is located just outside Abergavenny on the Brecon Road (A40).

Presbyterian Church Whitefield Chapel

On the wall to the left of the pulpit at the Presbyterian Church in Pen-y-Pound Road is a brass plaque inscribed -

To The Glory Of God And In Grateful Memory Of - Clifford Bowcott, Frederick Bowcott, Alfred Morgan Jenkins, Brynley Lewis Jones, William Morgan, William Rees, Charles Savagar - Who In The Great War Of 1914-1918 Heard Our Country's Call And Gave Themselves, Even Unto Death.

There is another plaque to the right of the altar commemorating Captain Robert Oswald Gardner of the 3rd Battalion, Monmouthshire Regiment who was killed near Ypres on 8 May, 1915. He was aged thirty-one and shot through the heart as his company ('B') went forward from support positions near Polygon Wood.

The church is also in possession of a framed and glazed Roll of Honour listing the names of fifty-five members who served in the Great War.

St Mary's Priory Church

The south wall of the nave at St. Mary's Church in Monk Street, Abergavenny bears a commemorative plaque to a local officer -

In Ever Loving Memory Of Charles Herbert George Martin, M.A., F.Z.S. Lieut. III Monmouthshire Regt., Killed In Action Near Ypres 2 May 1915. Aged 33. Greater Love Hath No Man Than This That A Man Lay Down His Life For His Friends. This Tablet Is Erected By His Wife And Son.

Charles Martin lived at The Hill, Abergavenny, now a residential college and the location for many years of the Western Front Association's annual seminar. Charles

Martin's name also appears on a memorial situated on the north wall of the nave. In white marble, and by W.D. Carîe, the plaque is headed with the words in gold letters - *In Memoriam 1914-1919* - and ends with the inscription -

These Made The Great Sacrifice For Their King And County. Their Names Are Here Set Up By Their Fellow-Worshippers In The Churches Of This Parish In Thankful Memory Of Them And Their Devotion To Duty.

The names are recorded on two black panels, twenty-nine under the heading - *Saint Mary's* - followed by eight for - *Christ Church*.

The first name recorded on the St. Mary's panel is that of Brigadier-General Randle Barnett Barker who won the Distinguished Service Order on the Somme in 1916 and again at Arras the following year. He was Colonel of the 22nd Battalion, Royal Fusiliers and in January, 1918, appointed as Commander, 99th Infantry Brigade. He was killed by a shell near Gueudecourt on 24 March, 1918. The General is also commemorated by the east window, which was installed by his wife in 1922.

The names that follow are listed in alphabetical order: Lance-Corporal W.E. Brown of the 9th Welsh; Rifleman Lionel Hubert Carr, who served with the 21st London Regiment; Sergeant Louis Coombey of the 6th Bedfords; Private William Henry Coombey, 3rd Monmouthshire Regiment; Lieutenant Leonard G. Cooper, mortally wounded during the 4th South Wales Borderers attack at Kabak Kuyu, Gallipoli on 9 August, 1915; Sergeant William Hayward Day, 3rd Monmouthshire; Second-Lieutenant James Graham Glendining, also of the 3rd Monmouthshire, but later transferred to the Royal Flying Corps and as an observer with 57th Squadron met his death in Belgium on 16 December, 1917; Drummer Ewart Goode, 3rd Monmouthshire; Corporal Henry Gwyther, King's Shropshire Light Infantry; Sergeant Ivor John Jackson of the Royal Air Force; Gunner James George Jones, Royal Garrison Artillery; Captain Jestyn LL. Mansel, 7th Dragoon Guards (see Caerleon memorial); Lieutenant C.H.G. Martin and Rifleman Thomas G. Meredith, both of the 3rd Monmouthshires; Second-Lieutenant Fotherergill L. Morgan, 7th London Regiment, who died on 3 December, 1917 from wounds received at Kangaroo Trench, Cambrai sector; Private Donald Morgn, 9th Welsh, then eight men from the 3rd Monmouthshire - Privates Joe Arthur Norton, Edwin Powell, Daniel Wyndham Powell, Arthur Price, George Roberts, Evan J. Reynolds, Second-Lieutenant C.L. Straker and Private Charles L. Savegar. Private Benjamin G. Weaver of the 3rd Worcestershire follows, then Sergeant A. Ivor White, 3rd Monmouthshire, followed by his officer - Captain William Walbeoffe-Wilson, who was the eldest son of Major William Henry Herbert Walbeoffe-Wilson, JP and before the war, Scout Master to the Abergavenny Boy Scouts. He was killed in action near Ypres on 2 August, 1915. The last name on the St. Mary's section is that of Private Robert Winney, also of the 3rd Monmouthshire.

The Christ Church tablet begins with Private C. Bailey, 3rd Monmouthshire, then Gus Evans, a private with 4th South Wales Borderers. Private James George Harding of the Grenadier Guards follows, then Trooper J.P. Howell of the 2nd Life Guards; Sub-Lieutenant Granville J. Mitchell who was killed with the Hood Battalion, Royal Naval Division in 1918; Sergeant Albert R. Morgan, awarded the Distinguished Conduct Medal while serving with 12th Field Company, Royal Engineers before his death on 13 February, 1916; Private Percy Staples, 2nd East Lancashire Regiment and Private George Williams of the 3rd Monmouthshire.

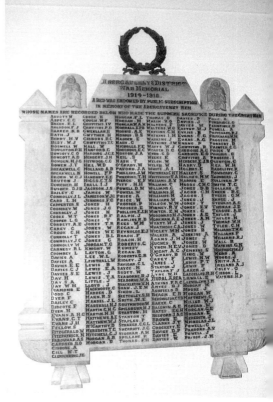

St Mary's Priory Church, Abergavenny, memorial.

Abergavenny Town Hall memorial.

Memorial plaque commemorating staff of the old Pen-y-Fal Hospital. Now at St Mary's, Abergavenny.

Also on the north wall, and to the right of the main memorial, is a brass plaque inscribed -

Gwell Angau Na Gwarth (Rather Death Than Dishonour) *In Memory Of The Following Men Of The Staff Who Fell In The Great War 1914 to 1918.*

There are four names recorded: William Ernest Evans of the King's Shropshire Light Infantry; Arthur Hall and Arthur Allan Hawker, both of the Grenadier Guards, and Sydney Rollings of the Gloucestershire Regiment. This commemoration was retrieved from the Pen-y-Fal Hospital upon its closure and placed in St. Mary's by the Royal British Legion on Palm Sunday, 1998.

The origins of the motto *Gwell Angau Na Gwarth* are explained in Captain G.A. Brett's, *A History Of The 2nd Battalion, The Monmouthshire Regiment.* Composed in English by the wife of Sir Benjamin Hall (afterwards Lord Llanover and Lord Lieutenant of Monmouthshire) the motto was taken into use by the county's volunteers around 1863.

Close to the Pen-y-Fal memorial is a small painted wooden shield in memory of those who lost their lives at sea.

Town Hall

There are two memorials located on the stairway of Abergavenny Town Hall in Cross Street. On a large marble tablet sculptured by Basil Evans, six columns of names appear below the inscription -

Abergavenny & District War Memorial 1914-1918. A Bed Was Endowed By Public Subscription In Memory Of The Abergavenny Men Whose Names Are Recorded Below Who Made The Supreme Sacrifice During The Great War.

Two hundred and nineteen names are recorded without rank or regiment. These are followed by a further one hundred and sixteen under the heading - *Rural Area.* The names appear in the following order:

1st column: W. Abbott, G.G. Aspey, R.L. Baker, J.J. Balsdon, R.B. Barker, J. Bath, H.V. Berry, W.J. Best, W. Boswell, R.H. Boughton, C.O. Bowcott, A.D. Bowcott, H.J.G. Bowden, J.T. Bowden, C. Breakwell, N. Breakwell, W.C.J. Brown, J. Bruton, H. Burcher, D.J.B. Busher, C. Bailey, J.L. Connolly, L.H. Carr, S. Carpenter, W. Coombrey, J. Connolly, W.T. Cooke, L.G. Cooper, A.E. Corbett, G. Carey, G.H. Crook, T. Connolly, J.C. Connolly, W. Connolly, R.L. Carnegy, L. Coombey, A. Davies, A. Davies, E.E. Davies, C.J. Davies, S.E. Davies, H. Day, S.A. Day, W.H. Day, E. Diamond, C. Dodd, F. Dyer, C. Dailey, F. Didcote, H. Dyer, A.H.C. Evans, C.T. Evans, J.H. Evans, S. Fellows, W. Fitzgerald, N. Fitzpatrick, A.S. Farouhar, R.O. Gardner, A. Gibbons, W.T. Gill, J.G. Glendinning.

2nd column: E. Goode, W.F. Gough, I.V. Griffiths, P.D. Griffiths, E. Gwenllan, H. Gwyther, R.C. Gibbons, T.C. Griffiths, W. Hall, G. Hanford, J.G.E. Harding, J.H. Herbert, C.G. Heywood, W.D. Hill, A.D. Holland, F.P. Howell, E.E. Hanbury, C.T.S. Higgs, I.J. Iball, J.S. Jackson, W. James, W.J.G. Jamieson, F.G. Jennings, H. Jones, J.C. Jones, N. Jones, R.F. Jones, T. Jones, T.R. Jones, W. Jones, W.E. Jones, B.L. Jones, G. Jones, T.G. Jordan, W. Knight, G. Layton, W.L. Lee, W. Leinthall, B. Lewis, E.A. Lewis, J. Lewis, T.A. Lewis, J. Little, J. Lloyd, C. Mackworth, D. Madden, R.S. Mann, J.L. Mansel, H.J. Marshall, C.H.G. Martin, H.H. Martin, A.E. Matthews, W.J.

Matthew, D. McCarthy, T.G. Meredith, G.J. Mitchell, A.R. Morgan, D. Morgan.

3rd column: F.L. Morgan, M. Morgan, W.A.H. Morgan, E.P.B. Morrall, A.E. Morris, D.S. Morris, E. Madden, C. Nash, F.E. Nicholls, E.C. Norgrove, J.A. Norton, S. Neil, T. Nash, W. O'Grady, J.A. Pavord, J.W. Phillips, T.H. Pickering, E.F. Pierce, H.H. Pitt, D.W. Powell, W. Powell, A. Price, W. Price, P. Prosser, E. Prosser, F.J.H. Phillips, J. Ralph, R.D. Rawlings, W.M. Rees, J. Regan, E.J. Reynolds, F. Roach, H. Roach, G. Roberts, Rumsey (no initials given), B. Regan, G.R. Roberts, J. Ridley, C.L. Savigar, H. Sayce, W. Scott, R.J. Seaborne, W.A. Seaborne, V.H. Shackleton, J.E.W. Shaw, L. Simon, S.H. Sketchley, W.E. Smith, W. Southwood, H.J. Spilsbury, H. Stanton, T. Stanton, P. Staples, C.C.L. Straker, J.C. Sherratt, A.W. Storrar, R. Spillane, F.H. Thomas.

4th column: O. Thomas, V.O. Walsh, F. Walters, W.G. Walters, C.H. Watkins, I.H. Watkins, J. Watkins, J.W. Watkins, W.J. Watts, B.G. Weaver, C.D. Webb, E. Weeks, W. Welsh, W. Welsh, A.I. White, C.H.T. Whitehead, T.A. Whitehouse, A.V. Williams, C. Williams, G. Williams, H. Williams, M. Williams, W. Williams, W.W. Wilson, R.V. Winney, E.H. Winter, H.J. Woodward, A.E. Worknan, W.J. Wyatt, C.A. Whatmore, W.H. Wigley, A. Walker, J.H. Adams, R. Hughes, H.E.V. Kynch, A.C. Knight, B. O'Grady, F. Casey, J. James, J. Stanton, F.J. Taylor, W.H. Lyne. *Rural Area* - F.R.C. Atkins, B.J. Amyes, R. Ashfield, E.B. Beach, C.T.D. Berrington, C. Baker, A.E. Baldwin, E.G.H. Bates, J.A.C. Bedford, E. Brown, J.T. Clarke, E. Crockett, D.P. Davies, E. Davies, W. Davies.

5th column: P. Davies, J. Davies, W. Davies, W.J. Eastup, B. Evans, C.G. Evans, A.G. Evans, P. Evans, R. Griffiths, A.G. Gibbons, E.O. Gardner, A. Griffiths, E.J.B. Herbert, D. Harry, E. Holmes, S. Hallet, M.W. Holmes, E. Harris, C.H.C. Hobbs, D.B. Jones, C.H. Jacob, I. Jacob, J. Jones, T. Jones, E.V. Jones, G. Jones, A.E. Jones, A.M. Jones, J. Jones, W. Jones, B. Jones, A. Jenkins, J. Jones, W. Jones, D. Jones, S. Jenkins, W. King, N.W. Lewis, P.T. Lewis, F. Lewis, J. Laker, R.H. Lascelles, E. Lilwall, I.M. Llewellyn, W. Morgan, J. Moore, W. Morgan, G. Matthews, W.J. Miller, W. Morgan, G.E. Morgan, E. Morgan, J. Meredith, J.L. Nicholas, C. Powell, A.V. Parsons, J. Powell, J.W. Preece.

6th column: A. Price, O. Pembridge, P. Pembridge, A. Powell, R.J. Pritchard, W.H. Pritchard, M. Prosser, R. Probert, C.G. Painter, V. Price, G. Pauling, I. Prosser, G. Quinton, W.H. Rea, R. Radcliffe, G. Rowberry, J. Saunders, P. Sullivan, T.C. Smith, P. Sollars, R.C. Sheen, G.W. Steen, J. Sayce, A.G. Stewart, J.D. Thomas, A.E. Teague, J. Taylor, H. Taylor, W.H. Thomas, C.H. Tyler, T.W.G. Williams, F. Williams, R.J. Williams, R. Wall, G.N. Watkins, J.J. Worthington, A. Webb, J. Woods, A.L. Smith, A.J. Ireland, G. Coley, L. Gibson, H.P. Watkins.

A framed hand-written version of the Abergavenny and District memorial can be found in the chapel of Nevil Hall Hospital just outside of the town.

The second memorial at the Town Hall commemorates sixteen men from the London and North Western Railway. On a brass tablet, the following inscription -

Erected By The Employees In The Locomotive Department L.& N.W. Rly. Abergavenny And Sub-Stations In Memory Of Their Fellow Workmen Who Lost Their Lives In The Great War 1914-1918.

The names appear without rank or regiment, but with detail of where and how each man died. Nine men - H.J.G. Bowden, N. Fitzpatrick, A.C. Knight, E.C. Norgrove,

H.J. Spilsbury, H.J. Taylor, A.I. White, A. Webb and W.D. Watkins are recorded as having been killed, died or mortally wounded while on active service in France. Two others, T.R. Jones and C.L. Savegar, are shown as - 'reported missing, presumed killed, France.' C.J. Booth died from illness contracted whilst abroad, R.C. Gibbons was drowned at sea, while J.A.C. Bedford, G.T. Evans and O.J. Morgan lost their lives in Egypt, Mesopotamia and Gallipoli respectively. The later being shown as - 'Died of Exposure.'

ABERTILLERY

The memorial to those men from Abertillery who fell in the Great War is located at the junction of Somerset and Queen Streets. A figure of a single soldier holding his rifle and tin hat aloft surmounts bronze panels affixed to three sides of the monument. Only names and regiments are recorded on the memorial. A booklet sold at the time of the unveiling ceremony, however, lists names, ranks and numbers (in most cases) in a series of regiment groupings:

Royal Navy: Signalman H. Flook, Signalman (2986) W.H. Hinds, Able-Seamen (549) E. Jones and (J75491) H.J. Lawrance, Gunner (13739) W.L. Owen, Able-Seaman (J81964) W.G. Phillips, Chief Engineer W.H. Saunders, Leading-Stoker (308593) J.T. Taylor.

Royal Naval Division: Able-Seaman (Z313) A. Morgan, Seamen (Z360) J. Morgan and (28805) W.T. Morgan, Able-Seamen (Z1404) T.D. Rees and (1401) S.G. Rogers, Signalman (Z312) H. Sterry (awarded Military Medal).

Welsh Guards: Privates (3834) R. Cook, (16681) B. Davies, (1355) G. Phillips and H.M. Porter.

Royal Welsh Fusiliers: Privates (61370) I.E. Bennett, (65901) B. Brown and (47245) D. Challenger, Corporal (38928) E. Eastey, Private (94232) F. Edwards, Drummer (7042) S. George, Privates (78328) W.J. Langley, (76549) G.W. Legg, (94266) F. Mason, (94150) G. Moore and (74767) E. Morgan, Corporal (15700) G.J. Reed, Privates (93738) S. Smith, (88830) M.H. Thomas and (17950) T. Thomas, Sergeant (29634) H.J. Tudor, Second-Lieutenant E.G. Williams, Lance-Corporal (54250) G. Williams, Private (47366) J. Williams.

South Wales Borderers: Privates (15440) S. Andrews and J. Ayland, Drummer J. Barnett, Privates (27195) P. Baker, (23045) E. Batton, (33098) E.B. Beard, (58713) T.H. Beddis, (21771) E. Bennett, (21122) A.J. Bevan, (33099) E.U. Bishop, J. Brian, (20971), J. Brickell, (20898) L. Challenger and (15168) T. Chapman, Sergeant (22484) R.J. Clarke, Corporal (12665) W. Close, Privates (20976) F. Coles, (33104) F.C. Coombes, (1893) W. Coombey and (14840) J.M. Cox, Signaller W.L. Davies, Privates (33058) W. Dobbins, (23194) E.W. Dyer and (25557) W.C. Edwards, Lance-Corporal (39288) F.J. Emanuel, Privates (21603) F. Fisher, (33248) A.E. Flowers, (12839) C.H. Ford and J.H. Fynn (awarded Victoria Cross), Captain E. Gill (awarded Military Cross), Private (23174) R. Griffiths, Lance-Corporal (1408) G.E. Halford, Private (15237) W.G. Hanbury, Sergeant (14706) W.J. Hodges (awarded Military Medal), Private (18088) I.A. Holland, Corporal (20982) J. James (awarded Military Medal), Privates (33234) J.C. Jenkins, (288030) A.J. Jones, (25174) A.R. Jones, (16098) A.R. Jones, (21951) I.W. Jones, P. Jones, (20171) T. Jones, (26825) W.J. Jones, (25055 R.J. Kibble, (13751) D. Lavender,

Abertillery memorial.

(53824) C.W.P. Lewis and (53821) F.M. Lewis, Corporal (23043) J.H. Lewis, Private (20188) P. Lewis, Lance-Corporal (20992) W. Lewis, Sergeant (16121) D.C. Llewellyn, Privates T.J. Llewellyn, (33119) D. Lloyd and (10606) J. Lloyd, Corporal (24962) W.P. Masey, Privates W.C. Masters, (11985) C. Meredith and (32156) M. Osland, Drummer (22443) S. Owen, Privates (2127) E. Parker, (21373) W.D.R. Parry, (23034) R. Pascoe, (13263) J. Peacock, (15447) W.G. Price, (31035) T.J. Probert, (1291) T. Purnell, (33190) T.J. Reed, (11616) L.H. Rees and (13954) P.A. Rees, Sergeant (627188) J.T. Richards (awarded Military Medal), Private (33273) J. Savage, Sergeant W.H. Savage, Privates (14604) A.E. Seeley, (29164) B.O.P. Short, (18069) J.E.W. Smith, (23208) F. Snellgrove, (53853) R.J. Stevens, (21408) A. Sweet, (12472) A. Tillings, (7964) H.A. Tombs, (33164) G.T. Venn, F.T. Ward, (18672) W. Weale and (5872) E.E. Whiteman, Sergeant (21999) W. Wigglesworth, Privates (9875) D.W. Williams, (9766) F. Williams, (21114) G.R. Williams, J. Withers, (25968) A.J. Wright.

Welsh Regiment: Private A.E. Beale, Corporal (1354) H. Blackwell, Privates (46491) O. Britton, (12788) I. Cole, (58191) T.H. Day, (682367) H.A. Edwards, (25694) J.T. Fletcher, (32691) I. Fraser, (22294) W. Fry and (25636) A. Grindle, Lieutenant G. Hobby (awarded Military Medal), Privates (35244) W.H. Howells, (36312) T.H. James and (11062) W.T. Jenkins, Lance-Corporal (26381) J. Jones, Privates (58212) E. Lewis, (18736) H. Lloyd and (22289) P. Luxton, Sergeant-Instructor (47317) J.V. Marston, Privates (58348) F. Matthews, (20100) R.J. Phillips, (25447) E.G. Rogers, (27774) W.H. Rose, (1516) S. Smith, (11079) W. Tanner, (309745) J.H. Thomas and (26508) C. Vaughan, Sergeant (53715) W.G. Venn, Private (74313) W. Weaver.

Monmouthshire Regiment: Privates (267595) T. Baynton, (1505) A. Bees and (2427) A.H. Bowden, Corporal (1296) H. Bowley, Privates (2118) J. Brown, (3135) J.E. Brown, (290882) F.C. Browning, (1058) A. Caines, (3405) S. Carpenter, (227903) W.T. Carter, (824) A. Close and (121) L. Coleman, Lieutenant W. Collings (awarded Military Cross), Private (1671) F. Crewe, Lance-Corporal (1240) G.L. Darvill, Privates (1324) E. Davies, (1616) J.T. Davies, (39298) W.H. Davies and (3070) A.J. Day, Lance-Corporal (2110) J.T. Denford, Private (2109) T.G. Denford, Lance-Corporal (193) W.J. Dimmick, Bandsman (1504) J. Ellis, Private (2423) C. Francis, Sergeant (493) A.J. Gatfield, Company Sergeant Major (69) J.T. Gill, Privates (1666) W. Gordon and (2488) B. Gough, Lance-Corporal (963) D.R. Griffths, Sergeant (54) W. Hailstone, Privates (1614) A.J. Harris, (266820) C. Henley and (2655) J.M. Howells, Quartermaster Sergeant (2491) T.P. Hughes, Private (290242) E. Humphries, M.Gunner (53807) J.T. Ireland, Private (2576) A.G. James, Corporal (800) A.W. James, Private (267645) B. James, Sergeant (75) R.C. Jones, Private (3129) W.O. Jones, Lance-Sergeant (2308) W.M. Keyse, Privates (1713) J. Lander, (2590) W.H. Lane, (3176) D. Langley, (2012) W.J. Lavender, H.J. Lee, (15134) J.A. Lewis, (3162) J.E. Lloyd, (2556) H. Martin, (227944) W. Mason and (82) W.J. McCarthy, Sergeant (132) T. Mercy, Privates (290012) T. Mercy, T. Morgan, (15768) T.E. Morris, (3103) W. Mutter, (2926) F.H. Nash, G. Newman, W.J. Ollis, (3618) G. Onions and (1365) L.A. Parfitt, Lance-Corporal (620) J. Phillips, Privates (1310) W.G. Pickford, (1818) A. Poore and (1025) P. Powell, Sergeants (266032) R.J. Powell and (961) G. Prewitt, Privates (1607) A. Pritchard, (2285) W. Prosser and (1593) M.E.W. Rancombe, Lieutenant C.S. Reed, Privates (3462) E.J. Reynolds, (119) W. Reynolds, (1215) W. Richards and (2622) G.H.

Rowe, Second-Lieutenant T.F.C. Salt, Privates (15811) S.E. Smith and (1600) T. Smith, Lieutenant W.V. Stewart, Private (1580) W.E. Stickler, Lance-Corporal (1074) B.G. Sturdy, Privates (1829) T. Taylor, (3118) W.B. Taylor, (1470) D. Thomas and (2490) S. Thomas, Sergeant (1822) G.W. Treharne, Private (2344) A. Werrett, Sergeant (290381) R. Whatley, Privates (2243) B. Williams and (1834) C. Williams, Acting-Sergeant (3439) G.W. Willis, Corporal (2863) G.A. Wood.

Dragoon Guards: Private (12459) C.E. Saunders.

Royal Hussars: Lance-Corporal (5203) G. Pilley.

Royal Field Artillery: Gunners (62634) A. Badham and (78153) H.A. Bruce, Corporal (20933) H. Cadwallader, Sergeant W.H. Cecil, Private (30613) S. Cooper, Gunners (189) J. Davies and (244834) E.L.R. Emanuel, Drivers (190773) J. Francombe, (4035) A.G. Hopkins, J. Jones and (195099) W. Kinnersley, Gunner (91473) W.C. Knock, Drivers (83258) G. Maggs and (6870) W.T. Meredith, Gunner (1063) J. Richards, Driver (43278) T. Rogers, Private (2416) G. Selby, Drivers (83259) F. Smith, (39782) J. Stafford and (39782) J. Stafford, Driver (461) E. Taylor, Gunners (43794) W.H. White, (19592) A. Williams and (97039) G. Wiltshire.

Royal Garrison Artillery: Gunner (275456) T. Hawkes.

Royal Engineers: Sapper (WR/50682) E. Cathew, Private (292270) W.H. Douglas (awarded Military Medal), Sappers (158234) F. Fielding, (1124) R.J.E. Hay, (158204) S.J. Holborn, (322987) G.H.F. James and (2450) L. Morgan, Corporal (382683) J. Phillips, Private (95961) G. Price, Sapper (164791) S.W. Skidmore, Privates (158227) A.J. White and (147269) W.H. Williams.

Grenadier Guards: Privates (24712) R. Bamford and (29916) A.L. Griffiths.

Royal West Surrey Regiment: Private (72552) W.G. Broom.

East Kent Regiment: Private (242404) J.T. Bryant.

Lancaster Regiments: Privates (51428) R.M. Ash, (13881) D. Jones and T. Kearton, Sergeant (12282) H. Parsons, Lance-Sergeant (9731) I. Rees.

Northumberland Fusiliers: Privates (44952) G. Drake and (45028) A. Sterry.

Royal Warwickshire Regiment: Private (235035) C.J. Aylesbury.

Lincolnshire Regiment: Lieutenant J.S. Metcalfe.

Devonshire Regiment: Private (67798) T.V. Westcott.

Cheshire Regiment: Privates (34188) F.J. Allaway, (18732) T. Brickell and (60850) F. Mason.

Gloucestershire Regiment: Sergeant (285189) J.H. Davies, Privates (6583) R.J. Maslin, (2031) A. Phillips and (285217) T. York.

Worcestershire Regiment: Privates (42062) W.J. Brooks (awarded Military Medal), (25452) F. Castle and (25189) C.T. Price, Lance-Corporal (40572) W. Probert.

Duke of Cornwall's Light Infantry: Private (7643) E.J. Stent.

Oxfordshire and Buckinghamshire Light Infantry: Private (25027) T. Brickell.

Hampshire Regiment: Private G.H. Payne.

Northamptonshire Regiment: Sergeant (5816) R. Reeve, Private (203560) E. Stowell.

Royal West Kent Regiment: Drummer (7043) S.G. Coombes.

King's Own Yorkshire Light Infantry: Private (3881) C. Smith.

King's Shropshire Light Infantry: Privates (27218) W.C. Bosley, (15770) H.E. Fairbard, (38603) R. Morgan and A. Oakley, Corporal (7396) E. Snell, Private (36474) C.M. Snellgrove.

King's Royal Rifle Corps: Private (11749) A.E. Morris.

Wiltshire Regiment: Private (6797) H. Bull.

York and Lancaster Regiment: Privates (47140) H.W. Fisher and (24487) J.H. Hitchens.

Argyll and Sutherland Highlanders: Private (22496) R. Clark.

Rifle Brigade: Privates (5521) M.S. Austin and (6050) A. Llewellyn.

County of London Regiment: Privates W. Perry, (682367) W.A. Smith and (204587) W. Stone.

Herefordshire Regiment: Private (5385) V. Barrell.

Machine Gun Corps: Privates (90450) R. Baker, O. Jenkins, (117658) M. Rees, (14011) E. Vines and (7875) T. Williams.

Royal Army Service Corps: Private (MT/047374) J. Hillier, Sergeant (54/084897) F. Mitchell, Private (MT/341331) W.H. Powell.

Royal Army Medical Corps: Private (48228) H.G. Boswell, Doctor W.H. Edmunds, Private (2963) I.J. Lewis, Corporal (48563) I. Phillips (awarded Military Medal), Doctor J.G. Sergent, Private (112016) A.E. Warlow.

Labour Corps: Privates (291414) E. Bond and (189017) E. Williams.

Royal Air Force: Second-Lieutenant G.A.H. Davies, 2nd Air Mechanic C.J.E. Jones.

Australian Imperial Forces: Driver (37907) R. Probert.

Units Unknown: J. Avery, H. Bishop, G. Bodley, W. Bull, J. Caines, J.F. Campbell, J. Carpenter, W. Cecil, A. Chaplin, T. Chorley, H. Clarke, H. Coles, S.J. Coombes, C. Cooper, G. Coveny, J. Coveny, S. Cox, G. Crockett, A.W. Crook, A. Day, J. Day, T. Dix, W.P. Dollin, S.F. Drew, B. Evans, D.R. Evans, E. Evans, T. Evans, F. Field, P. French, A. Gadfield, A. Gay, R. Gibbs, P. Gray, W.P. Gray, E. Green, A.L. Griffin, M. Hanbury, C.H. Hawkins, G.J. Hawkins, H. Herbert, A. Hopkins, F.C. Huntley, W.H. Hurd, W.A. Insley, S. Jenkins, T. John, R. Kingdom, A. Lane, L. Lewis, A.L. Lloyd, R. Lonsdale, A. Lovell, J. Manley, H. Morse, C.K. Munckton, W.M. Murphy, W.G. Nelmes, W. Newman, J. Parfitt, S. Peacock, A. Pennel, E. Perry, S.H.T. Pollard, H.O. Powell, J.A. Reed, P. Rees, W.J. Reeve, R. Rogers, J. Sherrard, E. Smith, T. Swaine, A. Thomas, F.D. Thomas, J. Thomas, W. Thomas, W. Tucker, T.W. Turner, A. Walker, H. Wellington, J. Whitely, S. Wilce, W.J. Williams, W. Willis, H.H. Wilson, R.G. Young, J. Young.

The names of two men, William John Morgan of the South Wales Borderers, and Jack Lowry, Royal Navy, have been added to the stone-work recently, along with panels listing those killed during the Second World War.

The memorial, which bears the inscription -

Their Name Liveth For Evermore - To The Glorious Memory Of The Men Of Abertillery Who Fell In The Great War 1914-1918. Greater Love Hath No Man Than This That A Man Lay Down His Life For His Friends

was unveiled by Field-Marshal The Viscount Allenby, GCB, GC, MC on 1 December, 1926.

Many of those mentioned on the memorial attended the Abertillery County School whose magazine, the *Tyleryan*, published the occasional 'In Memoriam' article. Remembered by 'O.N.R.' in the Spring, 1915 issue was - 'Wm. Mervyn Keyse or 'Willie' Keyse, entered school September 1908, and leaving in October

1909, became a clerk at the Abertillery District Council Offices. Like many more of those who 'fell in' at the first call to arms, he was an only son, being the only child of Mr and Mrs Thomas Keyse, Gladstone Street. He joined the Mon. Regiment August 1914, and on a never-to-be-forgotten morning of February, 1915, left Abertillery for the Front, in company with Fox, Prosser, Salt, Pritchard, Hepple, Hobby, and many more brave fellows, who later took part in the severe fighting in May 1915. He was returned as 'missing' on the fatal 8th, having just attained his 21st year. Nothing has been heard of him since.' Lance-Sergeant William Mervyn Keyse served with the 3rd Monmouthshire Regiment and was killed during the fighting at Frezenberg Ridge. He has no known grave, his name being recorded on the Menin Gate Memorial to the missing at Ypres.

The 'Salt,' referred to above, was Thomas Frederick Cyril Salt of Gwentland House, Oak Street, Abertillery who was on holiday in Devonshire when war was declared. Rushing home he first called on nine or ten of his friends and together they joined the 3rd Monmouthshire Regiment, Abertillery being the headquarters of 'E' and 'F' Companies of that battalion. After a short time on the Western Front, Salt would be commissioned in the field. Then on 3 April 1915, mortally wounded in trenches on the west slope of the Messines-Wytschaete Ridge near the village of Wulverghem. He died in hospital at Bailleul on the following day. In a letter sent to his parents (subsequently published in the *South Wales Gazette*), one of Salt's friends recalled how the evening that their son was shot, his platoon was relieving other troops in the front line. 'It was within twenty yards of his destination that the blow came. As the men of his platoon was filing by me I heard someone say, "Cyril is hit," and I immediately went out and found him, and, in company of three other fellows, took him to cover of our trench. The bullet had entered his temple, behind his right eye, and passed through parallel with his forehead.'

The writer recalls how it was some time before his friend could be taken away to hospital, 'I got coats, etc., and made him as comfortable as possible... . At intervals I would talk and try to cheer him up, and it was honestly grand to see the way poor Cyril would try to pull himself together.'

Abertillery Cemetery
The cemetery contains five war graves:

Private Joshua Ellis of the 3rd Battalion Monmouthshire Regiment was twenty-six when he died of pneumonia on 15 September, 1914.

Private George James Kite, 8th Battalion, South Wales Borderers. Born at Timsbury, Somerset, he resided in Crumlin and died 18 April, 1917.

Private R. Pascoe, 10th Battalion, South Wales Borderers and husband of Selina A. Pascoe of 99 Alexandra Road, Six Bells, Abertillery. Private Pascoe died, aged thirty-seven, on 29 January, 1920 having been gassed in France.

Private William Charles Smith served with the Welsh Guards and lived at 27 Penygraig Terrace, Aberbeeg. He returned home having been wounded on the Western Front and subsequently died, aged twenty-four, on 18 January, 1919.

Private Tom Thomas, 1st Battalion, Royal Welsh Fusiliers. Born in Neath, Glamorgan he died on 5 October, 1915, from wounds received on the Western Front. He was aged twenty-five.

BASSALEG

St Basil Parish Church

Inscribed over the lych gate to the churchyard are the words -

To The Honoured Memory Of The Men Of Duffryn, Graig And Rogerstone. They Were As A Wall Unto Us By Night And Day. 1914-1919.

Erected in 1926, the gate has two bronze panels, one either side of the entrance, and these bear the names of seventy-nine soldiers from the First World War and twenty-nine from the Second.

Left panel: This begins with the words -

In Honoured Memory Of The Men of Duffryn, Graig And Rogerstone Who Gave Their Lives In The Two World Wars.

James Arkinstall, Jim Bailey, Arthur Beeston, Fred. W. Beeston, Albert E. Berry, Wilfred Berry, William R. Blackwell, W.G. Courtney Bowen, Francis W. Buttle, George E. Champion, Alfred H. Collings, Timothy Connors, Charles G. Cooling, Stanley Court, Charles Cross, George Dabbs, Noet T. Daniel, Algernon Daniels, Edwin J. Davidge, A. Reginald Davies, D. Robert Davies, Robert E. Davies, Thomas C. Davies, John Dawson, William J. Deakin, Alexander Dillion, Ernest Dorking, W. Reginald Edwards, Frederick Evans, William H. Evans, John Fletcher, Stanley Ford, Christopher Griffiths, Alfred Harding, Alfred Haycock, William Hopkins, Stanley Jackson, George F. James, Harry S. John, David Jones, Frank W. Jones, Percy Jones, William H. Jones, Sidney St.C. King, George Lewis, Samuel Llewellyn, Thomas J. Lloyd, Sidney Long, John J. Millwater, Fred Morgan, Hugh Morgan, Ernest S. Parrish.

Right panel: Emlyn M. Powell, Leonard Price, Ashwell Rees, Theophilus G. Rees, Francis B. Ridout, Edwin Roberts, Fred Robinson, Edward Rowland, J. Basil P. Simms, Arthur Sisam, Sidney E. Smith, Henry Smithers, Albert Solkett, A. Augustine Sullivan, F. Cyril Taylor, Frederick T. Theobold, Edward R. Turner, David Walters, Sidney G. West, James White, L. Meredith Whitney, Charles J. Wilkie, Isaac Williams, Melville Williams, William Williams, Ivor C. Woolcock, Harry Woolrich. The panel concludes with the 1939-1945 names and the words - *We Will Remember Them.*

On the north wall of the church, the Commanding Officer and founder of the 17th Battalion, Welsh Regiment, Lieutenant-Colonel Charles Joseph Wilkie, is commemorated by a stained glass window. This shows the figures of St. George, St. David and St. Michael and bears the inscription -

Erected By The Officers, Non-Commissioned Officers And Men Of The 17th Welsh Regiment In Memory Of Their Original Expeditionary Force And Their Commanding Officer Lieut-Colonel Charles Joseph Wilkie Formerly Captain In The Oxford & Bucks 52nd L.I. He Served In The Tirah Campaign & In France & Was Killed In Action At Maroc Near Lens On Octr. 16th In The Year Of Our Lord 1916.

Colonel Wilkie lived at 'Derwallt', Rogerstone.

Below, and either side of the window there are large brass plates recording the names, ranks and numbers of the two hundred and fifty-eight officers and men of the Battalion who were killed.

Lych gate memorial, St Basil's Parish Church.

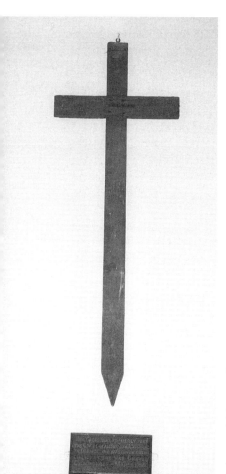

Centre plate: This begins with the dedication -

To The Glory Of God In Memory Of The Officers And Men Of The 17th Battalion The Welch Regt. Who Fell During The Great War 1914-1918.

Lieutenant-Colonel Charles Joseph Wilkie; Major Henry Percy Bright Gough, MC; Captains Percy Hier Davies, Clifford Martyn Dunn, Austin Joyce Elmitt, MC, William John Griffiths, MC, Frederick Stewart Higson, MC, Charles Vyvyan Lyne, Percy Kemp Ruttley, Colin Turner Young; Lieutenants John Collin Ensor, John Lawrence Hughes, Arthur Trevor Jones, Charles O`Malley, William Woolf; Second-Lieutenants Hubert Percy Andrew Bailey, Ernest Burtonwood, Arthur John Franklin, Greville Howard Hobby, Gerald Radcliffe Jackman, Victor Trevor Jones, Kelyth Pierce Lloyd Williams, John Harold Tudor Mathias, Robert Stuart McCartney, Hugh Neil O`Donnell, Leslie Andrew Tugby.

Left plate, 1st column: 55854 Private Stanley Baker Acres, 51668 Private Herbert Leslie Adams, 55852 Private Frank Amos, 46268 Lance-Corporal Thomas Edward Arthur, 37292 Private John Ashton, 26466 Private Fred William Atherton, 53748 Private Albert Edward Baldwin, 37849 Private John Banfield, 8138 Private William Alfred Baker, 25604

Marker cross from the grave of an unknown soldier buried in France. St Basil's Parish Church, Bassaleg.

Private Samuel Beddow, 51287 Private Frank Berry, 25602 Private Ernest Beynon, 25433 Lance-Corporal Thomas Boyland, 30161 Private Frank Brimble, 55132 Private Charles John Brown, 61021 Private William Brown, 48198 Private Bert Bucknell, 63665 Private Harold Budge, 28998 Private Ernest Jos Burrows, Private 51737 Alfred Ernest Burton, 26134 Sergeant Herbert Charles Caines, 25521 Private Henry Vincent Calkin, 46599 Private James Carroll, 54330 Private Charles Reginald Carswell, 25179 Sergeant Thomas Caswell, 25395 Lance-Corporal David Robert Chard, 36012 Private Charles William Clarke, 32591 Private Ernest Clarke, 291409 Private Fred. Clegg, 17433 Lance-Corporal Owen John Clement, 44192 Private George Cole, 54332 Private Phillip William Cole, 35443 Private Issaac Collins, 25511 Private John Ed. Collins, 26444 Private Alfred Cox, 63459 Private Frederick Cridge, 18161 Private William Cudby, 9119 Private James Cudby, 26078 Private William Curnock, 61043 Private George Cannon, 26334 Private Archibald Davies, 33342 Private Daniel Davies, 25987 Private David Davies, 202947 Private Evan Eph. Davies, 60713 Private George Hy. Davies, 25950 Private Harry Davies, 25219 Private John Davies, 1230 Lance-Sergeant John Elias Davies, 25471 Lance-Corporal John William Davies, 30652 Private Thomas Davies, 50558 Private Fred. Peter Deloghe, 47543 Private John Vincent Dornan, 26162 Private Patrick Downing, 54082 Private John Drew, 25897 Private Richard Edwards, 50547 Private George Ellis, 26172 Private Ebenezer Evans, 54080 Private Ivor Evans.

Left plate, 2nd column: 48589 Private Meredith Evans, 202658 Private Thomas Evans, 25481 Lance-Corporal Thomas Richard Evans, 55940 Private Arthur Edward Eyre, 25862 Private John Feaver, 26146 Lance-Corporal George Flack, 25824 Private Ivor Follett, 25786 Private Victor Thomas Ford, 25711 Private James Fowler, 54338 Lance-Corporal Joseph P. Fowler, 54034 Lance-Corporal Albert E. Godsell, 25507 Corporal James Gordon, 56980 Private Walter Gravenor, 25892 Sergeant George Gregory, 26476 Corporal Alfred Griffiths, 26088 Lance-Corporal John Griffiths, 60899 Private Ernest Grime, 44438 Private Edwin Hale, 32985 Lance-Corporal John Halford, 26198 Private Thomas Hanson, 25060 Private Ebenezer Harris, 57160 Private William Harrison, 25977 Sergeant Thomas Hawkins, 25343 Lance-Corporal Harold Higgins, 8867 Private William Highgate, 21909 Sergeant Trevor Hobby, 24118 Private Frederick Hole, 46417 Private Fred. Holland, 60729 Private Arthur H. Hollowood, 25387 Private Albert Hosking, 25033 Private William John Howell, 266782 Private Walter John Howells, 25078 Private Messach P. Hughes, 26467 Private William John Hughes, 37843 Private Harry Hunt, 43355 Private Hohn T. Ishmael, 25235 Private David William James, 54065 Private Lewis James, 44331 Private Thomas Henry James, 26206 Private Frederick Jenkins, 44267 Private William David Jenkins, 37848 Lance-Corporal Albert Jones, 25398 Private Allan David Jones, 44269 Private Brinley Richard Jones, 25246 Private Charles Thomas Jones, 8775 Private David Jones, 46609 Private David John Jones, 46342 Private Harold Glyn Jones, 26200 Private Henry Thomas Jones, 25488 Private Herbert Jones, 26381 Private John Jones, 46405 Private John Jones, 202667 Private John William Jones, 25042 Private Lewis Jones, 19293 Private Morgan Jones, 202955 Private Richard W. Jones, 46326 Private Thomas Rees Jones, 26035 Private James Kedward.

Right plate, 1st column: 54616 Private Albert Kendal, 46341 Private William James Kirby, 26219 Private Charles Langdon, 26068 Private Arthur S. Larcombe, 54075 Private Arthur James Lewis, 25222 Private Arthur Rufus Lewis, 17403

Private Daniel Lewis, 25705 Private Tudor Richard Lewis, 32669 Private Francis L. Lippett, 266712 Private John Lloyd, 25659 Private Thomas James Lowe, 25657 Private Thomas John Lytton, 57070 Private John Henry Mills, 25376 Private John James Mills, 290154 Private Charles Millward, 2763 Private William John Minton, 26234 Private Allan Morgan, 46102 Private Levi Richard Morris, 35084 Private William John Moses, 25530 Private Edward Mack, 46607 Lance-Corporal Albert Mallet, 55257 Private Montagu Matthews, 25106 Lance-Corporal Samuel Matthews, 25895 Private Thomas Maynes, 25934 Private Ernest N. Merrett, 46368 Private Alfred Merritt, 27472 Private Daniel Nelmes, 23035 Sergeant John Owen, 202669 Private John Owen Owen, 26249 Private William Charles Owen, 202670 Private William Glynne Owen, 39732 Private Owen Owens, 54354 Private James Parker, 26023 Private Harry Parkes, 18150 Lance-Sergeant Jonathan Parry, 25753 Private Owen Parry, 25280 Sergeant Edwin Parsons, 26492 Private William Parsons, 25457 Private Oswald Payne, 10807 Private William Peggrem, 25421 Sergeant Alex John Perry, 25469 Lance-Corporal John Perry, 51562 Private George Peters, 54113 Private Benjamin Phillips, 54084 Private Richard Thomas Phillips, 60956 Private Charles Pletts, 35131 Private James Victor Porter, 25957 Private David Powell, 26255 Sergeant Percy Powell, 45025 Private David John Price, 26029 Private John Price, 285124 Private John Priddy, 54087 Private John Pritchard, 202931 Private John Pughe, 24322 Private William Ralph, 25817 Private Alfred Rasman, 25420 Private Phillip John Rees, 25879 Private William John Rees.

Right plate, 2nd column: 25144 Sergeant William Rees Richards, 37865 Corporal Enoch Rist, 26349 Private Thomas Roberts, 53633 Private Thomas Roberts, 37494 Private William Roberts, 46267 Private William Roberts, 26388 Lance-Corporal Frank Rogers, 61085 Private Percy Rowley, 47501 Private Henry Samuel, 45286 Private Herbert E. Savage, 63259 Private Charles Seabourne, 26278 Private Albert Thomas Seal, 63710 Private Thomas Seddon, 25803 Private Albert Shepherd, 26281 Private Reginald Sheppard, 14226 Private John Henry Smith, 26479 Private John Spear, 61095 Private Francis Stafford, 26034 Private William Stanton, 25129 Private Samuel Starr, 25876 Private Llewellyn Stephens, 54372 Private W. Studholme, 56810 Private Frank Taylor, 25456 Corporal Harry Taylor, 60943 Private Peter Taylor, 26931 Private Gwilym Thomas, 54088 Private John Thomas, 25059 Private William Thomas, 26494 Private William Thomas, 202218 Private William James Thomas, 37828 Private Arthur Thompson, 16466 Private Arthur W. Thompson, 25189 Private William John Tobin, 202664 Private George Hy. Tompkins, 26027 Private John Trott, 202517 Private David Vaughan, 25127 Private Matthew Vaughan, 37804 Private Charles Walch, 24410 Private Timothy Whelton, 61108 Private Jack Wilkinson, 25577 Private Edwin John Williams, 47222 Private Herbert A.P. Williams, 26380 Private John Williams, 26118 Private Thomas Williams, 46255 Private Thomas Charles Williams, 267123 Private Thomas Henry Williams, 25475 Private William Williams, 266602 Private John Wilson, 23473 Private John B. Wilson, 202954 Private Edward Wood, 26350 Private William Wood, 58524 Private Edwin G. Woodman, 13439 Private Alfred Woods, 37900 Private Samuel Walley, 44825 Lance-Corporal Frank H. Walling, 30898 Private William Webber, 54379 Private Walter Webley, 63723 Wilfred Yardley.

On the wall just inside the entrance to the church is a plain wooden cross above a small plaque inscribed -

This Cross Was Formally Over The Grave Of An Unknown Soldier In France, And Was Given To The Church By The War Graves Commission - March 1930.

Four men of the First World War who were killed and buried in France are commemorated on the headstones of family graves within the churchyard. Second-Lieutenant William Jordan, 45th Squadron, Royal Flying Corps was killed while flying near St Omer, France on 8 November, 1916, and buried in Longuenesse Souvenier Cemetery. Rifleman James Arkinstall of the 1st Battalion, Monmouthshire Regiment died, aged eighteen, on 25 April, 1915 and Wilfred Berry, a member of 1st Royal Welsh Fusiliers, was killed on 25 September, 1915 at the age of nineteen. The last man, George Frederic James was thirty when he was killed on 15 May, 1916 while serving with the 6th South Wales Borderers.

There are two war graves in the churchyard, each with private headstones. Private Albert Edward Berry of the South Wales Borderers, who was born in Graig and awarded the Military Medal while serving with 'D' Company, 6th Battalion. He was twenty-four when he died on 23 September, 1918. Private Frank Wyndham Jones, also of the South Wales Borderers, who was wounded in France on 9 May, 1915 died at home, aged twenty-five, on 6 January, 1918.

BEDWAS

A stone pillar inscribed - *Erected To The Proud Memory Of The Men Of Bedwas & Trethomas Who Gave Their Lives In The Great War 1914-1918* - is situated in front of the Bedwas and Machen Urban District Council building in Newport Road. There are fifty-three names, each with rank and regiment, engraved into the stone-work:

Private G. Alcot, Welsh Regiment; Private J.H. Bright, Royal Army Service Corps; Corporal E. Brooks, Machine Gun Corps; Driver F.J. Brooks, Royal Field Artillery; Corporal A. Bundy, South Wales Borderers; Private J. Burt, Border Regiment; Private W.E. Cornish, South Wales Borderers; Sapper T.J. Davies, Royal Engineers; Private E.C. Dorking, Welsh Regiment; Private B. Evans, South Wales Borderers; Private W.G. Geeves, South Wales Borderers; Private F. Gilbert, Welsh Regiment; Private J. Havvock, Welsh Regiment; Lieutenant G.W. Hirst, King's Liverpool Regiment; Sergeant B. Holt, Welsh Regiment; Pioneer J. Horle, Royal Engineers; Private A.I. John, Machine Gun Corps; Private T. Jones, Welsh Regiment; Sapper T.M. Jones, Royal Engineers; Gunner A. Kimber, Royal Field Artillery; Private J. Lawerance, South Wales Borderers; Private H. Lee, Royal Welsh Fusiliers; Sergeant Major H. Manning, Indian Army; Private G. Marklove, Welsh Guards; Private J. Meyrick, East Kent Regiment; Company Sergeant Major W. Mitchener, South Wales Borderers; Rifleman W. Morgan, 1st Monmouthshire Regiment; Private W. Morgan, Oxfordshire and Buckinghamshire Light Infantry; Gunner D. Morris, Royal Garrison Artillery; Private T. Moyniham, Royal Munster Fusiliers; Corporal M. Macarty, Royal Munster Fusiliers; Private D. Nelmes, Welsh Regiment; Corporal G. Nicholas, Royal Engineers; Private A. Orchard, Welsh Regiment; Lance-Corporal S.L. Passmore, Welsh Regiment; Bombardier J.W. Peasey, Royal Field Artillery; Gunner F. Phipps, Royal Field Artillery; Private W. Prebble, London Regiment; Private T. Price, Welsh Guards; Private S. Purslow, Welsh Regiment; Signaller H. Rees, Royal Navy; Private W. Reynolds, Welsh Regiment; Lieutenant J.T. Richards,

6th Welsh Regiment; Private T. Richards, South Wales Borderers; Rifleman A. Roberts, 1st Monmouthshire Regiment; Signaller T.E. Roberts, King's Shropshire Light Infantry; Lance-Corporal S. Rose, Royal Welsh Fusiliers; Private W. Smith, South Wales Borderers; Private W. Vaughn, Devonshire Regiment; Driver A. Watts, Royal Field Artillery; Private E. White, Welsh Guards; Lance-Corporal S. Witts, South Wales Borderers; Private J. Williams, South Wales Borderers.

Company Sergeant Major William Mitchener won the Distinguished Conduct Medal with the 5th Battalion, South Wales Borderers and was killed in France on 30 May, 1918. His name also appears on the memorial at Trethomas.

An additional tablet bearing the names of those killed during the Second World War is located at the foot of the pillar.

St Barrwg's Parish Church
On the west wall of the church, an oak tablet with gold lettering records the names of those who were killed below the inscription -

Remembered With Love And Honour The Men Of The Parish Who Gave Their Lives In The Great War 1914-1919.

There are forty-nine names, each without rank or regiment, arranged in two columns:

Left column: G. Alcot, J.H. Bright, E. Brooks, P.J. Brooks, A. Bundy, J. Burt, W.E. Cornish, B. Evans, W.C. Greves, P. Gilbert, J. Havvock, G.W. Hirst, B. Holt, J. Horle, A.I. John, T. Jones, A. Kimber, J. Lawrance, H. Lee, H. Manning, G. Marklove, J. Meyrick, M. Morgan, W. Morgan, D. Morris.

Right column: T. Moynihan, D. Nelmers, G. Nicholas, A. Orchard, W.T. Owen, S.L. Passmore, J.W. Percey, P. Phipps, W. Prebble, T. Price, S. Purslow, H. Rees, W. Reynolds, J.T. Richards, T. Richards, A. Roberts, T.E. Roberts, S. Rose, W. Smith, W. Vaughan, A. Watts, E. White, S. Witts, J. Williams.

The memorial ends with the words - *All You Had Hoped For, All You Had You Gave. To Save Mankind Yourselves You Scorned To Save.* The same names and dedication, this time hand written and in a wood frame, appear on the wall to the left of the memorial.

A stained glass window on the south wall of the nave has the following dedication -

To The Glory of God And In Loving Memory Of Gerald William Hirst Of The King's Regiment Who Fell On Night Patrol In Picardy Feb. 26 A.D. 1917 Aged 19 Years.

The son of William and Rachel Hirst of the Bridge House, Bedwas, Gerald Hirst was killed on the Somme, near Flers. The window included the devices and battle honours of the King's (Liverpool Regiment).

In November, 1922, a carved oak reredos was erected in memory of another local officer. On the north chancel wall, a brass plate records

To The Glory Of God And In Loving Memory of Lieut. John Thomas Richards Of Penywain Farm In This Parish, Who Made The Supreme Sacrifice In The Great War, Nov. 6th 1917, Aged 21 Years. This Reredos Is The Gift Of His Mother.

Lieutenant Richards fell in Palestine while attached to the 24th Welsh Regiment. 'In

Bedwas and Trethomas memorial outside the council building in Newport Road, Bedwas.

Window commemorating Gerald William Hirst at St Barrwg's Parish Church, Bedwas.

Oak Tablet at St Barrwg's Parish Church, Bedwas.

Remember with love and honour
the men of this parish
who gave their lives in the
Great War 1914-1919.

G. Alcot	G. Moynham
J. H. Bright	Grimes
E. Brooks	W. Nicholas
R. J. Brooks	W. Orchard
J. Bundy	W. T. Owen
J. Buri	S. L. Passmore
W. E. Cornish	T. Pracey
B. Evans	H. Phipps
D. E. Clevers	W. Prebble
T. Gilbert	S. Price
J. Haycock	R. Purslow
G. W. Hirst	H. Rees
B. Holt	W. Reynolds
Horle	E. Richards
A. J. John	Richards
C. Jones	A. Roberts
A. Kimber	G. E. Roberts
J. Lawrence	S. Rose
H. Lee	Smith
H. Manning	W. Vaughan
G. Marklove	A. Watts
J. Meyrick	E. White
W. Morgan	S. J. Williams
W. Morgan	
D. Morris	

All you had hoped for, all you had you gave,
To save Mankind yourselves you scorned to save.

the assault,' records the historian of the Welsh Regiment, 'the 24th was prominent..' and later '...constantly counter-attacked and eventually had to be withdrawn.'

The churchyard contains five war graves:

Sapper Thomas John Davies, Royal Engineers, was attached to the RE Training Centre at Newark. He was born in Machen, resided at Pontllanfraith and died on 7 December, 1916.

Gunner Stephen Friend served with 29th Brigade, Royal Field Artillery and resided at 3 Standard Villas, Trethomas. He died, aged thirty-five, on 6 July, 1920.

Sapper J.H. Ham, Royal Corps of Signals, who died on 4 March, 1921 has a Commonwealth War Graves Commission headstone made from Welsh slate.

Private William Morgan, Machine Gun Corps (Infantry). Born in Cardiff and previously served with the Oxfordshire and Buckinghamshire Light Infantry, joining that regiment in Oxford. He died, aged forty-nine, on 3 May, 1918.

Gunner David William Pritchard, of 'D' Battery, 71st Brigade, Royal Field Artillery. The son of Griffith and Mary Pritchard of 4 Tydfil Road, Bedwas, he died, aged twenty-five, on 7 July, 1921.

BEDWELLTY

St Sannan's Church

Captain John Clarke was a medical practitioner in Aberbargoed. He joined the 1st Welsh Field Ambulance (Territorial Force) at Ebbw Vale and with that unit went to Gallipoli in July, 1915. He died in the following October from wounds received during the operations at Suvla Bay and is buried there at Hill 10 Cemetery. On the north wall of the church a window in his memory has the dedication -

Erected To The Memory Of The Late Dr. John Clarke Surgeon Aberbargoed By Friends And Members Of The Rhymney Valley Medical Association

and shows the figure of Christ upon the cross. To one side is a member of the Royal Army Medical Corps and, the other, a wounded soldier. A brass plate to the left of the window gives John Clarke's age as thirty-two, his parents as William and Mary Clarke of Ballymena, County Antrim, Ireland and date of death as 9 October, 1915. The tablet was erected by -

His Colleagues Of The Rhymney Valley Medical Association As A Token Of Their Esteem And Affection To One Who Gave His Life For His Country.

A much smaller brass plaque erected by the family of Sergeant William John Haskell of the 1st Battalion, Monmouthshire Regiment is located within the window recess. This memorial notes that he died of wounds on 25 May, 1915, is buried in Boulogne (Boulogne Eastern Cemetery), and - '*Is Also Depicted In This Window*'. William Haskell was a member of the St John's Ambulance, and lived at Tynewydd Cottage, Bedwellty.

Also on the north wall, and to the right of the window, is an illuminated Roll Of Honour comprising one hundred and twenty-seven names.

Another officer to lose his life at Gallipoli was Captain John Jordan of the South Wales Borderers. A brass shield, mounted on wood, and situated on the centre column of the north isle, has the inscription below the Regimental Crest -

Memorial shield to Captain John Jordan, St Sannan's Church, Bedwellty.

Memorial window to Doctor John Clarke at St Sannan's Church, Bedwellty.

In Loving Memory Of Capt. John Jordan - S. W.B. Who Died From Wounds Received In Action In The Dardanelles June 19th 1915. Aged 45. From His Wife And Children. Nearer My God To Thee.

He was mortally wounded during the fighting at Turkey Trench.

A wooden litany desk was presented to the church by the mother of John Morgan Norris who died in No.1 Casualty Clearing Station, France on St. David's Day, 1919.

The churchyard contains fifteen First World War graves:

Private H. Baddeley, Western Command Labour Centre, Labour Corps, served under the name of Scales. He died, aged twenty-four, on 19 November, 1918.

Private Joseph Beatson, South Wales Borderers, was the son of Joseph and Dina Beatson of 22 High Street, Blackwood. He died, aged twenty-five, on 2 March, 1919.

Sapper F.C. Carter, Royal Engineers, died 5 March, 1919.

Rifleman John Davies, 13th Battalion, King's Royal Rifle Corps, was born at Trehafod, Glamorgan. He lived in Bargoed, enlisted into the army at Tonypandy and died, aged twenty-one, on 25 July, 1916 from wounds received on the Western Front.

Private D. Donovan, Royal Defence Corps, was married to Elizabeth Donovan of 81 Jubilee Road, New Tredegar. He died, aged fifty, on 17 August, 1917.

Private Ernest Frank Higgs, 16th Battalion, Welsh Regiment, was from Bargoed. He died, aged twenty-seven, on 6 August, 1916 from wounds received in France.

Gunner David Jones, 43rd Battery, Royal Field Artillery, was born in Bargoed and enlisted into the army at Newport. He died, aged twenty-four, on 11 August, 1915.

Gunner Walter Adolphus Jones, Royal Garrison Artillery, was the son of Mrs Florence Parker of 42 Railway Terrace, Hollybush, Newport. He died, aged twenty-seven, on 22 November, 1919.

Private William Jones, 24th (Works) Battalion, King's Liverpool Regiment, was born in Wrexham. He lived in Tirphil, enlisted into the army at Bargoed and had previously served in the Welsh Regiment. William Jones died, aged forty-eight, on 15 October, 1916.

Corporal Daniel E. Murphy, Royal Engineers, was married to Mrs A. Murphy of 12 Albert Street, Merthyr Tydfil. He died, aged thirty-five, on 30 October, 1915.

Private Arthur Leslie Parsons, 3rd Battalion, South Wales Borderers, was born in Melksham, Wiltshire. He lived in Blackwood, enlisted into the army at Newport and died, aged twenty-two, on 12 October, 1918.

Private John Purnell, 'D' Company, 2nd Battalion, South Wales Borderers, was born in Geligaer, Tredegar and was the son of John and Ann Purnell. He died, aged thirty-three, on 10 October, 1915 from wounds received at Gallipoli.

Private G.A. Rock, Royal Welsh Fusiliers, was the son of Mrs Mary Ann Rock. He died, aged forty-eight, on 22 January, 1918 and is buried with his wife, Jane Rock.

Private N. Schofield, Machine Gun Corps (Infantry), was married to Rachel Schofield of 12 Elm Street, Aberbargoed. He died, aged twenty-five, on 25 December, 1918.

Private Albert Thomas, 16th Battalion, Lancashire Fusiliers, was born in Penrhiwceiber, Glamorgan and the son of Isaac and Annie Louisa Thomas of Coedybrain Cottage, Aberbargoed. He died, aged nineteen, on 26 September, 1918 from wounds received on the Western Front.

Bettws High School

The memorial tablet unveiled and dedicated by the Rt Revd Bishop Crossley in the hall of the Newport High School for Boys at Queen's Hill on 30 September, 1920 was designed by an Old Boy and practising architect of Newport - Mr Godfrey Stamp. Comprising an oak frame covered in beaten brass, the memorial was headed by the inscription -

To The Glory Of God And In Grateful Remembrance Of The Old Boys Of This School Who Laid Down Their Lives In The Great War A.D. 1914-1918.

In the centre of the panel is a cross, bearing within a laurel wreath the words - *Pro Patria.* Below the cross, and between the inscription - *Greater Love Hath No Man* - the Shield and Crest from the Arms of Newport together with the School motto - *Nid Da Lle Gellir Gwell.* The frame itself was decorated with national emblems, a Rose, Shamrock, Thistle and Leek, together with an anchor, crossed rifles and outstretch wings representing the armed services.

The names of those who were killed appear on two bronze panels, one being placed below each of the arms of the cross. There are eighty names recorded, each without rank or regiment.

Left panel: H.J. Ball, P. Baulch, H. Beck, E. Brewer, G.R. Brown, C.R. Campbell, R.E. Charles, W.E. Charles, H. Charrington, A. Cox, V.C. Cox, E.F. Davies, E.T. Davies, J.H. Davies, S.R. Duncanson, V.E.S. Edwards, C.E. Evans, P.C.W. Evans, W.H. Francis, F.D. Frost, W.F. Frost, H.B. Gibbs, B. Gill, A.R. Griiffiths, F.N. Groves, T.W. Haggett, R.H. Hammett, G.P. Harding, C.M. Harrington, N.L. Harris, A.W. Hartshorne, G.H.C. Hobbs, E.C. Holloway, F.H. Howard, C.P. Howells, G.D. Howells, W.H. Huggett, W.E. Jackson, T.W. James, W.S. Jeffries.

Right panel: E.W. Jones, H.T. Jones, J.S. Laurie, J. Lawless, A.S. Lewis, W.A. Luff, A.C. Moore, E.F.T. Morgan, G.L. Morris, N.C. Newland, W.B. Nightingale, A.D. Oliver, W.T. O'Connor, C.H. Owen, E. Pickett, F.R. Portnell, R.W. Price, C.M. Pritchard, J.M. Probert, W.G. Redshaw, C.N. Reed, A.R. Rees, A.C. Rogers, L.B. Simmonds, F.L. Spencer, S.H. Stevens, F.G. Sykes, E.R. Taylor, L. Taylor, T.A. Thomas, R.W. Thompson, E. Vaughan, O.T. Watkins, C. Welbirg, L. Wilkinson, E.H. Williams, F.J. Williams, I.G. Williams, L.D. Williams, G.P. Wright.

On 8 December, 1944 a fire destroyed the hall and much of the main building, including the First World War memorial. Rescued from the tragedy, however, were the two bronze name plaques and these were taken to St Mark's Church in Gold Tops for safe keeping. It was not until 1952 that a new memorial was erected in the restored school hall by the Old Boys Association. This time it was in the form of an organ and commemorated the fallen of both First and Second World Wars. A metal plate bears the inscription -

Newport High School For Boys - To The Glory Of God And In Remembrance Of Those Members Of This School Who Gave Their Lives In The Two World Wars - 1914-1918 - 1939-1945.

The dedication and unveiling ceremony of the organ was led by the Rt Revd The

Lord Bishop of Monmouth and took place on Friday 4 July. Just over two years later, on 7 November, 1954, two new bronze plaques bearing the names of those killed in both wars were placed either side of the organ. Four additional names - Arthur Ewart Bamford, John James Ellis, George Williams Hastings and John Crawford Wylie, had been added to the First World War list, making a total of eighty-four.

When Bettws High School was opened in the summer of 1972 a number of items from Queen's Hill, the old school having been closed, were lodged in its care. Included were the two new memorial plaques and organ, which were placed at the rear of the stage in the school hall. Towards the end of 1999, however, the plaques were moved to a new location in St Mark's Church.

Original memorial at Newport High School for Boys. Destroyed by fire on 8 December 1944, except for the two metal name-plates which are now held at St Mark's Church.

Organ installed at the Newport High School for Boys in 1952. Now in the care of Bettws High School.

BLACKWOOD

Unveiled in November, 1926, the Blackwood cenotaph in Pentwyn Avenue bears the inscription - *To The Memory Of The Men Of This Town Who Fell Serving Their Country 1914-1918 - 1939-1945*. The names of those who were killed appear, without rank or regiment, on a cast-iron panel, forty-three for the First World War: - W. Baker, J. Butler, W.J. Carey, O. Coles, J. East, O. Ebdon, A. Evans, C. Firr, J.H. Goodyear, S. Guest, W.R. Gwatkin, P.J. Gwilt, W.C. Halse, S.J. Hambleton, A.J. Harris, W.G. Hughes, R.T. Hutton, W.D. James, W. Jeanes, W.J. Jenkins, G.P. Jones, J.W. Jones, H.S. Lewis, S. Lewis, A. Meek, W. Milton, T.J. Morgan, W.J. Nethercott, H.N. Overton, H.G. Phillips, T. Price, A.E. Roberts, W.W. Smith, G.H. Snelgrove, J.H. Spence, A.R. Stephens, R. Stephens, W.J. Stokes, S. Walton, L.W. Watkins, A. Williams, A. Williams, T. Williams - and thirty-nine for the Second. Blackwood was the headquarters of 'H' Company, 1st Battalion, Monmouthshire Regiment (Territorial Force).

Blackwood cenotaph.

BLAENAVON

On 16 May, 1931 the foundation stone for a memorial clock tower was laid by Major-General Lord Treowen, CB, CMG, Lord Lieutenant of Monmouthshire, next to The Working Mens Institute in High Street, Blaenavon. The site was previously occupied by a captured German field gun which until then had served as a memento of the war. Unveiled by Colonel P.G. Pennymore, DSO, TD in the following November, the four-faced Portland stone tower incorporates a bronze panel inscribed -

> *Pro Patria - In Proud And Grateful Memory Of Those Men Of Blaenavon Who, Having Suffered Many Hardships And Dangers Finally Laid Down Their Lives In The Great War 1914-1918. This Memorial Is Erected By The People Of Blaenavon.*

Blaenavon was the headquarters of 'E' Company, 2nd Battalion, Monmouthshire Regiment (Territorial Force).

One hundred and fourteen men are recorded without rank or regiment. The names being arranged on the panel in three equal columns of thirty-eight.

1st column: - R. Ackroyd, H. Allcock, C. Andrews, G. Archer, J. Bailey, N.J. Baker, T. Barnes, A. Birkin, R. Bisp, J. Bourne, C.C. Brown, A.E. Burchell, L. Caddick, F. Caines, B. Carey, C. Catley, R. Clark, N. Clothier, F. Cook, F.J. Cudbey, N.B. Dancey, T.D. Dancey, A. Dando, R. Daniel, A. Davies, J. Davies, J.H. Davies,

Memorial clock tower at Blaenavon.

A. Dirkin, J.E. Edmonds, E.J. Eilson, D. Falvey, A. Filer, J. Gibson, E.J. Goodall, W. Goodall, W.H. Goodwin, J. Griffiths, E.J. Gulliford.

2nd column: E. Hadley, W. Hannaford, D. Harrington, G. Harris, W. Hart, A. Hill, J. Hill, W.J. Hill, D. Hirst, S. Holvey, W.G. Hopkins, I.J. Howells, W. Howells, D.J. Huish, R. Hurle, D.J. Jenkins, J. Jenkins, P.A. Jenkins, A. Jones, T.B. Jones, I. Jones, J.T. Jones, W. Jones, A.J. Kenvin, W. King, A.J. Lewis, E. Lewis, E.A. Lewis, G. Lewis, H. Lewis, J. Lewis, E. Mathews, D. Meredith, W.H. Miles, E. Morgan, T.H. Morgan, W. Morris, T.E. Nelmes.

3rd column: J. Nicholls, B. Parry, G. Parsons, C. Phipps, F.L. Pocock, O. Pointer, E.C. Preece, J. Price, T. Price, J.L. Pryce, J. Pugh, A. Redman, M. Regan, W.T. Reynolds, A. Roberts, J. Saunders, H. Shaw, H. Smith, T. Smith, I.E. Taylor, F. Thomas, J.L. Thomas, O. Thomas, S. Thomas, J.H. Tibbs, S. Vaughan, A. Whittaker, E. Wicks, A. Williams, D.J. Williams, R.J. Williams, T.G. Williams, T.J. Williams, W.A. Williams, W. Williams, W.J. Williams, H. Winwood and J. Woods.

Above these are four further names - Lieutenant-Colonel Maurice Nichol Kennard, who commanded the 18th West Yorkshire Regiment and was awarded the

Military Cross. He was killed 1 July, 1916 on the Somme; Major E.W. Edwards; Lieutenant John Paton Worton whose family home was at 48 Cwmavon Road, Blaenavon lost his life, aged twenty-four, during the fighting at Frezenberg Ridge on 8 May, 1915, and Company Sergeant Major Auron Letton of the 1st Battalion, South Wales Borderers. He was killed near Passchendaele during the 10 November, 1917 attack on the Goudberg Spur. Later, another panel was added to the memorial to commemorate those who died in the Second World War, and in 1979 a single name - that of Private J.A. Jones who was killed in Northern Ireland.

Blaenavon Cemetery
The cemetery contains one war grave. That of Sergeant Charles Harris, 'D' Battery, 62nd Brigade, Royal Field Artillery, who died on 19 May, 1917 from wounds received on the Western Front.

BLAINA

The new memorial in the park and sports ground at Surgery Road, Blaina, bears the inscription in both Welsh and English -

New memorial to the men and women of Nantyglo and Blaina at the sports ground, Surgery Road, Blaina.

Remember The Love Of Them Who Came Not Home From The Wars - To The Glory Of God And In Memory Of The Men And Women Of Nantyglo And Blaina Who Gave Their Lives In The Service Of Our Country.

Blaina was the headquarters of 'H' Company, 3rd Battalion, Monmouthshire Regiment. A piece of local stone rests on a paved platform, around the four sides of which black marble panels bear the names of those who were killed. There are one hundred and fifty names inscribed for the First World War by order of rank:

Captains: F.H.V. Bevan, J. Lancaster, J.H. Lewis.

Lieutenants: C.H. Adney (awarded Military Cross), A. Poulaine, W.H. Sutton, S.N. Williams.

Cadet: C.J.E. Jones.

Petty-Officer: W. Broome.

Company Sergeant Majors: G. Gomery, D.G. James.

Sergeants: R.J. Clarke, J. Gregson, W. Turner.

Corporals: G. Garbeth, E. Hunt, T.D. James, T.J. Williams.

Lance-Corporals: T.R. Allen, F. Andrews, G. Beck, I. Cole, G.H. Darvill, W.T. Keylock (awarded Military Medal), J. Pearce, J.H. Wilton.

Trooper: J.F. Williams.

Bombardier: H. Dimmick.

Drivers: G. Burton, W. Cook.

Gunners: W.H. Davies, G. Jones, W.H. Price.

Sappers: E.J. Maidment, R. Wills.

Able-Seaman: W.G. Phillips.

Air-Mechanic: C. Davies.

Ordinary-Seamen: F. Jeremiah, H. Willbert.

Privates: A. Abrahams, M.S. Austin, G. Baker, F.S. Bennet, A. Bond, J. Booth, T. Broughey, I. Britton, F.J. Brooks, S. Burton, T. Calvert, W. Carey, W.E. Carter, J. Chivers, W. Clark, W.H. Clarke, H. Compton, C. Corbett, E. Daniels, L. Davies, W.E. Davies (awarded Military Medal), A. Dimmick, W. Dimmick, F.W. Eacups, W.E. Earney, W. Edmunds, L. Edwards, P. Eustace, W.A. Evans, F. Fisher, T. Fletcher, F.W. Fowler, W. Fowler, T. Francis, G. Gittings, A. Gore, F. Hathaway, R. Hayes, G. Herrington, W.G. Hodges, W. Holder, E. Hole, A. Hughes, R. Isaac, S.C. James, F. Jeffreys, H.J. Jelly, W. Jenkins, W. John, F. Johncey, D. Jones, D.T. Jones, J. Jones, W. Jones, R.J. Kibble, J. Langley, W.J. Le Visconte, F.H. Lockstone, H.A. Lynes, J. Morden, D. Morgan, F.W. Morgan, T.L. Morgan, W. Morgan, W. Morgan, E. Morris, W. Morris, F.S. Newman, D. O'Brien, M. Osland, J. Padfield, R. Paul, A. Payne, J. Phillips, E.J. Powell, J.S. Price, W. Price, C. Pritchard, J. Pritchard, T. Prosser, W.H. Prosser, C. Pugh, S. Ralph, H. Richards, G.H. Riddle, E.J. Roberts, R. Rogers, E.C. Rowberry, D. Rowlands, C. Seymour, J.R. Sheargold, D. Smith, E. Smith, G. Smith, R. Smith, H. Sydenham, H. Teague, J. Thomas, J. Thomas, M.H. Thomas, T. Tuck, W.J. Turner, W.J. Vaughan, G. Wait, A. Walker, A.G. Weaver, F.J. Williams, G. Williams, W.T. Williams, E. Wiltshire, A. Wiltshire.

The memorial also includes the names of those who fell in the Second World War, and one soldier who was killed in Northern Ireland.

CAERLEON

The town memorial was dedicated on 29 May, 1921 and unveiled by the Commanding Officer of the 1st Monmouthshire Regiment, Lieutenant-Colonel C.A. Evill, DSO, TD. It was originally located at the junction of High and Cross Streets and moved to its present site, at the Memorial Gardens, High Street, in 1966. The gardens are situated next to the Town Hall. This building was formally the drill hall of the Caerleon Detachment, 1st Battalion, Monmouthshire Regiment. The memorial is made from Cornish granite, with bronze tablets, and takes the form of a lamp standard with drinking fountain. It bears the inscription -

In Grateful Remembrance This Memorial Was Erected By The Inhabitants Of Caerleon & District To The Memory Of The Men Who Fell In The Great War 1914-1919.

For Caerleon itself, there are twenty-eight names inscribed, six officers, by order of rank, then other ranks, which are arranged alphabetically. The officers are - Major Oswald Williams of the 1st Monmouthshire Regiment, who was killed on 13 October, 1915 at the Hohenzollern Redoubt near Loos; Captain Edmund Brewer of the 12th Battalion, South Wales Borderers, mortally wounded in January, 1918 while on patrol near Bullecourtand; Captain J. Llewellin Mansell, a regular soldier who served with the 7th Dragoon Guards in South Africa and was killed while leading a charge near Festubert on 20 December, 1914; Lieutenant W. Herbert and Second-Lieutenant Victor Stewart, both officers with the 1st Monmouthshire, and Lieutenant Leonard Williams, 1st South Wales Borderers.

Of the other ranks recorded, eight served with the 1st Monmouthshire Regiment - Riflemen Percy Baulch, who is buried in the churchyard at St. Cadoc`s, Edward Bowden, Albert Horton, Will Jones, George Lewis, Frank Moseley, J.H. Norris and Percy Scannell. Private Alfred J. Boulton served with the 10th York and Lancaster; Private Richard Cooke, 5th South Wales Borderers; Able-Seaman Mervyn Defries, the Mercantile Marine; Private Harry G. Hamblyn, 4th South Wales Borderers; Private Evan Hopkins, 6th South Wales Borderers; Corporal Charles Jones, 2nd South Wales Borderers; Private Harry Jones, 2nd Manchesters; Private Edgar Morgan, 13th Cheshire Regiment; Private Lewis Phillips, 6th South Wales Borderers; Lance-Corporal Fred Richards, 2nd Manchesters; Private Harold G. Stretton, 6th Queen's Own Royal West Kent Regiment; Private Horace B. White, Lancashire Fusiliers; Private John A. Williams, 9th Cheshire and Bombardier W. Wollen the Royal Marine Light Infantry.

The sections for the near parishes of Caerleon-Ultra-Pontem, Ponthir and Llanhennock provide a further thirty names:

Caerleon-Ultra-Pontem: Captain Leslie Phillips, 1st Welsh Regiment; Captain Stanley Spittle, Lieutenant Edward S. Phillips, Riflemen Albert Griffiths, Reginald Jeffries and Albert White, all of the 1st Monmouthshire; Private Benjamin Danks, 4th Welsh; Pioneer W.C. Dyment, Royal Engineers; Private Frederick Pattimore, Dorsetshire Regiment; a military policeman - Corporal Albert Rawlings and Able-Seaman Arthur Tooze of HMS *Revenge*.

Ponthir: Of the fourteen Ponthir men, four served with the Monmouthshire Regiment - Major Edmund S. Williams, 1st Battalion; Privates Samuel Berrow,

Town memorial outside old Drill Hall in High Street, Caerleon.

Memorial to the men of Caerleon parish at St Cadoc's Church.

Memorial window and dedication plaque to Oswald and Leonard Williams. Caerleon Catholic Church.

One of two dedication tablets inside the lych gate at St Cadoc's Church, Caerleon.

TO THE GLORY OF GOD
AND IN
SACRED MEMORY OF THE
UNDERMENTIONED OFFICERS
NON COMMISSIONED OFFICERS
AND MEN OF THE PARISH OF
CAERLEON WHO GAVE THEIR
LIVES DURING THE GREAT WAR
1914-1919

PERCY BAULCH	1st MONMOUTHS
WILLIAM BENNETT	S.S. ADRIATIC
ALFRED BOLTON	10th Y & LANCS
EDMUND BREWER	CAPT R GLOS YEO
RICHARD COOK	S.W. BORDERERS
HAROLD C COLLINS	ROYAL ENGINEERS
MERVYN DEFRIES	S.S. ADRIATIC
HARRY HAMER	6th D GUARDS
THOMAS W HERBERT	CAPT G DEW R E S
EVAN HOPKINS	S.W. BORDERERS
FREDERICK B JAMES	R.F.A.
CHARLES JONES	24 Bn S.W. BORD
IVOR SAMUEL JONES	CANADIAN CON
HARRY JONES	8th MANCHESTERS
WILLIAM JONES	1st MONMOUTHS
GEORGE LEWIS	1st MONMOUTHS
FRANCIS J S MACKWORTH	BRIGADE MAJ R A
FRANK MOSELEY	R E MONMOUTHS
JOHN HERBERT NORRIS	S.W. BORDERERS
J R NICOLLE	ROYAL ENGINEERS
FREDERICK A PATTIMORE	1st DORSETS
LEWIS PHILLIPS	S.W. BORDERERS
FREDERICK RICHARDS	R.A.F.
W VICTOR STEWART	1/3rd MONMOUTHS
PERCY SCANNELL	R MONMOUTHS
HAROLD G STRETTON	R W R REGT
ARTHUR O WILLIAMS	CHESHIRE REGT
OSWALD WILLIAMS	11th E S W BORD
OSCAR WHITE	24th MONMOUTHS
HORACE WHITE	LAM ASHIRE FUS
WILLIAM HOWLAND	R.A.F.

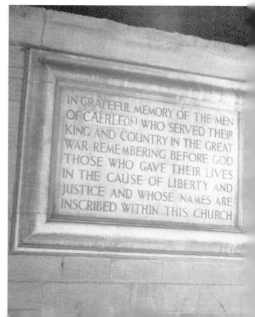

IN GRATEFUL MEMORY OF THE MEN
OF CAERLEON WHO SERVED THEIR
KING AND COUNTRY IN THE GREAT
WAR REMEMBERING BEFORE GOD
THOSE WHO GAVE THEIR LIVES
IN THE CAUSE OF LIBERTY AND
JUSTICE AND WHOSE NAMES ARE
INSCRIBED WITHIN THIS CHURCH

Edwin S. John and George Max Jarrett with the 2nd. Lieutenant Rupert Pilliner was killed while serving with the Royal Field Artillery; Second-Lieutenant Henry H. Stevens, the Royal Air Force; Lance-Corporal Albert Cording, 1st King's Shropshire Light Infantry; Gunners Arthur Cording and Sidney Daleymount, Royal Field Artillery; Private Phillip Ivor Lester, South Wales Borderers; Private Thomas E. Nicholls, King's Liverpools; Private Edward Roberts, South Wales Borderers; Quartermaster Sergeant Glyn Rowlands, Labour Corps and Private Alec Wheeler, South Wales Borderers.

Llanhennock: The remaining names on the memorial, those from the Llanhennock area, are - Major Francis J.A. Mackworth, Royal Field Artillery; Lieutenant Arthur C.P. Mackworth, of the 13th Battalion, Rifle Brigade, who died from illness and is buried in Holy Cross Cemetery, Oxford; Private Frank Harrhy, 10th Royal Welsh Fusiliers; Signaller John Alfred Jones, who served with the 1/19th London Regiment, and a member of the 2/7th (Cyclist) Battalion, Welsh Regiment - Private Reginald A. Nicholas.

Caerleon Catholic Church
The Church of Saints Julios, Aaron and David in High Street, Caerleon, has a stained glass window commemorating two local officers. A brass plaque below being inscribed -

> *To The Glory Of God In Thanksgiving For The Triumph Of Justice And In Memory Of Two Brothers Who Gave Their Lives. Major Oswald Michael Williams - 1st Monmouthshire Regt. - Killed In Action At The Hohenzollern Redoubt - 13th October 1915. R.I.P. - Lieutenant Leonard Williams 1st South Wales Borderers - Killed In Action Near La Bassée - 11 September 1915. R.I.P.*

Les Hughes and John Dixon record in their history of the 1st Monmouthshire, *Surrender Be Damned*, how Second in Command Major Williams was in the front line and rallying his men to the defence when he was shot and killed. He has no known grave and is commemorated on the Loos Memorial. Leonard Williams is buried in Vermelles British Cemetery and, records the history of the South Wales Borderers - 'was killed while supervising a working party.' The brothers' parents were Alfred and Amy Williams of The Mount, Caerleon.

St Cadoc's Church
Just inside the churchyard gate in Museum Street (on the right) lies the Rowberry family grave. Commemorated on the headstone is Petty Officer George Edwin Rowberry who was killed on 20 September, 1914 when his ship, HMS *Pegasus*, was sunk in Zanzibar Harbour by the German cruiser SMS *Königsberg*. He was aged twenty-eight and buried on Grave Island, Zanzibar. George Rowberry's name also appears on the Monmouth town memorial, on that for the King Henry VIII School, Abergavenny, and on a plaque commemorating those who lost their lives from the Parish of St Thomas' Church, Overmonnow.

The lych gate itself was completed on 28 June, 1919 and erected in memory of those men from Caerleon who served in the Great War, and as a thanks offering for the restoration of peace. Two stone panels record,

> (1) *This Lych Gate Was Erected To The Glory Of God As A Thank-Offering For The*

and

(2) *In Grateful Memory Of The Men Of Caerleon Who Served Their King And Country In The Great War Remembering Before God Those Who Gave Their Lives In The Cause Of Liberty And Justice And Whose Names Are Inscribed Within This Church.*

There are thirty-one names engraved on a brass plate just inside the church and close to the font. Seven of those recorded served with the 1st Monmouthshire Regiment - Percy Baulch, who is buried in the churchyard; Percy Scannell; Frank Moseley, who was mortally wounded in Belgium and died on 20 March; Major Oswald Michael Williams, the battalion Instructor of Musketry who was killed on 13 October, 1915 during the attack on the Hohenzollern Redoubt, and Lieutenant W. Victor Stewart and Privates William Jones and George Lewis who were all lost at the Battle of Frezenberg Ridge on 8 May, 1915.

Two men, William Bennett and Mervyn Defries, were shipmates on the SS *Adriatic*. This vessel, records Charles Hocking's *Dictionary Of Disasters At Sea*, left Newport on 21 October, 1916, for Marceilles with a cargo of coal - 'but was not seen again.'

Second-Lieutenant Edmund Brewer of the Glamorgan Yeomanry was mortally wounded on 12 January, 1918 while attached to the 12th South Wales Borderers and on patrol near Bullecourt in France. In the first year of the war, Major Francis Julian Audley Mackworth, Brigade Major of the 3rd Divisional Artillery and son of Sir Arthur Mackworth, was killed near Lacouture.

Others commemorated are - Alfred Bolton, 10th York and Lancaster; Richard Cook, Evan Hopkins, Charles Jones, John Herbert Norris, Lewis Phillips and Leonard Williams, all of the South Wales Borderers; Harold C. Collins and E.R. Nicholls, Royal Engineers; Harry Hamlin, 6th Dragoon Guards; Captain Thomas W.P. Herbert, 9th Welsh; Ivor Samuel Jones, who served with the Canadian Expeditionary Force; Harry Jones of the 8th Manchesters; Frederick B. James, Royal Field Artillery; Frederick W. Pattemore, 1st Dorsets; Frederick Richards, Army Service Corps; Harold G. Stretton of the Queen's Own Royal West Kent Regiment; Arthur J. Williams of the Cheshires; Horace White, Lancashire Fusiliers and William H. Wollan of the Royal Marine Light Infantry.

Second-Lieutenant William Victor Stewart is also commemorated, with other members of his family, on a brass memorial plaque, mounted on marble, located on the wall of the south aisle. He was eighteen when he fell and has no known grave.

The Commonwealth War Graves Commission note in their register for Monmouthshire (1930 edition) the existence in St Cadoc's Churchyard of a grave belonging to a German interned civilian. However this cannot be located. There are two First World War graves. Private Percy Baulch of the 3rd Battalion, Monmouthshire Regiment, who was born in Caerleon, the son of local undertakers William Henry and Ellen Baulch of 24 Gold Croft Common. He died, aged twenty-six, of pneumonia in Prees Heath Camp Military Hospital, Shropshire on 21 March, 1916 and is buried in a family grave. Another member of the Monmouthshire Regiment, Sergeant W.T. Friskney of the 2/1st Battalion, was twenty-nine when he died at home on 18 July, 1917.

CAERWENT

Eighteen names, together with ranks and regiments, are recorded below the dates - *1914-1918* - on two sides of a memorial lamp standard in the village square at Caerwent: Seaman T. Baker, Royal Navy; Private N. Bennett, Welsh Regiment; Captain J. Cropper, Royal Army Medical Corps; Lieutenant T.A. Cropper, Royal Field Artillery; Private A.H. Davies, Royal Naval Division; Stoker F. Gardener, Royal Fleet Reserve; Private J. Jones, Middlesex Regiment; Private J.H. Harris, South Wales Borderers; Rifleman W. Harris, Monmouthshire Regiment; Private W. Lewis, Lincolnshire Regiment; Corporal W. Morgan, South Wales Borderers; Private H. Peach, Welsh Regiment; Guardsman W. Thomas, Welsh Guards; Private R.J. Wheeler, South Wales Borderers; Private R.D. Wheeler, South Wales Borderers; Private J. Wood, South Wales Borderers; Private G.A. Humphries, Welsh Regiment and Private A.L. Williams, Machine Gun Corps.

Captain John Cropper was drowned on his way to Salonika, while his son, Lieutenant Thomas Andrew Cropper of "D" Battery, 75th Brigade, Royal Field Artillery, died, aged nineteen, in April, 1918 from wounds received on the Somme. (See also St Stephen and St Tathan's Church, Caerwent).

A third side of the memorial has the names of those from the Second World War, and the other, the inscription - *The Path Of The Righteous Is As The Shinning Light.*

St Stephen and St Tathan's Church

Eleven of the eighteen names recorded on the village memorial appear on an illuminated Roll of Honour kept in the church storeroom. The design incorporates several painted shields, depicting the flags and emblems of Britain's allies, with, in the centre, a hand-written list of those killed. Details of ranks, regiments, ages, dates and places of death are included with the names.

The same eleven names appear on the south wall of the chancel near the organ, this time on a brass tablet bearing the inscription - *This Organ Was Erected A.D. 1928 To The Glory Of God And In Grateful Memory Of* - Thomas Baker, Stoker H.M.S. *Caesar*; Norman Bennett, Private 9th Welsh; John Cropper, M.D., J.P., Captain R.A.M.C; Thomas Andrew Cropper, Second-Lieutenant Royal Field Artillery; Arthur Harold Davies, Private Royal Naval Division; Frederick Gardener, Stoker Royal Fleet Reserve; Joseph Jones, Private 1st Middlesex Regiment (awarded the Military Medal); William Lewis, Private 1st Lincolnshire Regiment; Ronald David Wheeler, Lance-Sergeant 6th South Wales Borderers (awarded the Military Medal); Robert James Wheeler, Private 1st South Wales Borderers; John Wood, Private 12th South Wales Borderers - *Who Fell In The Great War 1914-1919. 'Their Name Liveth For Evermore.'* The organ is situated to the left of the tablet.

A further commemoration, this time with the inscription - *Dedicated To The Glorious Memory Of The Eleven Men From Caerwent Who Made The Supreme Sacrifice In The Great War 1914-1919* - is on the north side of the church and takes the form of a stained glass window depicting various religious scenes.

The two officers mentioned on the village memorial, father and son - John and Thomas Cropper, are commemorated on the north wall close to the chancel -

In Loving Memory Of Captain John Cropper, R.A.M.C., C.M.A., B.C., M.D., J.P.

Caerwent memorial which includes the names of father and son, John and Thomas Cropper.

Memorial window at St Stephen and St Tathan's Church, Caerwent.

Memorial to father and son, John and Thomas Cropper on the north wall of St Stephen and St Tathan's Church, Caerwent.

IN LOVING MEMORY OF
CAPTAIN JOHN CROPPER, R.A.M.C.,M.A.,B.C.,M.D.,J.P.
WHO WAS DROWNED WHEN H.M.H.S.BRITANNIC, WAS TORPEDOED ON
NOVEMBER 21ST 1916.
"GREATER LOVE HATH NO MAN THAN THIS,THAT A MAN
LAY DOWN HIS LIFE FOR HIS FRIENDS."
ALSO OF 2ND LIEUT THOMAS ANDREW CROPPER, R.F.A.
ONLY SON OF THE ABOVE AND OF ANNE E.CROPPER,
WHO DIED OF WOUNDS RECEIVED IN ACTION ON APRIL 18TH 1918,
IN FRANCE AND WAS BURIED AT BEZAINCOURT.
"IF WE BELIEVE THAT JESUS DIED AND ROSE AGAIN, EVEN SO THEM
ALSO WHICH SLEEP IN JESUS WILL GOD BRING WITH HIM."

Who Was Drowned When H.M.H.S. Britannic, Was Torpedoed On November, 21st 1916. 'Greater Love Hath No Man Than This, That A Man Lay Down His Life For His Friends'.

The *Britannic*, was built in 1914 for the White Star Line and taken over by the Admiralty shortly after war was declared. Serving as a hospital ship, the vessel was travelling to Salonika when it struck a mine, laid by the German submarine *U-73* only an hour earlier, in the Zea Channel. The inscription goes on -

Also Of 2nd Lieut. Thomas Andrew Cropper, R.F.A., Only Son Of The Above And Of Anne E. Cropper Who Died Of Wounds Received In Action On April 18th 1918, In France And Was Buried At Bezaincourt. "If We Believe That Jesus Died And Rose Again, Even So Them Also Which Sleep In Jesus Will God Bring With Him."

The inscription misspells the grave location. Second-Lieutenant Cropper is in fact buried on the Somme at Bagneux British Cemetery, Gezaincourt.

A more recent commemoration to the fallen of both the First and Second World Wars was produced by local historian John Nettleship. The book, which includes photographs and biographical details of those from Caerwent who were killed, can be seen at the west end of the church.

CALDICOT

The new war memorial in Caldicot bears the inscription (in both Welsh and English) - *Caldicot Cross By Howard Bowcott 1995. Funded By Monmouth Borough Council And The Welsh Development Agency.* The cross is made entirely from single slates and was sponsored by Greaves Welsh Slate Co. Ltd of Blaenau Ffestiniog. The base of the memorial has the inscription - *Lest We Forget, They Gave Their Tomorrow For Our Today.* The names of the fourteen men who fell during the First World War (see St Mary's Church) follow, then those from the Second, and that of a single soldier who was killed in Iraq during the 1991 Gulf War.

Caldicot Methodist Church
On the north wall a small brass plaque has the inscription -

To The Glory Of God And In Memory Of James Alfred Tiplin, 1st Monmouthshire Regiment, Died 13th October, 1915, At Hulluch In France, Aged 20 Years. Greater Love Hath No Man Than This, That A Man Lay Down His Life For His Friends.

Private Tiplin, whose name is recorded on the Loos Memorial to the missing, was killed during the 1st Monmouthshire Regiment's attack on the Hohenzollern Redoubt.

St Mary The Virgin Parish Church
Kelly's Directory Of Monmouthshire & South Wales for 1926, records the existence at St Mary's of a window by Kempe, installed in memory of the men of Caldicot who fell in the Great War. On 5 November, 1950, records the *South Wales Argus*, Bishop Edwin Morris came to St Mary's to consecrate a war memorial to those who were killed during both the First and Second World Wars. Placed below the window, the

New war memorial, Caldicot.

Roll of Honour recording the names of over two hundred men and women serving in the armed forces. St Mary the Virgin Parish Church, Caldicot.

Altar and reredos commemorating the fallen of both World Wars at St Mary the Virgin Parish Church, Caldicot.

new memorial, an altar of Portland stone, was accompanied by a reredos in light English oak. This having a central crucifix on a square of inlaid marble, and the inscriptions - *Ad Majorem Dei Gloriam Et In Memoriam* - and - *Requiem Æeternam Dona Eis Domine*. Panels record the names of those who were killed, the 1914-1918 list comprising - George Andrews, Andrew J. Davies, Alfred W. Evans, Ernest C. Evans, Henry A. Parry, Percy S. Parry, Henry Peach, James A. Pride, Stanley S. Spencer, Charles W. Stringer, William H. Thomas, James A. Tiplin, Ernest R. Turner and Richard H. Williams.

Close to the altar, an illuminated Roll Of Honour records approximately two hundred and twenty hand-written names below the words - *For King, Country & Humanity. Pray For Those Who Are Fighting For Their King And Country* - and a display showing the flags of the several ally countries. The wording suggests that the list was compiled sometime during the war. The Stars and Stripes being among the flags shown, after April, 1917 with the entry of the United States into the war.

The churchyard contains one war grave, that of Lieutenant Reginald Herbert William Hardy, 3rd Battalion, Welsh Regiment, who was commissioned 5 May, 1915 and later attached, first to 1st Battalion, then 11th. He was the son of John William and Emma Sophia Hardy, and husband of Annie Hardy of 11 Pentre Gardens, Cardiff. Lieutenant Hardy died, aged twenty-nine on 4 November, 1918 and is buried alongside other members of his family.

CHEPSTOW

Unveiled on 8 January, 1922 by Commanding Officer of the 1st Monmouthshire Regiment, Lieutenant-Colonel C.E. Evill, DSO, the town war memorial by Eric Francis stands in Beaufort Square and includes two panels inscribed with the names of those from the area who fell during the First World War. There are eighty-three names, each with rank and regiment, recorded in the following order:

1st panel: Private J. Arthur, 18th Welsh Regiment; Lieutenant-Colonel H.W. Bircham, DSO, King's Royal Rifle Corps; Rifleman V. Bailey, 1st Monmouthshire Regiment; Lieutenant H. Ball, Royal Flying Corps; Private T. Barry, 1st Welsh Regiment; Rifleman S. Bevan, 1st Monmouthshire Regiment; Rifleman H. Carey, 1st Monmouthshire Regiment; Rifleman B.W. Collins, 1st Monmouthshire Regiment; Private W.G. Collins, 12th Gloucestershire Regiment; Private F.G. Coombe, 9th Cheshire Regiment; Private H.C. Curtis, Royal Army Medical Corps; Private W. Curtis, Australian Rifles; Rifleman J. Dade, 1st Monmouthshire Regiment; Rifleman H.J. Davies, 1st Monmouthshire Regiment; Private S.J. Davies, 3rd King's Shropshire Light Infantry; Private W.F. Dean, East Yorkshire Regiment; Private C.E. Dibden, Essex Regiment; Trooper G. J. Edwards, 12th Australian Light Horse; Rifleman D. Field, 1st Monmouthshire Regiment; Rifleman A. J. Fisher, 1st Monmouthshire Regiment; Private M.H. Fisher, 9th Welsh Regiment; Private W.E. Fisher, Durham Light Infantry; Private F. Fox, 1st Welsh Regiment; Corporal T.H. Griffiths, 1st Monmouthshire Regiment; Rifleman H.E. Hammonds, 1st Monmouthshire Regiment; Private J.J. Harrhy, 1st Devonshire Regiment; Rifleman C.W. Hobbs, 1st Monmouthshire Regiment; Able-Seaman J.H. Hobbs, Collingwood Battalion, Royal Naval Division; Corporal A. Holley, 1st South Wales Borderers; Private J. Hollins, Royal Army Medical Corps; Sergeant A. Howe, 2nd

Natal Regiment, South African Forces; Private W.J. Howell, South Wales Borderers; Stoker G. Hughes, Royal Navy; Rifleman J. Hughes, King's Royal Rifle Corps; Private B. James, 2nd Royal Welsh Fusiliers; Lance-Corporal G. Ll. Jenkins, 12th Gloucestershire Regiment; Private O.W. Jenkins, 12th Gloucestershire Regiment; Private A.J. Jones, 2nd Monmouthshire Regiment; Lieutenant D.R. Jones, Signal Service, Royal Engineers; Rifleman F. Jones, 2nd Monmouthshire Regiment; Rifleman J. Jones, 1st Monmouthshire Regiment; Rifleman W.B.G. Jones, 1st Monmouthshire Regiment.

2nd panel: W. Kelly; Private P.G. Kennedy, South Wales Borderers; Sergeant A.A. Kingsford, 8th Welsh Regiment; Major W.L. Lawrence, DSO, 1st South Wales Borderers; Private A.S. Lewis, 12th Gloucestershire Regiment; Private C. Lewis, South Wales Borderers; Private F.G. Lewis, 2nd South Wales Borderers; Sergeant C.E.J. Mansell, 2nd Royal Fusiliers; Lieutenant W. Martin, Royal Naval Division; Corporal A. Matthews, King's Royal Rifle Corps; G.W. Maddox, 1st Canadian Expeditionary Force; Private E.C. Morgan, 5th Welsh Regiment; Private S.J. O'Connell, South Wales Borderers; Rifleman J. O'Leary, 1st Monmouthshire Regiment; Rifleman M.W. O'Leary, 1st Monmouthshire Regiment; Rifleman T. O'Leary, 1st Monmouthshire Regiment; Driver C. Oakley, Royal Field Artillery; Rifleman J. Petheram, 1st Monmouthshire Regiment; Gunner M.I. Powell, Royal Field Artillery; Private A.G. Price, Gloucestershire Regiment; Lieutenant G.B. Price, South Wales Borderers; Sapper W.J. Price, Inland Waterways Transport, Royal Engineers; Rifleman C.F. Priest, 1st Monmouthshire Regiment; Lieutenant W.H. Proctor, Queen's Own Royal West Kent Regiment; Private A. Richards, 1st South Wales Borderers; Rifleman P. Richardson, 10th London Regiment; Private C. Rosser, Gloucestershire Regiment; Private H. Shurmer, 9th Welsh Regiment; Private W.H. Simnel, 2nd South Wales Borderers; Captain C.W. Stanton, 1st Monmouthshire Regiment; Corporal C. Stringer, 5th South Wales Borderers; Rifleman F.G. Warman, 1st Monmouthshire Regiment; Rifleman B. Wellington, King's Royal Rifle Corps; Private E.B. Wilkins, Gloucestershire Regiment; Private S. Williams, 4th South Wales Borderers; Able-Seaman W.C. Williams, VC, Royal Navy; Private W. Wootton, King's Liverpool Regiment; Sapper A. Wyatt, Royal Engineers; Private V.A.W. Wyatt, Royal Welsh Fusiliers; Rifleman G. Young, 1st Monmouthshire Regiment; Private L.L. Young, South Wales Borderers.

Able Seaman W.C. Williams won his Victoria Cross at Gallipoli (see gun memorial below and St Mary's Church) and Major W.L. Lawrence, DSO, was killed with the 1st South Wales Borderers during the fighting at Gheluvelt Chateau on 31 October, 1914. Lieutenant-Colonel Humphrey Bircham of the King's Royal Rifle Corps, a regular soldier (the son of Mr and Mrs F.T. Bircham of 'Gwentland' Chepstow) had served in South Africa where he commanded a Mounted Infantry Company. He was awarded the Distinguished Service Order after the March, 1915 fighting at Hooge and lost his life during an attack against German trenches at Pozières on 23 July, 1916.

Next to the town war memorial, and also unveiled on 8 January, 1922, stands a gun taken from a captured German submarine. An inscription on a small metal plate attached reads -

This Gun, Taken From A Captured German Submarine, Was Presented By His

54

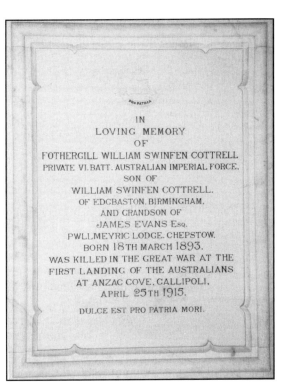

Memorial to Private Fothergill Cottrell.
Della Robbia Chapel, St Mary's Priory
and Parish Church, Chepstow.

Town memorial, Beaufort Square,
Chepstow.

Gun from German submarine presented to Chepstow in recognition of the award of the
Victoria Cross to Able Seaman William Charles Williams.

Majesty King George The Fifth To The town Of Chepstow In Recognition Of The Award Of The Victoria Cross To Able Seaman William Charles Williams, R.F.R. Of This Town, During The Landing From The 'River Clyde' At V. Beach, Seddul Bahr. He Assisted In Replacing In Position The Lighters Forming The Bridge To The Shore And Which Had Broken Adrift. Holding On To A Line In The Water For 'Over An Hour Until Killed (25th April 1915).'

The memorial was unveiled by Mrs Frances Smith, William Williams's eldest sister and next of kin.

Chepstow Cemetery

The cemetery is located just outside Chepstow in Mathern Road, Bulwark and includes the family grave of Able Seaman William Charles Williams, VC. There are eleven war graves (all with Commonwealth War Graves Commission headstones) - six of which belong to soldiers from the Inland Waterways and Docks section of the Royal Engineers. National Shipyard No.1 was constructed by the government at Chepstow during the First World War. The two Lewis brothers are buried in the same grave. Their headstone bears the badges of both regiments.

Pioneer Herbert Andrew, Inland Waterways and Docks, Royal Engineers, was born in Pendleton, Lancashire. He enlisted into the army in Manchester and served with the Lancashire Fusiliers before transferring to the RE. He died on 10 November, 1918.

Pioneer Patrick Carr, Inland Waterways and Docks, Royal Engineers, was born and resided in Glasgow. He enlisted into the army in Bristol and died 15 January, 1918.

Private A.J. Fisher, South Wales Borderers, was born in Chepstow, the son of James and Florence Fisher. He died, aged twenty-four, on 6 January, 1919.

Sapper Henry Grant, Inland Waterways and Docks, Royal Engineers, was from Ballymacarrett, Co. Down, Ireland. He enlisted in Belfast and died on19 April, 1917.

Able Seaman John Henry Hobbs, Collingwood Battalion, Royal Naval Division, was the son of George and Priscilla Hobbs of 6 Mounton Road, Chepstow. He was twenty-eight when he died of phthisis on 14 April, 1920.

Rifleman John Jones, 3/1st Battalion, Monmouthshire Regiment, was born and enlisted in Chepstow. He died 18 February, 1916.

Private E. Lewis, North Somerset Yeomanry, was the son of Mr F.W. Lewis of 9 Manor Road, Weston, Bath. He died, aged twenty-three, on 24 December, 1918.

Driver W.J. Lewis, 56th Divisional Signal Company, Royal Engineers, brother of Private E. Lewis above, died, aged twenty-two, on 25 December, 1918.

Sapper Henry McClean, Inland Waterways and Docks, Royal Engineers, was born in Shankhil, Co. Antrim, Ireland. He enlisted into the army in Belfast and died on 2 August, 1918.

Sapper John Brien Merrill, Inland Waterways and Docks, Royal Engineers, was the son of John Merrill and married to Emma Merrill. He died, aged thirty-two, on 6 December, 1918.

Sapper Francesco Portinari, Inland Waterways and Docks, Royal Engineers, was born in Italy. He resided in Poplar, London and died on 5 November, 1918.

Memorial Chapel, St Mary's Priory and Parish Church, Chepstow.

Reredos taken from the demolished St Luke's Church, Newport and now in St Mary's, Chepstow.

Old Drill Hall and parade ground of 'E' (Chepstow) Company, 1st Battalion, Monmouthshire Regiment. A memorial plaque was put up on the wall to the left in 1998.

Drill Hall

A blue oval plaque inscribed -

In Commemoration Of The Officers And Men Of 'E' Company (Chepstow) 1st Battalion, Monmouthshire Regiment (TF) Who Paraded Here 5th August 1914 Before Leaving For Active Service On The Western Front - Many Never Returned - Erected By The Chepstow Society

can be seen on the wall of the old Drill Hall in Lower Church Street, Chepstow. The parade ground referred to is now a car park. The Battalion moving first to its war station at Pembroke Dock, then via Oswestry and Northampton, landed in France on 6 November. The memorial was erected in 1998 and has white raised lettering.

St Mary's Priory and Parish Church

The Memorial Chapel on the north transept was created in 1955 and in this oak panels record the names of those from the parish who gave their lives in both world wars. As with the town memorial, there are eighty-three names for the First World War. Above the names are nineteen painted shields, including those for the Royal Navy, Army, Royal Air Force, St Mary and the Diocese of Monmouth, and the inscription - *To The Greater Glory Of God And In Proud Memory Of The Men Of The Parish Who Gave Their Lives In Two World Wars.*

Chepstow's Victoria Cross hero, Able Seaman William Charles Williams, is commemorated by Charles Dixon's paining of the landing from the *River Clyde* at 'V' Beach, Gallipoli on 25 April, 1915. The picture was purchased by public subscription and hangs between two ensigns. Close to this, and mounted on the wall, is the ship's bell from the minesweeper HMS *Chepstow*. This was presented to the town after the vessel was decommissioned in 1927 and originally hung in the

Charles Dixon's painting of the landing of the River Clyde *at 'V' Beach, Gallipoli. Purchased by public subscription in recognition of local hero, Able Seaman William Charles Williams, VC. St Mary's Priory and Parish Church, Chepstow.*

Town Arch. It was transferred to St Mary's in 1969 under the care of the Chepstow branch of the Royal Naval Association.

The reredos below the east window was sculpted by R.L. Boulton & Sons of Cheltenham and came from St Luke's in Newport which was demolished in 1994. Unveiled by the Venerable D.H. Griffiths, Archdeacon of Monmouth on 25 May, 1922, it was to commemorate the services of the women of Newport and the county of Monmouthshire during the Great War. After the closure of the church the reredos was re-erected in St Mary's by the Most Reverend Derrick G. Childs, Archbishop of Wales in 1985. A brass plaque situated on the wall near to the altar rail records -

> *To The Greater Glory Of God And In Grateful Commemoration Of The Sacrifices And Service Rendered By The Women Of Newport And Gwent During The Great War 1914-1918. The Reredos Is Dedicated As A Companion Memorial To The East Window Ascension Day 1922.*

The Della Robbia Chapel is on the south side of the church and this contains a white marble tablet in memory of Private Fothergill William Swinfen Cottrell. The memorial, which has the badge of the Royal Warwickshire Regiment above the words - *Pro Patria* - has the following inscription -

> *In Loving Memory Of Fothergill William Swinfen Cottrell - Private VI Batt. Australian Imperial Force. Son Of William Swinfen Cottrell Of Edgbaston, Birmingham And Grandson Of James Evans Esq. Pwllmeyric Lodge, Chepstow. Born 18th March, 1893. Was Killed In The Great War At The First Landing Of The Australians At Anzac Cove, Gallipoli, April 25th 1915. Dulce Est Pro Patria Mori.*

CHRISTCHURCH

The memorial granite cross inscribed - *Erected To The Memory Of The Fallen Of This Parish During The War 1914-1919* - stands opposite Holy Trinity Parish Church. There are fifty-one names recorded, each with rank and regiment, and in order of date of death. These include Major William Stanley Hern who was killed 10 August, 1915 at Gallipoli, four members of the Monmouthshire Regiment, who fell during the May, 1915 fighting at Frezenberg Ridge, and two men from the SS *Alfalfa*, torpedoed by the German submarine *UB2* off the Bay of Biscay on 27 April, 1917. The full list of names is as follows:

1914: Private H. Binning, South Wales Borderers, 26 September, 1914; H. Shyer, Royal Navy, 1 November, 1914.

1915: Private J. Blackmore, Scots Guards, 25 January, 1915; Private A. Royster, South Wales Borderers, 25 January, 1915; Private R. Jeffries, Monmouthshire Regiment, 25 April, 1915; Private F.W. Pattimore, Dorset Regiment, 2 May, 1915; Private A.J. James, Monmouthshire Regiment, 8 May, 1915; Private M. Morgan, Monmouthshire Regiment, 8 May, 1915; Private W. Blackmore, Monmouthshire Regiment, 8 May, 1915; Private A. White, Monmouthshire Regiment, 8 May, 1915; Lance-Corporal J.L. Stanley, South Wales Borderers, 9 May 1915; Private G. Turner, Welsh Regiment, 25 May, 1915; Major W.S. Hern, Wiltshire Regiment, 10 August, 1915; Private A. Griffiths, Monmouthshire Regiment, 13 October, 1915; Private R. Bevan, Norfolk Regiment, 23 October, 1915; Sergeant A. Miller, South Wales Borderers, 8 November, 1915.

1916: Private G. Morgan, South Wales Borderers, 9 February, 1916; Private H. Duffield, South Wales Borderers, 9 April, 1916; Sapper W. Watkins, Royal Engineers, 11 April, 1916; Sergeant A. Shotton, South Staffordshire Regiment, 1 July, 1916; Sapper A. Williams, Royal Engineers, 24 July, 1916; Private T. Griffiths, South Wales Borderers, 18 August, 1916; Corporal G. Tanner, Welsh Guards, 18 August, 1916; Private G.A. Stevens, Machine Gun Corps, 25 September, 1916; Lance-Corporal W.J. Thomas, Machine Gun Corps, 6 October, 1916; Gunner C.J. Turnbull, Royal Field Artillery, 16 October, 1916.

1917: Sergeant H.H. Harris, South Wales Borderers, 2 February, 1917; Private W.H. Byard, South Wales Borderers, 8 February, 1917; Chief-Engineer J. Anderson, SS *Alfalfa*, 6 May, 1917; Steward V.C. Cox, SS *Alfalfa*, 6 May, 1917; Sergeant I. Huggett, Gloucestershire Regiment, 8 May, 1917; Trooper L.H. King, Inniskilling Dragoons, 2 July, 1917; Private E.N. Merrett, Welsh Regiment, 10 July, 1917; Private P. Carman, Monmouthshire Regiment, 10 July, 1917; Driver W.H. Jones, Royal Field Artillery, 22 July, 1917; Gunner A. Jones, Royal Garrison Artillery, 25 July, 1917; Private W. Davies, South Wales Borderers, 31 July, 1917; E.F. Williams, Royal Navy, 22 September, 1917; Captain T.S. Spittle, Monmouthshire Regiment, 2 October, 1917; Gunner G.G. Luxton, Royal Navy, 18 October, 1917; Private G. Kerton, Welsh Guards, 1 December, 1917.

1918: Gunner G.H. Hay, Royal Garrison Artillery, 21 March, 1918; Private W. Dyment, Lancashire Fusiliers, June, 1918; Sergeant W.E. Dray, South Wales Borderers, 2 July, 1918; Private E.G. Ellis, Royal Scots, 4 August, 1918; A.H. Tooze, Royal Navy, 8 October, 1918; Private C.R. Johnson, Royal Welsh Fusiliers, 9 October, 1918; Private H. Masser, East Lancashire Regiment, 18 October, 1918;

Memorial cross, Christchurch.

Corporal A.E. Rawlings, Military Mounted Police, 23 November, 1918.

1919: Gunner B.F. Danks, Royal Field Artillery, 28 March, 1919; Private J. Trezise, Army Service Corps, 4 April, 1919.

Christchurch Cemetery

The cemetery is on the Christchurch Road just outside Newport and contains forty-nine First World War graves:

Rifleman W. Basford, 3/5th Battalion, King's Liverpool Regiment. Born Sandycroft, Flintshire in 1881, married to Mary E. Basford of 12 Denorben Street, Liverpool and died 20 December, 1918. Rifleman Basford is buried in the same grave as Private E. England (see below).

Driver Hubert Gerald Bayliss, 7th Brigade Ammunition Column, Royal Horse Artillery, died, aged twenty-five, on 12 March, 1919 after a period of sickness. Born in Co. Clare, Ireland, he served on the Western Front and was sent home from there suffering from shell-shock.

Lance-Corporal A.E. Bowen, South Wales Borderers. Died 24 July, 1916.

Lance-Sergeant Gustave Thomas Braithwaite, Royal Army Pay Corps. Born Leytonstone, London and died, aged forty-five, on 18 May, 1921 from phthisis. He was married to Ella Braithwaite of 12 Chapel Street, Mumbles and shares the same grave as Driver A.G. Russell (see below).

Private Thomas Bray, Royal Defence Corps. Died, aged fifty, on 5 June, 1920. He was married to Elizabeth Jane Bray of 16 Adelaide Street, Camborne, Cornwall.

Lance-Corporal Charles James Brown, South Wales Borderers, was attached to the depot at Brecon when he died, aged twenty-two, of pneumonia on 2 December, 1918. He had been returned home from France where he was wounded while serving with the 10th Battalion. Charles Brown was born in West Bromwich, Staffordshire and moved to Newport where he lived with his parents - Charles James and Sarah Brown at 28 Somerton Road.

Private L.E. Browning, Worcestershire Regiment, was the son of Joseph and Elenor Browning of Longhope, Gloucestershire. He died, aged thirty, on 11 December, 1917.

Rifleman Sidney Arthur Chidzey, Labour Corps, was born at Wrington, Somerset in 1892 and had originally enlisted into the 2/1st Battalion, Monmouthshire Regiment at Newport. His parents, James Thomas and Emma Chidzey, lived at 59 Sutton Road.

Private John Cowhen of the South Wales Borderers, was from Newport. He died, aged thirty-one, on 15 May, 1921.

Rifleman A. Davie, 6th Battalion, London Regiment. Died 28 May, 1918.

Gunner G. Davies, No.1 Siege Battery, Royal Garrison Artillery. Died, aged thirty-five, on 25 September, 1916.

Private W. Davies, Royal Defence Corps, lived at Abergavenny and originally served in the Monmouthshire Regiment. He died on 30 April, 1918.

Second-Lieutenant A.P. Duncan, 1st Battalion, Monmouthshire Regiment, died 26 May, 1918. He was forty-two and married to Ethel M. Duncan of 25 Church Road, Maindee, Newport.

Worker Gertrude Winifred Allam Dyer, Queen Mary's Army Auxiliary Corps, died 27 January, 1918. She was thirty-eight and the daughter of Frederick and Sarah Dyer of 14 Richmond Road, Newport.

Private E. England, 10th Battalion, East Yorkshire Regiment, is buried in the same grave as Rifleman W. Basford (see above). He died, aged twenty-one, on 4 December, 1918 and was the son of Amos England of Ratley, Warwickshire.

Lance-Corporal Frank Evans, 9th (Reserve) Battalion, South Wales Borderers, having been wounded in France subsequently died on 20 March, 1920. He was forty-one, the son of John and Martha Evans, and left a widow, Sarah, who lived at 11 Dudley Street, Corporation Road, Newport.

Corporal G.J. Fielder, 1st London Field Ambulance, Royal Army Medical Corps, was born in Paddington, London and died, aged thirty, of phthisis on 2 March, 1920. He was married to Alice Fielder of 'Lackenhurst' in Shipley, Sussex.

Private Joseph Thomas Goodreid, 1st Battalion, South Wales Borderers, died 20 August, 1920. He is buried in a private family grave, the headstone of which records that he was 'Accidently Shot' whilst on duty at Drogheda Barracks in Ireland. He was nineteen years old and the son of John Goodreid.

Private Robert Henry Hammett, 16th Battalion, Royal Warwickshire Regiment, was born in Monmouth and lived in Newport. He enlisted into the army in Birmingham and died 25 September, 1916 from wounds received in France.

Lance-Corporal T. Hourahine, Royal Army Medical Corps, died 24 March, 1919.

Gunner G. Hughes, Royal Field Artillery, died 13 May, 1917.

Ordinary Seaman Walter Percival Hughes, Royal Navy, of HMS *Vivid* and the son of Ernest and Rachel Hughes of 194 Corporation Road, Newport. He was nineteen when he died on 5 November, 1915.

Petty Officer Motor Mechanic Ernest Ethelbert Hurn, Royal Naval Air Service, died 15 February, 1918.

Private W. Jackson, Royal Army Service Corps, died 7 April, 1920.

Sapper R. Jones, Royal Engineers, was born in Holyhead and thirty-six when he died on 15 June, 1916. He was married to Sarah Ann Jones of 3 Penywerlod Terrace, Markhams Village, Argoed and the son of Robert and Jane Jones.

Private W. Jones, Pembroke Yeomanry, died 4 December, 1915. The headstone to Private Jones' grave is the usual Commonwealth War Graves Commission type. However an error has been made in the pattern of badge used. The badge worn by the Pembroke Yeomanry consists of the Prince of Wales' plumes above a scroll inscribed - *Fishguard*. The plumes are shown, but the inscription reads - *Welsh Guards*.

Sergeant F.W. Lennox, 91st Company, Royal Army Ordnance Corps, died 9 December, 1918.

Driver Frances Mary Dulcie Llewellyn-Jones, Women's Royal Air Force, was the daughter of the Revd David Ernest and Frances Eliza Sophia Llewellyn-Jones of The Vicarage, St. John's Road, Maindee, Newport. The Revd Llewellyn-Jones was the vicar of Maindee and Rural Dean of Newport. Frances Llewellyn-Jones was twenty-four and died on 13 November, 1918.

Private Albert Edward Mapps, Army Service Corps, was attached to the Remount Depot at Ormskirk and died, aged thirty-three, on 19 March, 1916. He was the son of John Edward and Sarah Mapps and married to Mary Ann Mapps of 6 Wells Terrace, Cwmbran.

Lance-Corporal R. Martin, Dorsetshire Regiment, died 1 November, 1918.

Able Seaman Richard Martin was a member of the Drake Battalion, Royal Naval Division, and having been wounded on the Somme died at home on 3 December, 1916. He was thirty-seven and married to Ellen Martin of 34 Dudley Street, Newport.

Private George Osmond, 1st Battalion, Welsh Regiment, was the son of Samuel and Sarah Osmond of 37 Dewstow Street, Newport. He died, aged thirty-seven on 17 February, 1919.

Sergeant E.E. Parrington, Royal Army Ordnance Corps, served on the Western Front where he was Mentioned In Despatches. He was born in Islington, London, the son of William and Susan Parrington of 50 Seymour Road, Harringay, and married to Maud Parrington. The couple lived at 2 London Road, Pembroke Dock. Sergeant Parrington died, aged thirty-nine, of phthisis on 5 December, 1918 and is buried in the same grave as Private A.Pullin (see below).

Driver W. Phillips, Army Service Corps, was twenty-nine when he died on 27

December, 1918. He was the son of John and Bessie Phillips of Paul, Cornwall and married to Edith Gertrude Phillips. The couple lived at 71 James Street, Trethomas.

Sapper Harry Glyn Poole, Royal Engineers, was attached to the Signal Service Training Centre and died on 7 June, 1919. He was born 6 August, 1898 and the youngest son of Henry and Mary Poole of 50 Somerset Road, Newport.

Gunner William Richard Pratt, Royal Navy, of HMS *Vernon* who died 21 July, 1916. He was thirty years old and the son of William and Alice Pratt of 1 Longcroft Road, Westham, Weymouth in Dorset.

Private A. Pullin, No. 3 Company, Labour Corps, is buried in the same grave as Sergeant E.E. Parrington (see above). He previously served with the Royal Berkshire Regiment and died on 10 February, 1919.

Lance-Corporal A.E. Rawlings, Military Mounted Police, died 23 November, 1918. He was twenty-nine.

Private George Reece, 1st Battalion, Wiltshire Regiment, was the son of George and Eliza Reece. He died, aged twenty-three, on 19 May, 1917.

Private H.J. Richards, 'D' Company, 8th Battalion, South Wales Borderers, died on 26 December, 1916. He was thirty-one and the son of Frederick John and Emily Annie Richards of 34 Chepstow Road, Newport.

Private E. Rose, Gloucestershire Regiment, died 16 June, 1918.

Driver A.G. Russell, Royal Army Service Corps, died 20 September, 1920 and is buried in the same grave as Lance-Sergeant G.T. Braithwaite (see above).

Private E.E. Scotcher, Worcestershire Regiment, died 6 October, 1918.

Lance-Sergeant John Alfred Small, 19th Battalion, Lancashire Fusiliers, was the son of Charles Henry Small of 5 May Street, Newport. He served originally with the Monmouthshire Regiment and died from wounds received in France on 24 April, 1918.

Corporal L. Stevens, 35th Company, Royal Army Ordnance Corps, served at Gallipoli and died, aged thirty-nine, on 26 November, 1920. He was married and lived at 3 Bamborough Gardens, Shepherds Bush, London. Corporal Stevens is buried in the same grave as Private F.H. Ward (see below).

Private J. Trezise, 45th Company, Royal Army Service Corps, died 4 April, 1919.

Private Ernest William Vincent, Royal Army Service Corps, was the son of William and Alice Vincent of 4 Ivor Street, Newport. He was born in London and died, aged twenty-one, on 11 May, 1920.

Private F.H. Ward, Royal Wiltshire Yeomanry, was the son of Francis William Ward of 24 St Margaret's Road, Stoke, Coventry. He died, aged twenty-nine, on 15 May, 1919. Private Ward is buried in the same grave as Corporal L. Stevens (see above).

Private J. Watts, 57th Battalion, Training Reserve, died 13 October, 1918.

The cemetery also contains two war graves, both with the standard pattern Commonwealth War Graves Commission headstone, but neither is inscribed with name or any other detail.

Holy Trinity Parish Church
The stained glass window put up in the Lady Chapel in memory of men from the parish that fell during the Great War was lost, when, on 5 November, 1949, a fire almost completely destroyed the church. The bronze tablet that accompanied the window, however, survived, and this can now be seen on the wall of the choir vestry

at the west end of the church. The inscription reads - *The Window In This Chapel Was Erected In Memory Of The Following* - there are forty names: J. Anderson, R. Bevan, H. Binning, J. Blackmoore, W. Blackmoore, W.H. Byard, T.P. Carman, V.C. Cox, W. Davies, W.E. Dray, W. Dyment, E. Ellis, A. Griffiths, T. Griffiths, W.S. Hern, I. Huggett, A.H. James, R. Jeffries, C.R. Johnson, A. Jones, C. Kerton, H. Masser, E.N. Merrett, A. Miller, G. Mogford, M. Morgan, F.W. Pattemore, A.E. Rawlings, A. Royster, W. Shotton, H. Shyer, J.L. Stanley, G.A. Stevens, G. Tanner, W.J. Thomas, A.H. Tooze, G. Turner, W. Watkins, A. White and A. Williams.

Also lost in the November, 1949 fire was the window erected by the family of a local officer. Once again, the metal plaque that accompanied the memorial survived and can be seen in the choir vestry -

In Loving Memory Of Major W. Stanley Hern - Wiltshire Regt. Fought In The Matabelle Rebellion 1896-97 - Wounded In The South African War 1899-1902 - District Commissioner In West Africa - Killed Suvla Bay Gallipoli 10th Aug. 1915. This Window Was Erected By His Father & Family A.D. 1919.

Attached to the 5th Battalion, Wiltshire Regiment, Major William Hern was killed during the fighting at Chunuk Blair. Having advanced up the Chunuk, the Wiltshires were met by the enemy who attacked over the crest of the hill. Lieutenant-Colonel F.E. Whitton recorded in his history of the Leinster Regiment, who were holding the apex, how three companies of the Wiltshire were caught in the open and annihilated. Another record of the engagement noted how - '...more than half the officers and men were never seen again.' William Hern has no known grave, his name being recorded on the Helles Memorial.

The choir vestry also holds a framed Roll of Honour featuring a drawing by Wilfred Pippet of a soldier kneeling before Christ on the Cross. Around the illustration is a quotation from *St Matthew* (Chapter 24, Verse 7) -

And You Shall Hear Of Wars & Rumours Of Wars. See They Ye Be Not Troubled - and below - *Of Your Charity Pray For The Souls Of The Gallant Dead.*

Thirty-two hand-written names follow, these being set out according to year of death - 1914 (two), 1915 (fifteen), 1916 (five), 1917 (five), 1918 (five). Thirty of the names recorded are those listed on the bronze plaque that previously accompanied the memorial window. This time Christian names are given in full. The two additional names are those of Captain Thomas Stanley Spittal, an officer of the 1st Battalion, Monmouthshire Regiment who died in France on 2 October, 1917, and Private Lionel Henry King, 6th (Inniskilling) Dragoons, killed exactly three months earlier on 2 July, 1917.

The churchyard contains two war graves: Gunner Benjamin Fredrick Danks, Royal Field Artillery, was the son of Mr H.B. and Mrs Elizabeth Danks of Cromwell House, Caerleon. He died, aged nineteen, on 28 March, 1919. Gunner Danks is buried in a private grave alongside other members of his family.

A member of the Royal Air Force, Air Mechanic 2nd Class, Frederick Harris died on 21 July, 1918 at a Volunteer Aid Detachment Hospital in West Hartlepool. Frederick Harris was thirty-five. He is buried in a family grave and referred to on the headstone as 'Sculptor of Newport.'

CROESYCEILIOG

Gwent Constabulary Headquarters

Designed by Herbert Wauthier and made by F. Osborne & Co. Ltd of London, the small copper tablet located in the reception area of the Gwent Constabulary Headquarters at Croesyceiliog has the following inscription -

To The Proud And Honoured Memory Of The Members Of The Monmouthshire Constabulary Who Gave Their Lives For Humanity In The Great Wars 1914-1918 - 1939-1945. This Tablet Is Erected By Past And Serving Members Of The Monmouthshire Constabulary.

There are eight names listed for the Second World War and seven - P.Cs A. Little, A. Jay, T.H. Davies, H. Plaistow, H. Hughes, S. Pucknell and W.O'Brien for the First. The wording is flanked by flambeaus with sprigs of laurel attached.

Gwent County Hall

The two First World War memorials now displayed in County Hall, Croesyceiliog can be seen in the balcony area, outside the council chamber. Originally located in the main entrance of the old County Hall in Pentonville, Newport, an ornate brass tablet mounted on black wood bears the inscription - *To The Members And Staff Of The County Council Who Fell In The Great War 1914-1919.* Below this, there are six names recorded - Major Lord Llangattock, who served with the 1st Monmouthshire Battery, RFA and died in October, 1916 from wounds received on the Somme; three Newport men - Rifleman Stanley Langmaid of the 1st Monmouthshire Regiment, who was taken prisoner and died in German hands on 20 July, 1915, Ivor Henry Vivian Williams, also of the Monmouthshires, and Arthur Reginald Griffiths who was mortally wounded while serving in France with the 1/7th Middlesex Regiment, and from Usk, Private Eric Saunders of the Royal Engineers also fell in France. The remaining name is that of a Royal Gloucestershire Hussars officer - Captain Hon. Elidyr John Barnard Herbert, who was killed in Palestine on 12 November, 1917. The memorial was unveiled by his father, Major-General the Right Hon. Lord Treowen, CB, CMG, on Wednesday 3 May, 1922 (see also Llanover).

Next to the County Council memorial is that to seven teachers who were killed -

To The Glory Of God And In Honoured Memory Of The Teachers In The County Intermediate Schools Of Monmouthshire Who Laid Down Their Lives In The Great War 1914-1918.

Engraved on an oak tablet, the men's names are recorded along with their school: Brinley L. Jones and William C. Raymond, who were colleagues at the Abergavenny Intermediate School in Harold Road; Rene P.M. Gardeur, Charles S. Reed and Owen Jenkins, all from the school in Oak Street, Abertillery; John W.Taylor of Pontywaun and Owen G. Jones who taught at Tredegar.

Pontrhydyrun Baptist Church

The stone memorial in the churchyard at Chapel Lane, Croesyceiliog, comprises a small Celtic cross mounted on a pedestal. The inscription reads -

Monmouthshire Constabulary memorial, Gwent Constabulary Headquarters, Croesyceiliog.

Pontrhydyrun Baptist Church memorial, Chapel Lane, Croesyceiliog.

Roll of Honour, St Mary's Church, Croesyceiliog.

County Council Staff and Intermediate Schools memorials, Gwent County Hall, Croesyceiliog.

*Erected To The Memory Of The Glorious Dead Of This Church And Congregation
Who Gave Their Lives For King And Country In The Great War 1914-1919.*

The remaining three sides of the pedestal record twenty-three names without rank or regiment:

Clifford Bowles, Raymond Dart, Ralph Fisher, Lionel John George, Frank Holcombe, William Jones, Daniel Jones, Bert King, Archie Lee, Lewis Leigh, T.J. Lewis, Charles Morgan, Joseph Morgan, George Osborne, Raymond Pauling, Robert Pask, Alfred Price, Clifford Thomas, Richard Vizard, Arthur Wassel, Tom Waters, John Watkins, William Williams.

St Mary's Church

The church holds in store an illuminated and framed Roll Of Honour commemorating some twenty-four members of the parish that served in the Great War. There are four columns with the headings - *Name - Rank - Regimental No. - Regiment or Ship* - and the information recorded is:

Joe Jenkins, Private, 315864, 1st Monmouthshire Regiment; Albert Charles, Private, 63482, South Wales Borderers; Percy Watkins, Gunner, 186464, Royal Garrison Artillery; Stanley Jones, Gunner, H.M.S. Iron Duke; John Hopkins, Gunner, 186385, Royal Garrison Artillery; John Watkins, Private, 11896 (Killed In Action); Gilbert Hornsby, Private, 2475, 2nd Monmouthshire Regiment; Arthur Hawkins, Gunner, 54269, Royal Garrison Artillery; Reginald Hawkins, Private, 38552, L.B; Fred Cooper, Private, 2371, 2nd Monmouthshire; David Cooper, Private, 312821, Tank Corps; Alfred Lloyd, Private, Welsh Guards (Died In England); Bert King, Private, 11896, Welsh Guards (Killed In France); Victor King, Private, 91444, Durham Light Infantry; Geo. Matthews, Private, 39178, South Wales Borderers; Fred Matthews, Gunner, Tank Corps; Arthur Matthews, Private, 59707, Royal Welsh Fusiliers; William Bishop, Private, 15838, Grenadier Guards (Killed In France); Albert Bishop, Private, 31952, 1st Monmouthshire; Lionel George, Private, (Killed In France); Chas. Hancock, Private, 20124, South Wales Borderers; Geo. Homewood, Private, 15644, A.P.W.O; Arthur Bossworth, Lance-Corporal, 1277 (Killed In France); Chas. Passat, Private (Killed In England).

The design includes the wording -

For King And County - below a Union Jack, and - *St. Mary's Church, Lower Pontnewydd. Subscribed For By The Members Of The Above Church.*

CROSSKEYS

Crosskeys Methodist Church

The church in High Street, Crosskeys, formally known as Pontywaun Wesleyan, has in the church hall, two memorials. Made from oak, and with gold painted letters, the tablets commemorate those who served, together with those who were killed. On the left wall, a crown is displayed between the words - *Pontywaun Wesleyan Church & School* - and below this a quote from Bunyan's *The Pilgrim's Progress* - *"So They Passed Over, & The Trumpet Sounded For Them On The Other Side."* Twelve names follow, each accompanied by date of death:

Edwin Budgett, 18 March 1917; Richard Morris, 1 August 1917; James Morris,

Memorial boards showing the names of those killed and those that served from the Pontywaun Wesleyan Church, now Crosskeys Methodist.

22 June 1918; Abner Lewis, 22 May 1918; Reggie Gill, who lost his life on the last day of the war - 11 November 1918; Joseph Godden, 25 March 1918; Henry Haynes, 8 September 1918; Arthur Edwards, 30 May 1918; Willie Green, 22 October 1918; Willie Webb, 18 September 1918; Herbert Robbins, 27 October 1918; Herbert King, 18 September 1918.

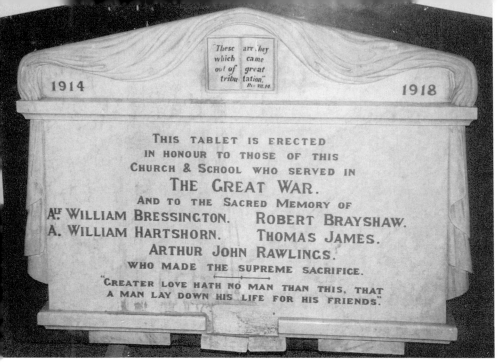

Memorial from the old Gladstone Street Methodist Church, now in the care of Crosskeys Methodist Church.

The memorial on the right side of the hall is once again headed by the name of the church. This time either side of the Royal Arms, and above the inscription - *In Honour Of Our Heroes Who Answered The Call Of King & Country 1914-1918*, seventy-six names follow, the last being those of four women:

G.H. Stock, G. Mansell, H. Nicholas, A. Mountain, W. Mountain, W. Sainsbury, T. Yeoman, F. Forward, W.A.J. Price, W. Richards, E. Huntley, J.J. Stokes, J. Stokes, C. Thomas, J. Jeffries, T. Prosser, S. Prosser, H. Lewis, H. Nicholas, P. Hurn, E. Southall, T. Downs, F. Hayes, A. Hayes, S. Hitchcocks, T.A. Bateman, W.G. Davies, B. Hill, G.H. Hill, T.J. Williams, A. Williams, J. Hall, T.J. Beckington, A.W. Hibbs, T. White, G. Sainsbury, E. Sainsbury, E. Sainsbury, G. Godden, T. Godden, O. Godden, W. Godden, V. Godden, F. Sharman, A. Sharman, W. Lewis, W. Jones, W. Lush, G.A. Lush, F.V. Lewis, W.D. Gill, H.A. Sheppard, W.T. Edward, T. Lee, I. Lee, A. Lee, J. Mainwaring, I. King, G.M. Tayler, G.H. Williams, L. Jeffries, P. Phillips. C. Hurn, C. Parfitt, L. Sutton, G. Huntley, H. Brayley, F. Hawkins, S. Hawkins, W.H. Parry, H. Thompson, B.J. Rogers, Miss S.J. Powell, Miss F. Forward, Miss M. White and Miss D. Green.

The church is also in possession of the memorial belonging to the old Gladstone Street Methodist Church which was closed down in 1975. At the top of a white marble tablet, an open book placed between the dates - *1914-1918* - quotes a passage from *The Revelation* (Chapter 7, Verse 14) - '*These Are They Which Came Out Of Great Tribulation*'. Below this is the following inscription -

This Tablet Is Erected In Honour To Those Of This Church & School Who Served In The Great War. And To The Sacred Memory Of - Alf. William Bressington, A. William Hartshorn, Robert Brayshaw, Thomas James, Arthur John Rawlings -

Who Made The Supreme Sacrifice. 'Greater Love Hath No Man Than This, That A Man Lay Down His Life For His Friends.'

Hope Baptist Church

A brass and copper plaque mounted on an oak backing to the left of the pulpit has the inscription -

Pro Patria - To The Glory Of God And In Ever Abiding And Grateful Memory Of The Men Of This Church And Sunday School Who Fell In The Great War - 1914-1918.

Five names follow: Captain William Jones-Evans of the Royal Army Medical Corps, who died from wounds received on 13 September, 1917. He was attached to the 2/1st South Midland Field Ambulance and is buried in Vlamertinghe New Military Cemetery, Belgium. Lance-Corporal Oliver Brown served with the Machine Gun Corps, and died in France on 20 November, 1917, as did Bombardier Charles McGregor, Royal Field Artillery, who fell on 3 August, 1917. He was awarded the Military Medal. Private William R. Lott, Army Service Corps, died at home on 14 October, 1918, and was buried in Risca Cemetery. The last name is that of Private Frank Dollery. The words - *'Greater Love Hath No Man Than This'* follow the names.

The same five names also feature in an illuminated Roll of Honour by C. Winmill of Abercarn and Crosskeys displayed to the right of the pulpit. The list, hand-written in Gothic script, contains seventy-one names, mostly with regiments, and appears blow the following dedication -

Hope Baptist Church, Crosskeys - Names Of Members Of The Above Church & Sunday School Who Served With The Forces In The Great War 1914-1918.

At the bottom, and within a wreath of laurels flanked by the Union Jack and Royal Ensign, the words -

For King And Country. Two other quotations - *'Fight The Good Fight'* and *'Hitherto Hath The Lord Helped Us'.*

are shown, one either side of the names. Those who were killed are indicated by a cross. Other information recorded is the award of the Serbian Cross to Sergeant Major J.G. Collier of the Royal Army Medical Corps, and the Croix de Guerre and Star to Lieutenant T.R. Benson, Royal Engineers. A.C. Jones appears without rank or regiment and is indicated as having served at a 'Wireless Station.'

CRUMLIN

A Roll Of Honour in the form of a bronze panel set into the wall close to the old Mining School gates in Mining School Hill bears the names of eighty-eight men that died in the First World War. Many were local Territorials from 'H' Company, 2nd Battalion, Monmouthshire Regiment. The names are arranged alphabetically, without rank of regiment, in three columns:

1st column: - R. Andrews, T. Arthur, J.H. Barkwell, D. Bessant, R. Bullock, A. Carter, G. Charles, F.A. Clements, E. Coles, W. Coles, N. Cousins, S. Cross, W. Curnuck, B. Davies, L. Davies, A.H. Downes, H. Edwards, F. Elias, R. Elias, R. Ellis,

Crumlin war memorial, Mining School Hill.

E. Evans, A. Griffiths, P. Griffiths, J. Haines, W.J. Hale, H.J. Haley, J.W. Hall, R. Harrhy, H. Herbert.

2nd column: W.J. Holder, J. Hollister, T. Hurley, H. James, H. James, H.R. James, W. James, T. John, J. Jones, J. Kenvyn, A. Kettley, J.G. Kite, R. Knight, W.J. Lane, H. Lloyd, W.S. Lloyd, J. Maclarney, J.W. Magee, A.R. Maidment, G. Martin, J. Merry, W. Mogg, E. Morgan, O. Morgan, T.G. Morgan, G. Morris, M. Morris, C. Neale, D. O'Keeffe, F. Owen.

3rd column: F.G. Palmer, A. Perry, W. Porter, A. Pritchard, J. Pritchard, D. Prothero, C.O. Purchase, T. Purnell, D. Roberts, J. Rogers, G. Seabourne, A.J. Seager, J. Sherman, G. Smith, W. Smith, E. Targett, E. Taylor, R.J. Taylor, W.H. Thomas, T.J. Trow, R. Trumper, S. Vigars, W. Vowles, W. Waite, T. Walker, A.H. Walwyn, G. Watkins, F.E. Williams, G. Worthing.

The fallen of the Second World War are recorded above.

CWM

There are three memorials in the forecourt of the branch library in Canning Street, Cwm, all of which have been erected in recent years to replace the original cenotaph put up shortly after the end of the First World War. Lying flat on the top of stone work, a brass plate bears the inscription -

> *Remembering - All Who Gave Their Lives In Two World Wars 1914-1918 & 1939-1945 - And All To The Present Day So That We May Live - When You Go Home Tell Them Of Us And Say For Your Tomorrow We Gave Today - We Will Remember Them.*

Dedicated on Sunday 5 October, 1997 is the memorial to the left - a Dragoon carved into stone, together with the inscription - *3rd Batt. Monmouthshire Regt. South Africa 1900-02*. Now a memorial to Cwm's local Territorials, the town was the headquarters of 'C' Company, 3rd Monmouthshire Regiments. The stone work was taken from the front wall of the recently demolished drill hall. The Battle Honour was awarded in recognition of those members of the regiment who volunteered for active service during the Boer War. A brass plate on the right side of the memorial has the inscription -

> *This Monument Is Dedicated To The Men Who Served In The 3rd Battalion Monmouthshire Regiment And In Memory Of Those Who Paid The Supreme Sacrifice. 'They Never Flinched Or Faltered'.*

The third memorial, a plain stone Celtic Cross, stands in the centre.

Three memorials remembering the dead of Cwm in the forecourt of the branch library in Canning Street.

Cwm Cemetery

The cemetery at Cwm contains the graves of nine First World War soldiers:

Private James Gordon Craig, 10th Battalion, South Wales Borderers, who died 3rd May, 1918.

Private Albert William Hall, 10th Battalion, South Wales Borderers, was born in Peterstow, Herefordshire. He lived in Cwm and died 25 July, 1916.

Sergeant William George Hamblin, South Wales Borderers, was the son of Alfred and Annie Hamblin of 6 Bailey Street, Cwm. He died, aged twenty-seven, from wounds received on 6 February, 1919.

Sergeant T.W. Hatton, 1st Battalion, South Wales Borderers, was the son of John and Mary Hatton and husband of Elizabeth. He died, aged forty, from wounds received in France on 1 December, 1918.

Private T. Johns, 21st Company, Royal Defence Corps, died 28 January, 1919.

Private D.J. Morgan, Monmouthshire Regiment, was the son of William and Mary Morgan of 49 Atlas Road, Canton, Cardiff. He transferred to the Labour Corps and died, aged twenty-eight, on 3 July, 1918.

Private J. Tabbot, 17th Battalion, Royal Welsh Fusiliers, died 3 October, 1917.

Private Windsor Virtine, 3rd Battalion, Monmouthshire Regiment, lived in Cwm and was the son of Samuel and Charlotte Virtine. He was wounded in Belgium and died, aged twenty-two, on 27 May, 1915.

Private W.J.P. White, 21st Company, Royal Defence Corps, died 23 May, 1920.

Tallistown Congregational Church

The memorial at the church in Marine Street, Cwm is situated behind the pulpit and comprises a white marble tablet recording the names and regiments of those killed within an oak surround. Under the heading - *1914-1918 - Fell In The Great War* - there are ten men listed:

David Clist, who enlisted into the 10th (1st Gwent) Battalion, South Wales Borderers, but later transferred to the 3rd Monmouthshire Regiment. He was killed at the Battle of Frazenberg Ridge on 8 May, 1915 and has no known grave. His brother, Stanley, also served with both battalions. He would be lost a few months after David, losing his life during the first phosgene gas attack on 19 December, 1915. His body lies in Bard Cottage Cemetery, Boezinge, Belgium.

The Clist brothers are followed by Thomas Henry Edwards, also of the 10th South Wales Borderers, and Gilbert Harris who served on HMS *Monmouth* (see St Mary's, Monmouth). Killed on the Somme on 26 September, 1916, was George Hoare, who enlisted into the 2nd Monmouthshire Regiment and later transferred to the 6th Welsh. Another member of the Hoare family, James Hoare, served with the 3rd Monmouthshire Regiment and was awarded the Distinguished Conduct Medal. He was killed while attached to 171st Tunnelling Company, Royal Engineers on 3 August, 1917.

Two other members of Monmouthshire Regiment are also shown. William S. Lewis and John Henry Pickford. The latter fell on 31 July, 1917 while trying to save a wounded friend: the second time the battalion records note an act of bravery by this man. The two remaining soldiers are - Richard Lloyd of the 13th Royal Welsh Fusiliers, killed in action on 20 October, 1917, and Albert Jones who is recorded on the memorial as having served with the Bedfordshire Regiment.

The oak surround has two panels, one either side of the marble tablet, recording the names, ranks and regiments of those members of the church who served in the Great War. Engraved in gold letters are the following:

Left panel: Lieutenant E. Evans, 13th Welsh Regiment; Second-Lieutenant T.H. Parry, Welsh Regiment; Sergeants E. Stephens and W.G. Thomas, Privates H. George, D. Owens, J. Griffiths, M. Morgan, W.J. Rule and A.J. Watckins, all local Territorials from the 1st Welsh Field Ambulance; Sergeant H.R. Clist, Privates G. Mandley, A. Mandley and G.J. Graig, of the 10th South Wales Borderers; Sergeant

W. Morgan, Privates W. Harris, E. Williams and G. Hancock, 3rd Monmouthshire Regiment; Privates C. Coles, E. Thomas, S. Mills, C. Barnes, G. Morgan, F. Rule and A. Morgan, of the South Wales Borderers; Private C.I. Jones, 5th Welsh Regiment.

Right panel: Privates I. Tuck, R. Worthing and T. Rule, Royal Welsh Fusiliers; Corporal J.H. Williams, Privates W. Drisoll and J.H. Miles, 1st Monmouthshire Regiment; Private C. Smith, 2nd Monmouthshire Regiment; Privates L. Michard and T.P. Morgan, both of the Army Service Corps; Private I. Peters, 5th King's Liverpool Regiment; J. Buckler, 3rd

Marble and oak memorial at Tallistown Congregational Church.

Devonshire Regiment; T.P. Morgan, 21st Dragoons; Private V. Daniels, Gordon Highlanders; Private C. Burgess, 2nd Welsh Regiment; Lance-Corporal R.E. Clist, 6th Lancashire Fusiliers; Private G. Williams, Welsh Guards; Private R. Price, 4th Welsh Regiment; Private M. Williams, Royal Field Artillery; Petty Officer A. Bosley, Royal Naval Division; R.J. Evans and H. Mathews, of the Royal Naval Volunteer Reserve. The last names are those of four women - M. Edwards, R. Edwards and B. Lewis, who served with the Women's Army Auxiliary Corps, and Gertrude Tuck who was a member of the Women's Royal Air Force. Her brother is also mentioned.

CWMBRAN

Within a few years of the war ending, the local firm of Guest, Keen and Nettlefolds (GKN) produced a set of cast iron plaques recording the names of employees who lost their lives. Originally located in the Work's administrative building, notes W.G. Lloyd in his book *Roll of Honour*, the three plaques, two large and one small, were moved when the GKN Nut and Bolt Works was closed down in 1962, to the storage department of the Company's Iron Foundries in Clomendy Road. Further closures saw a move to GKN (Shotten) Ltd and from there to a safer home at the local Royal British Legion.

It was in 1949 that the town of Cwmbran opened a Garden of Remembrance to commemorate the dead of both world wars. A plain Cross of Portland stone was added in November, 1952. As part of the 50th anniversary of the formation of Cwmbran New Town, the unveiling of the Cwmbran War Memorial by Sir Richard Hanbury Tenison, KCVO, HM Lord Lieutenant of Gwent and Doug Henderson, MP, Minister of State (Armed Forces), took place at Cocker Avenue Park on Sunday 6 June, 1999.

Refurbished and rededicated, the Cross and GKN plaques are now together and situated in a paved area of the park. The base of the Cross bears the inscription - *To The Fallen. At The Going Down Of The Sun And In The Morning We Will Remember Them* - and the dates - *1914-18 - 1939-45.*

Below this, and affixed to a pedestal, a tablet of Welsh Slate records the date of the ceremony and a list of locations where the names of those who made the supreme sacrifice are recorded and honoured -

> *All Saints Parish Church, Llanfrechfa - Croesyceiliog Cricket And Rugby Club - Ebenezer Baptist Church, Two Locks - Holy Trinity Parish Church, Pontnewydd - Mount Pleasant Baptist Church, Henllys - Penywaun United Reformed Church - Pontrhydyrun Baptist Church, Pontnewydd - Richmond Road Baptist Church, Pontnewydd - Salvation Army, Cwmbran - St. Gabriel's, The Parish Church of Cwmbran - St Mary's Church, Croesyceilog - St Michael And All Angels Church, Llantarnam.*

The GKN plaques are now located on a specially built wall behind the Cwmbran Memorial Cross. One hundred and fifty names are listed, without rank or regiment. Both the larger

Cwmbran memorial clock.

right and left-hand tablets bear the inscription -

In Ever Grateful Recognition Of The Splendid Patriotism And Heroic Self Sacrifice Of The Employees Of Guest, Keen & Nettlefolds Ltd Who Gave Their Lives For Their King And Country In The Great War 1914-1918.

The left-hand plaque records in three columns the names of eighty-four men from the Cwmbran Colliery:

1st column: J. Atkins, J. Atkins, A. Bates, W. Brinkworth, W. Chapman, F. Chatman, C. Collier, S. Cook, J. Crimmins, R. Dart, L.J. Davies, W. Daw, H. Driscoll, T. Drummond, J. Edwards, C. Evans, J. Evans, A. Fishlock, R. Hawkins, A. Hiscock, A. Hughes, T. Hughes, J. James, J. Jenkins, J. Johnstone, C. Jones, F. Jones, F. Jones.

2nd column: J. Jones, T. Jones, H. Lawrence, L. Leigh, H. Lewis, I. Lewis, C. Linney, J. Linney, W. Luffman, T. Lyons, J. Meyrick, C. Morgan, J. Morgan, P. Morgan, T. Morgan, W. Newells, J. Nicholas, G. Osborne, S. Pattimore, T. Payne, T. Payne, R. Powell, A. Price, W. Pritchard, J. Raisey, J. Ramsden, W. Rawlings, J. Reynolds.

3rd column: W. Richards, J. Roach, E. Ruddick, F. Skillman, E. Smith, T. Smith, D. Spanswick, J. Spanswick, H. Stanley, G. Taylor, F. Thomas, G. Thomas, W. Thomas, W. Tilton, W. Toms, H. Turner, J. Vince, H. Virgo, P. Virgo, R. Vizard, H. Walker, D. Waters, J. Watts, W. Watts, G. Whitby, F. Williams, R. Williams, A. Woods.

The plaque on the right has the names of the fifty-nine men who died from the Cwmbran Works:

1st column: W. Andrews, W.W. Bennett, A. Bosworth, J. Butcher, R. Cantle, R. Coles, H. Cordier, R. Cumbley, J. Davies, J. Desmond, T. Dodman, D. Driscoll, T. Fielding, C. Findlay, J. Flello, J. Francis, P. Gimblett, G. Holmes, T. Hulbert, A. Jenkins.

2nd column: C. Jones, J. Jones, K. Jones, J. Kilday, W. Leyshon, W. Maile, R. Morris, A. Nurden, D. O'brien, W. Parker, R. Pask, C. Pessant, S. Pattimore, A. Powell, R. Powell, W. Prangley, H. Price, J. Pym, P. Regan.

3rd column: T. Relihan, A. Richards, W. Rosser, J. Rowlands, F. Skinner, M. Skyrme, W.C. Stevens, C. Stiff, J. Tamplin, C. Thomas, W.H. Tomkins, C. Virgo, R. Wall, F. Watkins, J. Watkins, F. Weldon, A. Wheeler, D. Williams, W. Wood, H. Woodward.

The centre and smallest plaque has just seven names: J. Bartlett, T. Jones, M. Landers, A. Lewis, J. Price, J. Ryan and H. Soloman. These men were employees of GKN's Newport Wharf.

The origins of the memorial clock tower in Ventnor Road, Cwmbran, where a service of remembrance is held each November, is explained in W.G. Lloyd's book about the Eastern Valley of Gwent in the First World War - *Roll Of Honour.* Sometime after the armistice the Cwmbran branch of the British Women's Total Abstinence Union began a fund. The purpose of which was to provide a building in memory of those from the area who were lost. By 1935, however, the required target had not been met, and in that year the BWTAU handed over to the Council what moneys had been collected to date. This was to be used on a war memorial in the form of a public clock. The clock tower was put up in February 1936 and unveiled in the following June by the BWTAU's oldest member, Mrs Annie Kelly. The small plaque

attached to the clock makes no mention of its origins. The inscription reading simply
- *Clock Tower Erected By The Urban District Council Of Cwmbran February 1936.*

Cwmbran Cemetery

The cemetery is on the Llantarnam Road and contains eleven war graves:

Private P. Desmond, 2/2nd Battalion, Monmouthshire Regiment, enlisted at Pontypool under the name of John Shea. This is the name shown on his Commonwealth War Graves Commission headstone. He was born in Cwmavon, lived at Cwmbran, and died on 3 October, 1916.

Driver H. Head, 3rd Monmouthshire Battery, 4th Welsh Brigade, Royal Field Artillery, died 7 November, 1918. He had transferred to the Labour Corps.

Private Frank Holmes, Royal Army Service Corps, died, aged thirty-four, on 17 January, 1921.

Private John Jenkins enlisted into the Monmouthshire Regiment at Pontypool. He later transferred to 587th Area Employment Company, Labour Corps and died 11 March, 1918. He lived in Cwmbran and was married to Elizabeth Kate Jenkins.

Private John Meredith, Welsh Regiment, was twenty-seven when he died 9 June, 1917.

Private George Penn, 14th Battalion, Welsh Regiment, was born in Oakfield and enlisted into the army at Newport. His parents were Thomas and Polly Penn and he lived with his wife, Elsie Penn, at 20 Tranquil Place, Cwmbran. Private Penn died, aged twenty-nine, on 17 September, 1918 from wounds received in France.

Private Gwyn Pugh, 17th Battalion, Royal Welsh Fusiliers, was the son of Frederick and Mrs M. Pugh of Holly Bush, Cwmbran. Buried in a private family grave, his date of death is shown as 19 March, 1919. The records of the Commonwealth War Graves Commission, along with *Soldiers Who Died In The Great War*, gives 2 March. He was twenty-one.

Private Mark Skyrme, 3/1st Battalion, Herefordshire Regiment, was born at Vowchurch, Herefordshire. He died of phthisis on 12 April, 1916, aged twenty-nine, and is buried in a private family grave. His parents, Stephan and Emily Skyme, lived at 31 Llandowlias Street, Cwmbran.

Sergeant Percy Virgo, 9th Battalion, South Wales Borderers, was twenty-six when he died on 3 August, 1916. He was born in Newport.

Private F.C. Walby, Royal Army Service Corps, died 10 February, 1919.

Private Joseph Weyman, 'B' Company, 1st Battalion, Welsh Regiment, was gassed in France and died at home on 14 March, 1919. He was thirty-two and the son of Daniel and Annie Weyman of Blaenavon.

St Gabriel's Church

In January 1925, an organ was installed in St Gabriel's, Clomendy Road, Old Cwmbran, in honour of those from the area who had been killed during the First World War. On the 11 November, 1926, notes W.G. Lloyd in his book *Roll Of Honour*, the second part of the memorial was unveiled by Colonel Sir Joseph A. Bradney, CB, TD, DL. This being a tablet of British oak, which was attached to the side of the organ, and a lectern. Surmounted by the figure of Christ on the Cross, the tablet has the following dedication curved and highlighted in gold -

Original memorial cross, together with the three plaques formerly at the Guest, Keen and Nettlefolds works now on a new site at Cocker Avenue Park, Cwmbran.

IN MEMORY
OF OUR COMRADE
PTE. C.R WOODWARD
.A.S.C.
DIED ON ACTIVE SERVICE
FRANCE 7th MAY 1917

Memorial to Charles Rupert Woodward. St Gabriel's Church, Cwmbran.

Oak tablet commemorating the men of Llantarnam and Cwmbran who fell in the Great War. St Gabriel's Church, Cwmbran.

Memorial lectern, St Gabriel's Church, Cwmbran.

TO THE GLORY OF GOD AND IN PROUD MEMORY OF THE MEN OF LLANTARNAM AND CWMBRAN WHO MADE THE SUPREME SACRIFICE IN THE GREAT WAR 1914-1918.

ANSTEY T.J.
ATKINS JAS.
ATKINS JNO.
BATES A.
BENNETT W.
BISHOP W.H.
BUMSTEAD L.
BUTCHER J.
CHAPMAN W.H.
COLE R.H.
COLLIER C.
COOK S.
CUMBLEY R.C.
DAVIES A.G.
DAVIES L.I.
DAVIES L.J.
DAWSON W.E.
DESMOND J.
DRISCOLL D.
DRUMMOND T.
FIELDING T.
FISHER R.

FLELLO J.
HEASTIE W.K.
HINTON A.G.
HOLMES G.
HOWELLS C.
HUNT S.G.
JAMES J.
JAMES T.W.
JOHNSON J.
JONES C.
JONES J.W.
JONES K.
LAWRENCE H.
LEWIS H.W.
LEWIS T.
LEYSHON W.
LUFFMAN W.
LYONS T.
MARTIN T.
MEREDITH J.
MORGAN J.
MORGAN P.

MORGAN
ORPWOOD
PARKER
PARKER
PATTENON
PHILLIPS
REECE
RICHARD
RICHARD
ROWLAND
SALTER
SCAMMEL
SEYMOUR
SKILLMAN
SKYRME
SKYRME
SPANSWICK
SPANSWI
STEER G.
STIFF G.
TAMPLIN
THOMAS

THOMAS C.F.
THOMAS W.
TOMKINS W.G.
TROTMAN W.A.
TURNER H.D.
VAUGHAN E.
WALL B.
WATKINS D.J.
WAYGOOD P.G.
WEEKS H.J.
WELDON F.
WHATLEY C.E.
WHITBY G.
WILLIAMS A.E.
WILLIAMS C.G.
WILLIAMS R.
WILLIAMS W.E.
WOODS W.J.
WOODWARD C.R.
WOODWARD H.

"Lest we forget."

MAKE THEM TO BE NUMBERED WITH THY SAINTS:

To The Glory Of God And In Proud Memory Of The Men Of Llantarnam And Cwmbran Who Made The Supreme Sacrifice In The Great War 1914-1918.

Eighty-six names, arranged alphabetically and in four columns, follow:

1st column: T.J. Anstey, Jas. Atkins, Jno. Atkins, A. Bates, W. Bennett, W.H. Bishop, L. Bumstead, J. Butcher, W.H. Chapman, R.H. Cole, C. Collier, S. Cook, R.C. Cumbley, A.G. Davies, I. Davies, L.J. Davies, W.E. Dawson, J. Desmond, D. Driscoll, T. Drummond, T. Fielding, R. Fisher.

2nd column: J. Flello, W.K. Heastie, A.G. Hinton, G. Holmes, C. Howells, S.G. Hunt, J. James, T.W. James, J. Johnson, C. Jones, J.W. Jones, K. Jones, H. Lawrence, H.W. Lewis, T. Lewis, W. Leyshon, W. Luffman, T. Lyons, T. Martin, J. Meredith, J. Morgan, P. Morgan.

3rd column: W.F. Morgan, W.S. Orpwood, G.F. Parker, W. Parker, S. Pattemore, E. Phillips, L. Reece, A. Richards, W.J. Richards, J. Rowlands, C. Salter, W.F. Scammels, S. Seymour, F. Skillman, J. Skyrme, M. Skyrme, D. Spanswick, J. Spanswick, G.P. Steer, C. Stiff, J. Tamplin, C. Thomas.

4th column: C.F. Thomas, W. Thomas, W.G. Tomkins, W.A. Trotman, H.R. Turner, E. Vaughan, R. Wall, D.J. Watkins, P.G. Waygood, H.J. Weeks, F. Weldon, C.E. Whatley, G. Whitby, A.E. Williams, C.G. Williams, R. Williams, W.E. Williams, W.J. Wood, C.R. Woodward, H. Woodward.

Along the bottom of the memorial the quotations - *'Lest We Forget'* and *'Make Them To Be Numbered With The Saints'*..

The eagle lectern is also in oak and has the inscription -

In Proud And Glorious Memory Of Our Loved Ones Who Fell In The Great War 1914-1918 - carved into the stem.

On the north wall of the church, a small grey marble tablet commemorates the death of one of the men whoes name appears on the Roll of Honour -

In Memory Of Our Comrade Pte. C.R. Woodward - A.S.C. - Died On Active Service France 7th May 1917.

Charles Rupert Woodward served with 8th Field Bakery, Army Service Corps and was twenty when he died of pneumonia. He is buried in Janval Cemetery, Dieppe.

CWMCARN

Erected by inhabitants of the district and unveiled on 5 March, 1922 by Major Sir John Wyndham Beynon, Bart, the town memorial in the square at the bottom of Ivor Street, Cwmcarn, bears the inscription -

To The Glory Of God And In Everlasting Memory Of The Men Of Cwmcarn And Pontywaun Who Gave Their Lives In The Great War 1914-1918.

There are eighty names, together with ranks and regiments, recorded on two bronze panels:

Front panel: Lieutenants John William Taylor and Ellerton Davies of the 2nd Monmouthshire Regiment, both killed in Flanders, 1915 and buried in Calvaire (Essex) Military Cemetery, Ploegsteert; Sergeant Major W.J. Stroud of the Royal Army Medical Corps; Sergeant T. Callagan, Welsh Guards; Sergeants L. Edwards,

D. Harper, W.E. Landers (awarded the Military Medal), G.H. Smith and Corporals W.J. Brinkworth, W.H. Cunnick and P. Griffiths, all of the South Wales Borderers; Corporal W. Crabb, 2nd Monmouthshire; Corporal A. Griffiths, Welsh Regiment; Corporal W. Williams, who served with the Grenadier Guards; then seven Lance-Corporals - W. Duffield and T.J. Gooding of the South Wales Borderers, T.H. Roberts, A. Short, D.H. Thomas and G. Whateley, all members of 2nd Monmouthshire, and W.J. West who was killed while serving with the Royal Army Medical Corps. Signalman T.W. Hands was originally from Manchester and was awarded the Military Medal while serving with the Royal Berkshire Regiment. Another Signalman - D.F. Rowlands served with the Royal Field Artillery, as did Gunners T.G. Holtham, W.H. Maisey, B. Willits, Drivers J. Brown, E.A. Davies and Bombardier T.J. Whateley. The next name on the front panel of the memorial is that of Sapper W.R. Burns, another holder of the Military Medal. Men from the local Territorial Force Battalion, the 2nd Monmouthshire Regiment, complete the first panel and begin the second - Drummer W.T. Stroud, Privates S.V. Burns, A. Davies, J.W. Evans, J.J. Foley, O. Harrison, A. Jenkins, W.H. Morgan, S.T. Rogers, W.J. Sage.

Rear panel: W. Simmonds, W.J. Stone and D. Thomas. Two men from the 1st Monmouthshire follow - Privates T. Roberts and R.D. Tudor, then fourteen from the South Wales Borderers - Privates J. Birt, E. Broad, H.V. Duffield, R. Franklyn, H.P. King, T.J. Matthews, M. Moseley, C. Petherson, W. Pye, J. Titt, T.H. Walters, F.W. Westcotte, J. Greenslade (he served with the 10th Battalion) and A. Hopkins. Next come five gunners from the Royal Field Artillery - H.J.J. Burge, T. James, D.T. Mantle, J. Rowlands and P. Thomas; then a Royal Welsh Fusilier, B. Lovell; two men from the Royal Army Medical Corps - T. Nicholas and W.H. Smith; a Scots Guardsman - B.

Davies; W.J. Evans, Gloucestershire Regiment; W. Harper of the 7th Worcesters; G.M. Hern of the Royal Irish Rifles; W.R. Lott, who served with the Motor Transport section of the Army Service Corps; G. Price, listed as 'R.S.L.I.', but thought to have served with the King's Shropshire Light Infantry; G.G. Welsh, Durham Light Infantry; O. Kenna of the Royal Engineers; J. Sheppard, Rifle Brigade and T. Pike, Grenadier Guards. The last names on the memorial are those of three members of the Royal Naval Division - Stokers F.L.J. Coles and A.R. Roberts and Seaman P.C. Thompson.

The rear panel of the memorial, which ends with the quotation from *St John* (Chapter 15, Verse 13) - '*Greater Love Hath No Man Than This, That A Man Lay Down His Life For His Friend*' - also includes information regarding the date of unveiling and the several members of the Memorial Committee - Councillor A.E. Meredith (President), J. Richards (Chairman), D. Evans (Treasurer) and F. Charlotte (Secretary). The memorial also includes the names of those killed in the Second World War and that of a single soldier of the Welsh Guards who was killed in Northern Ireland in 1979.

Cwmcarn memorial.

EBBW VALE

A single soldier raising his helmet into the air in victory and standing on a pedestal, fixed to which are four copper panels, forms the Ebbw Vale war memorial in Libanus Road. The front of the pedestal, which is mounted on a base of unpolished Cornish granite, bears the inscription -

Erected In Memory Of Our Glorious Dead 1914-1918 - 1939-1945 By The Inhabitants Of The Ebbw Vale Urban District Area. Their Name Liveth For Evermore.

The remaining three sides are dedicated to, and bear the insignia of, The Royal Navy and Mercantile Marine (left), Royal Army Medical Corps and Nursing Service (right), Royal Air Force (back). The work and design of the Craftsmen's Guild, London, the Ebbw Vale memorial was unveiled on 24 September, 1924 and originally occupied a site in the middle of the town. It was moved to its present position in April, 1950, where, on the following 10 May, it was rededicated and unveiled by Lord Raglan, Lord Lieutenant of Monmouthshire. Many of those killed from the Ebbw Vale area served in one or other of the town's Territorial Force units. 'B' Company of the 3rd Monmouthshire Regiment was located there, as well as the 1st Welsh Field Ambulance and a detachment of the Royal Gloucestershire Hussars.

Ebbw Vale Comprehensive School
The memorial formerly at the Ebbw Vale County School in Beaufort Road (now closed) is now held in store at the new comprehensive in Waun-Y-Pound Road.
The intertwined letters - EBCS - with the words - *Dall Pob Anghyfarwydd* - in Welsh, then the Latin school motto - *Palma Non Sine Pulvere* (the palm is not obtained without labour) - appear within a double circle at the top of an oak surround. The dedication, followed by the names of those old boys who were killed, is recorded in raised letters on a bronze tablet within the surround -

This Tablet Has Been Erected By The Old Pupils Of This School To Perpetuate The Memory Of Those Who Fell In The Great War 1914-1919. 'Their Sacrifice Our Inheritance Their Remembrance Our Inspiration'.

There are thirteen names, each listed without rank or regiment: E.W. Briscoe, W. Briscoe, G. Davies, A. Griffiths, B.L. Jones, D.T.A. Jones, I. Newcombe, W.I. Pembrey, W. Riddell, A.G. Samuel, D.J. Stokes, W.F. Ward and J.P. Worton.

Ebbw Vale Cemetery
The cemetery is located on the Waun-Y-Pound Road (A4046) and contains fourteen First World War graves:
Private I.A. Booth, 3rd Battalion, Monmouthshire Regiment, was married to Annie May Booth of 30 Charles Street, Tredegar. He died, aged thirty, on 21 August, 1919.
Assistant Cook Mary Ann Evans, Queen Mary's Army Auxiliary Corps, was the daughter of Isaac and Hannah Evans of 11 Armoury Terrace, Ebbw Vale. She died on 23 March, 1919.

Ebbw Vale County School memorial.

Ebbw Vale memorial.

Private A. Harper, 2nd Battalion, Monmouthshire Regiment, was the son of Henry and Rose Hannah Harper of 5 Hart Street, Ebbw Vale. He died, aged twenty-two, on 17 November, 1918.

Private Dan Higgins, Depot, South Wales Borderers, was born in County Kerry, Ireland. He died on 8 September, 1914.

Staff Sergeant Gwyllym Hoskins, 321st East Anglian Field Ambulance, Royal Army Medical Corps, was the son of Herbert Henry Hoskins and married to Beatrice Bessie Hoskins of 50 Western Terrace, Ebbw Vale. He was born in Bedwellty and died, aged forty-six, on 6 March, 1918.

Sergeant H.C. Jenkins, 10th Battalion, South Wales Borderers, won the Military Medal in France. He died on 12 March, 1919.

Sergeant Mechanic Dafelyn Tawelog Austin Jones, 1st Aircraft Acceptance Park, Royal Air Force, previously served with the Machine Gun and Tank Corps. He was due to be commission on 1 October, 1918, but was killed on that day while flying. He was the son of Mr and Mrs J. Orton Jones of 22 Eureka Place, Ebbw Vale.

Private Rosser Davies Lewis, 10th Battalion, South Wales Borderers, was born in Bedwellty and was the son of Thomas and Elizabeth Lewis of 32 Beech Terrace, Ebbw Vale. He died, aged forty-four, on 14 March, 1915.

Private F.J. Martin, 1st Battalion, West Yorkshire Regiment, died on 21 February, 1919.

Corporal William John Maynard, Royal Army Service Corps, died 29 January, 1919. He is buried in a private grave with Victoria Maynard.

Private George Alexander Pocock, 3rd Battalion, Monmouthshire Regiment, was born in Hammersmith, London and was the son of George Pocock of Mountain House, Pontsticill, Merthyr Tydfil. He died, aged sixteen, on 28 March, 1915, having been wounded in Belgium two weeks earlier. Janet and John Dixon include in their book - *With Rifle And Pick*, part of a letter sent home by Sergeant Major T.E. Banks of 'B' Company - 'We have just come out of the trenches. We went in last Friday so we had a fair share of it...I am pleased to tell you I have just been congratulated for bringing a wounded man out of the trenches and taking him back to the dressing station - a mile back - in broad daylight and above all who do you think it was - Young Pocock. He was with another sergeant in a support trench, behind my fire trench and he got shot right through - the bullet passing through his lung.'

Private Meredith Probert, 4th Battalion, South Wales Borderers, was married to Emily Probert of 42 Victoria Road, Ebbw Vale. He served under the name of Wilcox and died, aged thirty-seven, on 27 January, 1916.

Petty Officer C.W. Rees, HMS *Colleen*, Royal Navy, died 21 March, 1920.

Private J. Seaborne, 2nd Battalion, Monmouthshire Regiment, died, aged thirty-six, on 10 December, 1918.

Recently three old sections of the cemetery were cleared and, as a result, the headstones of five graves (four First World War, one Second World War) were grouped together near the entrance and alongside a memorial stone inscribed -

Those Commemorated By The Memorial Stones Erected Here Died In The Service Of Their Country And Lie Buried Elsewhere In This Cemetery.

The four First World War soldiers are: Mary Ann Evans, Gwyllym Hoskins, Dan Higgins and Rosser Lewis.

GOLDCLIFF

St Mary's Church

A small brass plaque on the north wall of the nave has the inscription - *To The Glory Of God And In Memory Of* (three names follow) *Who Sacrificed Their Lives In The Great War, 1914-1918. 'Lest We Forget'*. The names recorded are: Private Joseph W. Barratt of the 1st Battalion, Nottinghamshire and Derbyshire Regiment, who was killed on 27th May, 1918 during the fighting at the Chemin Des Dames in France; Driver Ivor J. Huggett, Royal Field Artillery, and Private T. Reginald Waters, South Wales Borderers, who is buried in the churchyard at St Mary's Nash.

Memorial plaque to three men at St Mary's Church, Goldcliff.

GOVILON

Christchurch

To the left of the chancel arch, a stone tablet records in red letters the names of the eleven men and one woman from Govilon who died in the Great War. The dedication reads -

To The Glory Of God And In Honoured Memory of - (the names follow) - *Of This Parish Who Laid Down Their Lives In The Great War 1914-1919.*

Three quotations follow -

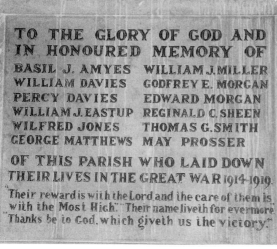

Memorial plaque, Christchurch, Govilon.

'Their Reward Is With The Lord And The Care Of Them Is With The Most High' - 'Their Name Liveth For Evermore' - and - 'Thanks Be To God, Which Giveth Us The Victory'.

The twelve names are as those recorded on the King George's Playing Field entrance pillars (see below).

Roll of Honour tablet in the King George's Playing Field gates, Govilon.

King George's Playing Field

The dates *1914* and *1918* are engraved (one on each) into the two stone pillars at the entrance to King George's Field in Merthyr Road, Govilon. On the right-hand side, and carved into a stone tablet, is the inscription -

To The Glory Of God And In Memory Of Those From This Parish Who Laid Down Their Lives For King And Country In The Great War This Entrance Is Erected.

On the left pillar there are twelve names: Basil J. Amyes, William Davies, Percy Davies, William J. Eastup, Wilfred Jones, George Matthews, William J. Miller, Godfrey E. Morgan, Edward Morgan, Reginald C. Sheen, Thomas G. Smith, May Prosser. A third, and smaller pillar on the right side of the entrance, has the inscription - *At The Going Down Of The Sun And In The Morning We Will Remember Them.*

GOETRE

St Peter's Church

Kelly's Directory Of Monmouthshire & South Wales for 1926 records that the nave of St Peter's had been panelled in oak in memory of the men of Goetre who fell in the Great War. Also forming part of the memorial, and situated on the north wall above the panelling, is a white marble tablet with the following inscription - *1914-1918 - The Oak Panelling In This Church Was Erected To The Glory Of God And In Memory Of*

Memorial marble tablet and oak panelling, St Peter's Church, Goetre.

- R. Baker, E.J. Davies, G. Dobbs, J. Dobbs, E. Evans, H. Guest, E. Harper, S.H. Kirby, C.E.V. Knight, E.O. Morgan A. Parsons - *Who Made The Supreme Sacrifice In The Great War And As A Thank Offering For The Providential Return Of The Following* - W.C. Andrews, G. Bandfield, W.H. Belcher, R. Bowen, I. Charles, W.J. Charles, F. Collins, R. Cornish, A. Cotterill, C. Cox, E.B. Cuthbertson, F.C. Day, T. Day, D. Edmunds, A. Edwards, G. Evans, W. Evans, G. Gwatkin, R. Harding, S.E. Harding, E.A. Jenkins, I. Jenkins, P. Jenkins, W.J. Jenkins, E. Lloyd, C.W. Merrick, B. Morris, E. Morris, S. Morris, V. Morris, A. Parsons, G. Parsons, W. Parsons, A.T. Phillips, F.J. Phillips, I.C. Phillips, A. Probert, A. Powles, R.J. Rosser, W. Summers, L.D. Whitehead. The names of those who fell are written in gold, those who served, and the dedication, in black.

On the south chancel wall, a brass plaque bears the inscription -

In Loving Memory Of Walter James Robinson - Woodbine House, Pinchbeck, Lincs. Killed In Action In Flanders, October 12th 1917, Aged 37 Years. The Souls Of The Righteous Are In The Hands Of God.

Walter Robinson was engaged to Muriel Davies, the daughter of the Revd Joseph Davies, Rector of St Peter's. He enlisted into the army at Newport, where he worked for Lloyd's Bank, and subsequently served with 'A' Company, 7th Battalion, East Kent Regiment. During the 12 October attack at Poelcappelle, 'A' and 'B' Companies advancing in support, records the war diary of the 7th Buffs - 'came in their turn under intense machine gun fire.' Walter Robinson's name also appears on the Newport Town Roll of Honour, the memorial for the Newport Athletic Club and that for St John the Baptist Church, Newport.

Also in the chancel, this time on the north wall, another brass plaque has the inscription - *Pro Rege Et Pro Patria* - over the badge of the Border Regiment. This is followed by -

In Loving Memory Of Sidney Henry Kirby 2nd Lieut: 10th Border Regt. Att: 1/5th H.L.I. Grandson Of Colonel Henry Byrde, Kandy. Killed In Action At Krithia Nullah, Gallipoli. December 19th , 1915 - Aged 24. 'I Am The Resurrection And The Life'.

The battalion records of the 1/5th Highland Light Infantry note that the objective on 19 December was two enemy trenches known as 'G12' and 'G11a.' Sidney Kirby was involved in the assault by 'C' Company on the latter, and was killed while leading a party that had been sent to deal with an enemy barricade.

A family headstone in the churchyard commemorates the death on 20 June, 1917 at Messines, France, of Ernest Oliver Morgan. He was aged thirty-five and served with the 144th Battalion, Australian Expeditionary Force. An inscription below his name reads - *Upright In Life. Noble In Death.*

GRIFFITHSTOWN

St Hilda's Church

There are eighty-eight names, each recorded together with rank and regiment, carved into three oak panels at the west end of the church. Below the names, which are highlighted in gold, the inscription -

> *To The Glory Of God And The Honoured Memory Of The Men From The Parish Who Gave Their Lives For Their County In The Great War 1914-1919. 'They Were A Wall Unto Us Both Night And Day'.*

The memorial was unveiled by Colonel H.D. Griffiths in March, 1921. Sixteen of the names appear under the heading - *Members Of The Church Lads' Brigade.* Over half of those listed on the three panels served with Welsh regiments, including seventeen men from the local Territorial Force battalion, the 2nd Monmouthshires, and one man, Trooper Edward John Humphreys, who died at Gallipoli with the Welsh Horse Yeomanry. There are a number from the Royal Field Artillery, Griffithstown being the headquarters of the 3rd Monmouthshire Battery.

St Hilda's Church, Griffithstown memorial.

Other regiments represented are the 7th Queen's Own Royal West Kents, in which Miles John Sterry won both the Military and Distinguished Conduct Medals - he was killed during the attack at Mount Carmel in France on 27 October, 1918; the 1/8th London Regiment (Post Office Rifles), who on 15 September, 1916 attacked Flag Lane on the Somme, where Harold Wheeler was killed, and the 3rd Dragoon Guards. Lance-Corporal Stanley Benjamin Williams of this regiment was awarded the Military Medal before he fell on 26 August, 1918 near Montrelet in France. Both Frank and Arthur Wilkey were originally from Bristol, Arthur being killed with the 1st Gloucestershire Regiment on 23 December, 1914, while holding trenches running from Le Plantin to La Quinque Rue, two days after the attack on Givenchy, while Frank was one of several hundred who fell with the Tyneside Scottish when they attacked south of La Boisselle on the first day of the Battle of the Somme - 1 July, 1916. Two men, A.R.J. Brown and R.C. Farrington served with the Australian Forces, and John Herbert Harris was lost when his ship - HMS *Defence* was sunk at Jutland on 31 May, 1916. The full lists is as follows:

Left panel: Private A.V. Benfield, Worcestershire Regiment; Staff Sergeant J. Bond, Royal Field Artillery; Private A.R.J. Brown, Australian Forces; Private T.Brown, 2nd Monmouthshire Regiment; Private F. Collier, Royal Welsh Fusiliers; Sapper L.C. Comer, Royal Engineers; Private S. Congram, 3rd Royal Fusiliers; Private J. Davies, 4th South Wales Borderers; Private J.T. Dudley, 11th South Wales Borderers; Private J.M. Dykes, 1st South Wales Borderers; Private A. Edwards, 8th Welsh Regiment; Corporal T.H. Edwards, 10th Scottish Rifles; Corporal R.C. Farrington, 5th Australian Division; Gunner W.T. Gardner, Royal Garrison Artillery; Private J. Green, 2nd South Wales Borderers; Private S.W. Gregory, Northumberland Fusiliers; Lance-Corporal J. Griffin, 4th South Wales Borderers; Gunner J.H. Harris, HMS *Defence;* Private C.J.H. Hemming, Royal Welsh Fusiliers; Sergeant J.H. Herbert, Oxfordshire and Buckinghamshire Light Infantry; Gunner I.J. Hiley, Royal Naval Division; Driver W.H. Hughes, Royal Field Artillery; Trooper E.J. Humphreys, Welsh Horse; Quartermaster Sergeant B. Jacob, Royal Welsh Fusiliers; Private J. James, 2nd South Wales Borderers; Private A.J. Jones, 2nd Monmouthshire Regiment; Sergeant F.J. Jones, 3rd South Wales Borderers; Private W.S. Jones, Army Service Corps; Private E. Jukes, 4th South Wales Borderers; Gunner C.G. Kilby, Royal Naval Division.

Centre panel: Sergeant H.W. Kilminster, 2nd Monmouthshire Regiment; Private A.H. King, 1st King's Own Yorkshire Light Infantry; Gunner W. King, Royal Field Artillery; Sergeant C.E. Knipe, 2nd Monmouthshire Regiment; Bombardier W. Lane, Royal Garrison Artillery; Gunner R.V. Lavis, Royal Field Artillery; Private S.R. Lawrence, King's Shropshire Light Infantry; Sergeant S. Lewis, 8th Welsh Regiment; Driver G. Lovegrove, Machine Gun Corps; Private C.A. Millard, 2nd South Wales Borderers; Private J.F. Mills, 10th South Wales Borderers; Gunner D.J. Moore, Royal Field Artillery. *Members of the Church Lads' Brigade:* Lance-Corporal A. Ball, 2nd Monmouthshire Regiment; Private A.S. Britton, 3rd Royal Welsh Fusiliers; Gunner W.H. Clapham, Royal Field Artillery; Driver A. Davies, Machine Gun Corps; Private W.A. Day, 2nd Monmouthshire Regiment; Private W.T. Higgs, 2nd Monmouthshire Regiment; Private C.H. Kirtland, 2nd Monmouthshire Regiment; Corporal R.K. Lewis, 2nd Monmouthshire Regiment; Trumpeter F.J. Lovejoy, Royal Field Artillery; Ordinary Seaman R.H. Mason, Royal Naval Division;

Company Sergeant Major R.S. Morgan, Royal Engineers; Private A.H. Parry, 2nd South Wales Borderers; Corporal C.A.Payne, 2nd Monmouthshire Regiment; Private A. Rees, Royal Welsh Fusiliers; Private W. Wilkey, 2nd South Wales Borderers; Private H.J. Williams, 5th South Wales Borderers.

Right panel: Private H.A.P. Morgan, 23rd Welsh Regiment; Private E.W. Parry, 2nd Monmouthshire Regiment; Gunner C.J. Phillips, Royal Navy; Private B.T. Powell, 5th South Wales Borderers; Private B.E.C. Price, 2nd Monmouthshire Regiment; Private T. Price, 1st South Wales Borderers; Sergeant J.S. Rowe, Royal Field Artillery; Private A. Russell, 1st South Wales Borderers; Sergeant M.J. Sterry, DCM, 7th Queen's Own Royal West Kent Regiment; Signaller A. Thomas, 13th South Wales Borderers; Bombardier C.E. Thomas, Royal Field Artillery; Bombardier G.J. Thomas, Royal Field Artillery; Private J.H. Thomas, 5th South Wales Borderers; Sapper E. Traves, Royal Engineers; Sergeant C. Trehearne, 5th South Wales Borderers; Private W. Tunley, 2nd Monmouthshire Regiment; Lance-Corporal I. Turner, 2nd Monmouthshire Regiment; Private A. Vaughan, Royal Welsh Fusiliers; Private R. Watt, 4th South Wales Borderers; Sergeant A.L. Watts, Royal Field Artillery; Private J.R. Watts, 2nd Monmouthshire Regiment; Corporal E. Weare, 12th South Wales Borderers; Rifleman H. Wheeler, 8th London Regiment; Private H.H. Whittington, 2nd Monmouthshire Regiment; Private H. Wigmore, 6th South Wales Borderers; Private A.C. Wilkey, 1st Gloucestershire Regiment; Private F. Wilkey, 3rd Tyneside Scottish; Gunner H.H. Williams, Royal Field Artillery; Lance-Corporal S.B. Williams, MM, 3rd Dragoon Guards; Private A. Wilson, 2nd South Wales Borderers.

HAFODYRYNYS

In 1921 the fallen from the area were commemorated on the Hafodyrynys Miners' Welfare Association gates at the entrance to a memorial garden and community hall. In 1926, and during the General Strike, the Hafodyrynys miners extended the area to include a recreation park. There are two panels incorporated into the gates. On the left, and headed by the date - *1914* - one bears the inscription - *To The Everlasting Memory Of The Men Of This District Who Gave Their Lives In The Great War.* The other records, below *1918*, thirty names, together with rank and regiment:

Company Sergeant Major A.H. Walwyn, Sergeant S. Cross, Privates J.H. Barkwell, E. Brown, A. Hall, H. Herbert, J.G. Kite, T. Taylor and F. Williams all served with the South Wales Borderers and Privates L. Davies, A. Downes, A. Griffiths, P. Griffiths, E. Mullarney, J. Murray, J. Rogers and D.J. Roberts were members of the local Territorial Force regiment, the 2nd Monmouthshire. N. Cousins, W.L.I. Edwards, R. Elias and E.G. Palmer all served with the Royal Naval Division while J. Pritchard and G. Worthing enlisted into the Royal Air Force. The remaining seven men are - Gunners A. Carter and F. Elias of the Royal Field Artillery; Corporal A.I. Davies and Private G. Charles who served with the Welsh Regiment; W. James, a trooper with the 11th Hussars; Grenadier Guardsman, A.G. McGillvery and Private E. Taggett who was killed while serving with the Royal Dublin Fusiliers. A small brass plaque to the right of the gates records their restoration in June, 1996 by Gwent Mechanical Handlings Ltd of Risca.

Hafodyrynys Miners' Welfare Association memorial gates.

ITTON

St Deiniol's Church

A stone Celtic Cross in the churchyard has the following inscription -

To The Glory Of God And In Honour Of The Men Of This Parish Who Fell In The Great War 1914-1919. 'Their Name Liveth For Evermore'.

There are three names recorded - Private Jesse L. Stephens of the 2/8th Sherwood Foresters; Henry R. Stump, who served with the 4th Mounted Rifles of South Africa, and James H. Hughes, a Bombardier with 70th Brigade, Royal Field Artillery.

Itton memorial, St Deiniol's Churchyard.

89

LLANBADOC

St Madoc's Church

The memorial to those from the parish who were killed is located at the entrance to the chancel and takes the form of a Rood Beam. On the left stone rail is the inscription -

To The Glory Of God In Thanks Giving For Victory And In Memory Of All Those Who Gave Their Lives For Us In The Great War Of 1914-1919.

The rail on the right side records nine names, without rank or regiment, in the following order: William Carey, George Davies, Edgar Harrhy, George Ll. Jenkins, Tom Parry, Eric S. Saunders, Geoffrey Webb, Charles Edward De La Pasture and McVeagh Crichton. Charles Edward de la Pasture was the son of the Marquis de la Pasture, and was killed with the 1st Battalion, Scots Guards near Ypres on 29 August, 1914. He commanded the right flank company, notes the Battalion records, which was surrounded by the enemy between Becelaire and the Menin Road. His name also appears on a family grave in the churchyard.

Memorial in the form of a Rood Beam at St Madoc's Church, Llanbadoc.

LLANDDEWI SKIRRID

St David's Church

On the north wall of the church, a white marble plaque mounted on a black surround bears the inscription -

In Loving Memory Of Albert E. Teague, Dearly Beloved Son Of C. And A. Teague, Of This Parish, Who Fell In The 2nd Battle Of Ypres May 1915, Aged 20 Years. 'He Gave His Life'. Erected By His Parents, Brothers And Sisters.

Private Teague served with the 3rd Battalion, Monmouthshire Regiment and was killed on 5 May during the fighting at Frezenberg. He has no known grave, his name being recorded on the Menin Gate at Ypres.

Albert Teague, along with five other men, is also commemorated on the south wall of the church. A brass plaque mounted on wood and engraved by F. Osbourne and Co. Ltd of London, has the following inscription -

To The Glory Of God And In Grateful Memory Of The Following Who Fell In The Great War 1914-1918.

The names are given with regiments: G.W. Steen and A.G. Powell, both South Wales Borderers (the former having previously served in the 3rd Monmouthshire); F.R.C. Atkins, who was killed in France with the Canadian Expeditionary Force; E.V. Jones, 5th South Lancashire Regiment and local Territorials - T. Jones and A.E. Teague of the 3rd Monmouthshire Regiment. The inscription ends - *R.I.P. Erected By Parishioners And Friends.*

LLANDOGO

The village memorial at Llandogo, a Celtic Cross of Cornish granite, bears the simple inscription - *1914-1918 - To The Glorious Memory Of* - then the following names and regiments: Lieutenant C.D.W. Rooke, Cameronians; Lieutenant A.E. Ashton, 4th Dragoon Guards; Private A. Burden, Border Regiment; Private G.V. Butchers, Welsh Guards; Able Seaman W. Lambert, Royal Navy and Able Seaman A. Williams, Royal Naval Division. These are followed by - *'Their Names Liveth For Ever'* - then six names belonging to those who were killed in the Second World War.

Charles Douglas Willoughby Rooke was the son of a local Justice of the Peace and was killed, aged twenty, on 19 June, 1915. While holding trenches at La Vessée, France, records the war diary of the 1st Battalion, Cameronians, Lieutenant Rooke went out with a patrol during the evening of 19 June. Badly wounded, he was hit in three places over the heart and he lay out in No Man's Land for some time before he could be brought in. He died shortly afterwards. Both Privates Antonio Burden and George Butchers also fell in France. The former on 28 April, 1918, in the Battle of the Lys, while the latter was killed during a raid on enemy positions at Mortaldje, near Ypres, on 2 July, 1916.

LLANELLEN

St Helen's Church

Commemorated in a family plot in the churchyard at St Helen's, is Captain William Walbeoffe-Wilson of the 3rd Monmouthshire Regiment. Killed on 2 August, 1915, he had joined his battalion in the Kemmel sector just one week earlier. Aged thirty-three, Captain Walbeoffe-Wilson is buried in Lindenhoek Chalet Military Cemetery, Kemmel.

LLANFIHANGEL CRUCORNEY

St Michael's Church

A white marble plaque on the south wall of the nave, and sculpted by R. Price & Sons of Abergavenny, has the inscription -

To The Glory Of God In Honoured Memory Of The Men From This Parish Who Laid Down Their Lives In The Great War, 1914-1918.

Eight names follow:

Captain Algernon Foulkes Attwood and Edward Russell-Clarke Esq., both commemorated elsewhere in the church; Sub-Lieutenant Leslie Morgan Thomas, mortally wounded on the Somme while serving with the Anson Battalion, 63rd (Royal Naval) Division during the February, 1917 operations on the Ancre; Sergeant John Price, a member of 116th (Railway) Company, Royal Engineers who lost his life in Egypt on 3 November, 1918; Lance-Corporal George Aaron Johnson of the 2nd Battalion, South Wales Borderers, mortally wounded during the November, 1914 fighting at Tsingtao, China; Private Ernest Arthur Meek of the 2nd Monmouthshire Regiment; Private Henry James Beechey, killed with the 8th Welsh Regiment in Mesopotamia, and Sapper Charles Price Thomas of the Royal Engineers.

On the north wall of the nave, a brass plaque has the following inscription -

In Ever Loving Memory Of Edward Russell-Clarke, C.B.E. Naval Intelligence Division Who Sacrificed His Life For His Country And Died At Penbydwl On The 17 October, 1918. Born 31 January 1871.

Records held at the Buckingham Palace Office give an award of the MBE on 4 June, 1917 for work as an aviation electrician and telegraphist for the Admiralty. The CBE was conferred on Edward Russell-Clarke, this time in recognition of his work as an adviser to the naval staff on wireless telegraphy, six months later.

Patrick Beesly, in his book - *Room 40, British Naval Intelligence 1914-1918*, notes how in September, 1914, Russell-Clarke, a barrister by profession, informed the Admiralty that he and a friend had for some time been intercepting German coded messages on their equipment in Wales and London. Both men were amateur 'radio hams,' and, with others, were responsible for the formation at Hunstanton on the Norfolk coast, of the first of many intercepting stations throughout the British Isles.

In the chancel, and on the north wall, a brass plaque bears the following inscription -

In Remembrance Of Algernon Foulkes Attwood. Captain Royal Fusiliers. Only Son

Of Llewellyn Carless Foulkes Attwood Of This Parish And Of Rachel Edith, Nee Corsellis, His Wife. Who Laid Down His Life For His King And For His Country At The Battle Of The Aisne On The 14th Day Of September 1914, In The 35th Year Of His Age. He Died Unmarried And Was The Only Male Of The Last Generation Of The Family Of Attwood, Formerly Of Hawne House Corngreaves Hall And The Leasowes Near Halesowen In The County Of Worcester. 'Possunt Quia Posse Videntur'.

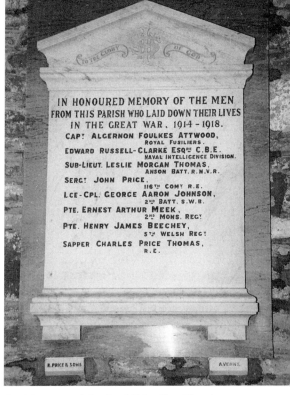

Captain Attwood served with the 4th Royal Fusiliers. This battalion, records H.C. O'Neill in his regimental history, took up a position just after midnight of 13 September at the Rouge Maison Spur. Attwood's company held an outpost line, but the Fusiliers' position had, in the dark of night, been set too close to the enemy. The Germans could, in one place, be heard talking. 'The Germans immediately

Parish memorial, St Michael's Church, Llanfihangel Crucorney.

profited by this mischance to take the Fusiliers' right flank in enfilade with machine guns, and many casualties were suffered'.

LLANFOIST

St Faith's Church

The top section of a brass plaque located on the north wall of the church is inscribed -

In Proud And Grateful Memory Of The Men From The Parish Of Llanfoist Who Gave Their Lives For Their Country In The Great War 1914-1918.

Sixteen names follow:

Captain Brynley Lewis Jones of the 3rd Monmouthshire Regiment, who died at home and is buried in Abergavenny New Cemetery; Captain G.F. Pauline, Grenadier Guards, who won the Military Cross on the Somme in 1916 and was killed by a shell in March, 1918; Second-Lieutenant Geoffrey Harland Chapman Hobbs, 7th Dorsetshire Regiment, who fell on the Somme during the attack on Gird Trench on 16 September, 1916; Sergeant Major I. Iball, who served with the 3rd Monmouthshire Regiment; Sergeant A.D. Bowcott of the Royal Welsh Fusiliers; Corporal D. Jones, 4th South Wales Borderers; Lance Corporal I. Prosser, Royal Army Medical Corps (buried in the churchyard); Lance Corporal R. Ashfield, 9th Duke of Wellington's (awarded Military Medal); Sapper T.J. Bowen, Royal Engineers; Gunner J. Meredith, Royal Garrison Artillery; Private S. Jenkins, 3rd

Monmouthshire Regiment; Lance-Corporal A. Jenkins, 3rd Monmouthshire Regiment; Private E. Lilwall, 2nd Monmouthshire Regiment; Private C.O. Bowcott, ALI; Private J. Saunders, Somerset Light Infantry and Private A. Webb of the 3rd Monmouthshire Regiment.

A further forty-eight names are inscribed at the bottom of the plaque under the inscription -

And As A Thanks-Offering To Almighty God For The Safe Return Of The Following Men From This Parish Who Served In His Majesty's Forces.

The names are recorded with ranks and regiments in the following order:

Lieutenant-Colonel H.J. Miers (awarded Distinguished Service Order), Corporal F.B. Prosser and Private J.H. Reed, all of the 2nd Monmouthshire Regiment; Lieutenant R.V. Smith, 7th Worcestershire Regiment; Regimental Sergeant Major C. Morgan, Lance-Corporal S. Lewis, Sappers J.H. Barnes, H. Meredith and Farrier G. Newgent, all of the Royal Engineers; Corporal E.A. Wilson, Privates R. Greenaway, W.H. Llewellyn, I. Watkins, R. Gwatkin, J. Prosser and J. Forty of the 3rd Monmouthshire Regiment; Corporal T.H. Williams, Privates S. Jones and F. Stradwick, Army Service Corps; Lance-Corporal F. Edge, 8th Welsh Regiment; Private W. Edge, 51st Welsh Regiment; Lance-Corporals B. Walby and J. Webb, both of the South Wales Borderers; Private F. Vaughan, 6th Leicestershire Regiment; Private W. Jones, 2nd Devonshire Regiment; Private W.W. Vaughan, Cheshire Regiment; Rifleman R.L. Williams, 1st Monmouthshire Regiment; Rifleman F.E. Watkins, Royal Irish Rifles; Rifleman T. Jones, RLAR; Rifleman H. Greenaway, Royal Field Artillery; Driver W.E. Williams, Royal Field Artillery; Gunners H. Walby, F.L. Manns and B.J. Tye, of the Royal Garrison Artillery; Air Mechanics F. Sheppard and B. Jones, Royal Air Force; Privates R. Walters, W. Barber and T. Jenkins, Royal Welsh Fusiliers; Rifleman H. Thomas, King's Royal Rifle Corps; Private A. Morris, Tank Corps; Private W. Morgan, Machine Gun Corps; Private J. Williams, 733rd Labour Company; Private H.C. Mills, Royal Marines; Able Seamen A. Howells and H.J. Pritchard, Royal Navy; Able-Seaman G.S. Kingsbury, Royal Naval Volunteer Reserve and Private H. Prosser of the South Lancashire Regiment.

The churchyard contains two war graves: Lieutenant Charles Ferdinand Reiss Hanbury-Williams, 2nd Battalion Oxfordshire and Buckinghamshire Light Infantry who was the son of Major-General Sir John Hanbury-Williams, GCVO, KCB, KCVO, CB, CMG of Henry III Tower, Windsor Castle. Born 9 November, 1890, educated at Wellington College and Gazetted Second-Lieutenant on 22 May, 1912, he was placed on half-pay list due to ill-health on 26 May, 1914. He re-joined the establishment as Lieutenant on 6 August, 1914 and was posted to the 5th (Service) Battalion, Oxfordshire and Buckinghamshire Light Infantry. Unfit for overseas service and transferred to 9th (Reserve) Battalion in May, 1915, Charles Hanbury-Williams died in London, aged twenty-six, after a long illness on 19 December, 1916. Lieutenant Hanbury-Williams has a Commonwealth War Graves Commission headstone and is buried alongside a family grave.

Buried in a private family grave is Lance Corporal Ivor Prosser who served with 3rd/1st Welsh Field Ambulance, Royal Army Medical Corps. He died, aged twenty-three, on 29 March, 1919.

LLANFRECHFA

All Saints Church

A brass plate commemorating forty-six men of the Parish of Llanfrechfa is situated on the south wall of the nave. The dedication reads -

To The Glory Of God And In Grateful And Honoured Memory Of The Men Of Llanfrechfa Parish Who Made The Supreme Sacrifice In The Great War. The Are In Peace.

The names are listed in rank order: Major E.S. Williams, Lieutenant R.C.L. Pilliner, Second-Lieutenant H.H. Stephens, Second-Lieutenant C.L. James, Quartermaster Sergeant G. Rowlands, Sergeants W. Knight and G.M. Jarrett; Corporals J. Morgan, A.A. Lee and T.J. Lewis; Lance-Corporals A.R. Bosworth, S. Berrow, Albert Cording, R. Fisher, A.W. Price and J. Rees (awarded Military Medal); Bombardier M. Robbins, Gunners Arthur Cording and S. Daleymount; Privates R.C. Dart, C. Morgan, E. Way, W.H. Bishop, Ivor Lewis (awarded Military Medal), F.J. Lewis, A. Lloyd, L.J. George, C. Passant, E.G. John, P.I. Lester, A. Wheeler, E. Roberts, G. Price, T.E. Nichollas, A. King, G.H. Brain, S. Pattimore, C. Bowles, H.G. Lowe, J. Watkins, R.C. Vizard, A.J. Wassall, T. Hardy, A. Nurden, W.J. Prosser and R.J. Carpenter. Both S. Daleymount and F.J. Lewis were change ringers at All Saints.

Also on the south wall the badge of the Royal Artillery features in a white marble plaque inscribed -

In Thankful Remembrance Of Rupert Colerick Laybourne Pilliner 2nd Lieut. Royal Field Artillery Who Fell In Action At Armentières France 4th Nov. 1914 Aged 23. Dear Elder Son Of Alfred M. & Edith M.E. Pilliner Of Llanyravon In This Parish. 'The Master Of All Good Workmen Has Put Him To Work Anew'. 'LÆtus Sorte Mea'.

Rupert Pilliner served with 127th Battery, 29th Brigade, RFA, which as part of the 4th Division crossed to France on 22 August, 1914. It took part in the retreat from Mons, the Battles of the Marne and Aisne before being engaged at Armentières.

A stained glass window by William Pearce on the north wall, showing Christ looking down on a wounded officer, records the death at Frezenberg Ridge of an officer of the 1st Monmouthshire Regiment -

To The Glory Of God And In Loving Memory Of Major Edmund Styant Williams. Killed In Action At The Second Battle Of Ypres May 8th 1915.

This officer, records Les Hughes and John Dixon in their book - *Surrender Be Damned*, was killed while directing the remnants of the battalion in the front line trenches in an attempt to organise the defence of the right flank.

The churchyard contains five war graves:

Private Alfred Lloyd, Welsh Guards, was born at Croesyceiliog, the son of Thomas Henry and Lucy Lloyd of Ashford Farm. He enlisted into the army at Pontypool and died, aged twenty-three, on 25 July, 1918. Alfred Lloyd is buried in a family grave with his mother, father and Joan Lloyd.

Private C. Passant, Monmouthshire Regiment, was born in Shropshire and as a regular soldier served in South Africa with the South Wales Borderers. He was married to Annie Agnes Passant of 39 The Highway, Croesyceiliog and died, aged forty-two, on 14 October, 1914.

IN THANKFUL
REMEMBRANCE OF
RUPERT·COLERICK
LAYBOURNE · PILLINER
2ND LIEUT. ROYAL FIELD ARTILLERY
WHO FELL IN ACTION AT
ARMENTIERES FRANCE 4TH NOV. 1914
AGED 23. DEAR ELDER SON OF
ALFRED M. & EDITH M.E. PILLINER
OF LLANYRAVON IN THIS PARISH
"THE MASTER OF ALL GOOD WORKMEN
HAS PUT HIM TO WORK ANEW."
"LÆTUS SORTE MEA."

Memorial to Rupert Colerick Laybourne Pilliner. All Saints Church, Llanfrechfa.

Memorial window to Edmund Styant Williams. All Saints Church, Llanfrechfa.

Private S. Pattemore, South Wales Borderers, was twenty-two when he died on 20 July, 1918.

Lance-Corporal John Rees, 6th Battalion, South Wales Borderers, served in France and Flanders where he was awarded the Military Medal. Wounded, he returned home and subsequently died on 28 October, 1918. He was born in Llantrisant, lived in Llanfrechfa and enlisted into the army in Newport.

Private Robert Thorne, 5th Battalion, South Wales Borderers, was married to Rosanna Thorne of 5 Chapel Row, Ponthir. He died, aged forty-five, on 27 October, 1919.

LLANGIBBY

St Cybi's Church

A stone Celtic Cross in the churchyard has the following inscription -

In Grateful And Glorious Memory Of The Men Of Llangibby And Coed-Y-Paen Who Fought And Of The Following Who Laid Down Their Lives In The Great War 1914-1918. 'Their Name Liveth For Evermore'.

The names recorded are without rank or regiment: D. Arthur Addams Williams,

Arthur Bishop, Ernest Griffiths, James Payne, Frank Lewis, Thomas Barton, Ralph Lewis, William Payne, Godfrey Lewis, Arthur Charles.

Inside the church, and on the south wall, there is a white marble memorial sculpted by Maile and Son of London commemorating the death of a young officer at Gallipoli. Below a cross, draped with a sword-belt and sword, the inscription -

In Proud And Loving Memory Of A Brave And Gallant Soldier - Donald Arthur Addams-Williams. 2nd Lieut. South Wales Borderers, Beloved Only Son Of The Revd. Herbert Addams-Williams, M.A. Rector Of This Parish And Grace, His Wife, Who Was Killed At The Dardanells August 11th 1915, Aged 19 Years When Leading His Men Into Action After Having Been Three Times Wounded. 'Go To Thy Grave; At Noon From Labour Cease, Rest On Thy Sheaves, Thy Harvest Work Is Done. Come From The Heart Of Battle, And In Peace, Soldier Go Home. With Thee The Fight Is Won'.

Buried in the 7th Field Ambulance Cemetery, Donald Arthur Addams-Williams served with 'A' Company, 4th Battalion, South Wales Borderers and was killed during the attack on Kabak Kuyu. 'The advance,' records C.T. Atkinson in his history of the South Wales Borderers, 'was timed for 7 pm, at which hour Lieutenant Bell and Second-Lieutenants Addams-Williams and Owen, took out a covering party of 120 men. Moving in skirmishing order they at once came under rifle and machine-gun fire but reached the intended positions nevertheless, despite heavy casualties.'

LLANOVER

Captain, the Hon. Elidyr John Bernard Herbert, Royal Gloucestershire Hussars, was attached to the 19th Squadron, Machine Gun Corps (Cavalry) when he was killed in Palestine on 12 November, 1917. In his memory, his father, Lord Treowen, conceived the idea of the 'settlement garden city' of Tre'elidyr, to be built on his estate at Llanover and to include a school, chapel, village hall and green. On the green stands a cross, and close by a stone seating area containing three engraved brass tablets.

The centre tablet has the inscription, first in Welsh, then in English,

This Cross Is Erected In Memory Of Those Who Answering The Call Of Duty Fell In The Service Of Their King Giving Their Lives That The Cause Of Justice & Liberty Might Prevail ++ May It Remind Those Who Look Upon It That They Too Are Summoned Daily By Duty To Loyalty And Self-Sacrifice.

The tablets to the left and right record, in addition to Lord Treowen's son, a further seventeen names, all connected with the Llanover estate, and who fell during the Great War: Second-Lieutenant James Tony Clarke of the 2nd Royal Sussex Regiment was aged twenty-three when he was killed on the Somme in September, 1916. He has no known grave, his name being recorded on the Thiepval Memorial in France. Another young officer, Second-Lieutenant Dion P. Davies is shown as having served with the Jamaica Contingent, and Cadet J.L. Nicholas with the Royal Air Force. There is a Grenadier Guardsman, Private Noel W. Lewis, and two members of the Welsh Guards - Privates Benjamin Evans and Edwin B. Beach.

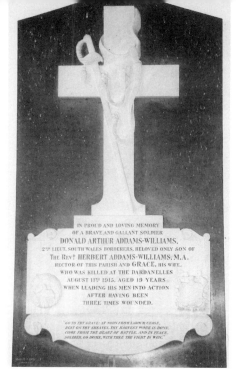

Memorial plaque, entirely in Welsh, to two workers from the Llanover estate. Presbyterian Church, Llanover.

Memorial to Donald Arthur Addams-Williams, St Cybi's Church, Llangibby.

Other Welsh regiments are represented by Private Corris G. Evans, Royal Welsh Fusiliers; Sergeant W.J. Rea, Lance-Corporals David B. Jones, Percy T. Lewis, T.W.G. Williams, Privates John D. Thomas and Reg. Griffiths, all of the South Wales Borderers, and Privates Wilfred Morgan, Ivor Jacob and Charles H. Jacob who were killed while serving with the Welsh Regiment. The last man is Lance-Corporal D. Harry of the King's Shropshire Light Infantry. For each of the eighteen men who fell, a tree was planted. These were arranged in a curved line between the cross and memorial plaques.

Hanover United Reform Church

An oak tablet bearing both the names of those who were killed, and those who served, is situated in the Sunday School room. At the top of the memorial, the inscription in gold letters reads -

This Roll Of Honour Commemorates Those Connected With This Church And

The green at Llanover 'settlement garden city'.

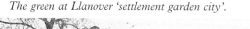

Sunday School Who Bravely Fought And Those Who Nobly Fell In The Great World-War Of 1914-1918.

Below this dedication is a colour print showing various troops climbing the steps of a temple where an angel awaits them at the entrance. The men carry the flags of the United Kingdom, France, the United States and other allied countries.

The names of nine men are recorded in gold letters under the heading - *Killed* - Second-Lieutenant T. Clarke, Sergeant William Ray, Lance-Corporal David Harry, Private I. Jacob, Private W. Morgan, Private C. Jacob, Lance-Corporal P.T. Lewis, Lance-Corporal R. Griffiths and Cadet L. Nicholas who is buried in St Bartholomew's Churchyard and recorded as having died of pneumonia at home.

Those that - *Served* - are shown in the following order - Second-Lieutenant D.P. Davies, Sergeant William Harry, Corporal David Price, Privates David Griffiths (awarded Military Medal), William Jenkins, E. Jenkins and F. Alexander, Bombardier G. Williams, Privates R. Roberts, C. Durham, P. Jenkins, R. Price, J.T. Evans, P. Edwards, William Morgan, J. Morgan, S. Francis, D.J. Griffiths, I. Williams and W. Evans, L/S E. Morris, L/S D.H. Morris, Privates T. Morris, A. Griffiths, F. Griffiths, G. Powell, V. Jones, William Griffiths, J. Davies, A. Williams, A. Phillips, C. Price, F. Ray, R. Jones, W. Jones and F. Jones.

Inside the church, a brass plaque mounted on white marble to the right of the pulpit shows the Crest of the South Wales Borderers. Below this is the inscription -

In Ever Loving Memory Of Lce. Cpl. Percy Thomas Lewis Of Ty-R-Ewrn-Goytrey Who Was Killed By Enemy Shell At Headquarters Of 10th Batt. S. W.B. France On His 22nd Birthday July 2nd 1918. Interred At Varrennes British Cemetery Near Albert. "While He Walked The Paths Of Youth. He Walked In Wisdom Too."

The war diary of the 10th South Wales Borderers records the 2 July and the direct hit that also killed two officers and wounded two others.

Presbyterian Church

A memorial to two workers on the Llanover Estate is situated on the east wall of the church. All in Welsh, the brass plaque has the inscription -

'Yr Arglwydd Bia'r Clod' Cysegredig I Goffadwriaeth Dau O Aelodau Yr Eglwys Hon A Gollasant Eu Bywydau T ra'n Amddiffyn Eu Gwlad (The Lord has the glory. Sacred to the memory of two members of this church who lost their lives defending their country) - *Benjamin Evans Yn Ffrainc. Medi 27air 1915 - David Benjamin Jones - Yn Mesopotamia. Chwef 15fed 1917. 'Maer Nos Ar El Barrau I Gyd Yr Oleuri'* (The darkness continues to give light).

Private Evans served with the Welsh Guards and was killed at the Battle of Loos on 27 September, 1915. His workmate, who joined the South Wales Borderers, became a lance-corporal, and fell during the 4th Battalion's attack at Dahra Bend, Mesopotamia, 15 February, 1917.

St Bartholomew's Church

On the north wall of the nave, a brass tablet mounted in a stone surround has the inscription -

To The Glory Of God And In Grateful Remembrance Of The Following Communicants Of This Church Who Fell In The Great War 1914-1919.

Six names are recorded, each with rank and regiment: Noel W. Lewis, Private, Grenadier Guards; William J. Rea, Sergeant, 2nd Gwent, South Wales Borderers; John J.T. Clark, Second-Lieutenant, 2nd Royal Sussex Regiment; John D. James, Private, 2nd Gwent, South Wales Borderers; Burgess Beach, Guardsman, Welsh Guards; Cornis G. Evans, Lance-Corporal, Royal Welsh Fusiliers. The inscription ends with the quotation - *'Let Those Who Come After See To It, That Their Names Are Not Forgotten'*.

Noel Lewis was killed quite early on in the war, being mortally wounded during the September, 1914 fighting near La Cour de Soupir Farm in France. William Rea of the 11th (2nd Gwent) Battalion, South Wales Borderers was killed on 7 July, 1916. His battalion had gone forward in an attempt to clear the enemy from Mametz Wood on the Somme.

The churchyard contains two graves belonging to servicemen of the Second World War, and one from the First - Cadet Joseph Leonard Nicholas, Royal Air Force. Born 28 May, 1899, he died 19 December, 1918 and is buried in a family grave.

LLANTARNAM

St Michael and All Angels Church
St Michael and All Angels Church is on the Newport Road, close to the junction with Llantarnam Road. In September, 1915, Captain Gordon Pemberton Steer of the Somerset Light Infantry, and son of Edward and Augusta Steer of Woodlands, Malpas, left for France. Attached to the 2nd Wiltshire Regiment, he joined the Battalion at Les Harisoirs on 14 October and was soon in the firing line at Givenchy. On the 25 November, records the Battalion war diary, two mines were blown under the German front line opposite the Wiltshires. Very quickly men from 'A' Company charged forward, but during the operation Gordon Steer was mortally wounded. Featuring the figures of Christ, St Peter and St Michael, the east window of the church commemorates his death. An inscription in the bottom right-hand corner of the window reads -

Remember Ye In Your Prayers, Gordon Pemberton Steer, Captain, Somerset Light Infantry, Who Was Mortally Wounded At Givenchy 25th November, 1915, And Died At Wimerenx, France, 26th December, 1915, Aged 30 Years, And Also All Others Who Have Laid Down Their Lives For Their King And Their Country In The Great War.

Opposite the east window, and on the north side of the chancel arch, a marble tablet bears the inscription -

Sacred To The Memory Of Thomas John Anstey Born August 28 1884 Fell In Action At Gallipoli October 6 1915 In The Great War.

Thomas Anstey, whose cameo portrait forms part of the memorial, was living in Wandsworth, London when war broke out. He joined the City of London Yeomanry (Roughriders) and on 18 August, 1915 landed with his regiment at Suvla Bay, Gallipoli. After dark on 5 October, records A.S. Hamilton's history of the City of

London Yeomanry, an attempt was made to wire round part of the Roughriders' trench that was exposed to the enemy. It was during this operation that Corporal Anstey was posted as missing. His body was later found and buried in Green Hill Cemetery, Suvla.

A third memorial in St Michael and All Angels takes the form of an oak lectern. Presented by Mrs Russell Trotman to commemorate the death of her brother, it was dedicated on 25 December, 1918 and bears the inscription -

Sacred To The Memory Of Edgar Vaughan, 49th Canadian Battn. Edmonton Regiment, Who Was Killed In Action At Passchendaele Oct. 30th 1917. Age 28.

Edgar Vaughan was formally a chorister at the church.

The churchyard contains one war grave, that of Private P. Morgan of the 1st Battalion, Grenadier Guards who died 31 March, 1915. He was twenty-six.

Memorial to Thomas John Anstey, St Michael and All Angels Church, Llantarnam.

LLANTILIO CROSSENNY

St Teilo's Church

Kelly's Directory of Monmouthshire and South Wales for 1926 records that an ancient cross in the churchyard of St Teilo's has been restored as a memorial to the men connected with the parish who fell in the Great War. The names of the men are inscribed on the cross. Today, only the base of the cross remains. This has attached a tablet of Welsh slate inscribed - *In Memory Of The Men Who Fell In The Wars*, under the dates - *1914-1918*. There are ten names recorded, each without rank or regiment: John Brown, Ernest Fisher, George Fisher, George Heseltine, Edward Jeffreys, Arthur Mardon, Henry Plaistow, Charles Radford, Charles Ruck and Oliver Watkins. There are two names for the Second World War.

Private George Fisher served with the 3rd Monmouthshire Regiment and was awarded the Distinguished Conduct Medal on 26 January, 1918. He was attached to the 9th Battalion, Royal Welsh Fusiliers when he died on the following 30 May from wounds received during the Battle of the Aisne.

LLANTILIO PERTHOLEY

St Teilo's Church

Some time in the 1920s, the steps forming the base of the ancient cross in St Teilo's churchyard were used as a location for four memorial plaques bearing the names and regiments of those from the parish who were killed during the Great War. On the uppermost step the inscription reads -

To Our Glorious Dead This Cross Has Been Restored In Memory Of Capt. William Humphrey Thomas, M.C. And Bar, Mentioned In Despatches - 1/1st Berks. Yeomanry, Very Dearly Loved Son Of Mr And Mrs William Lloyd Thomas Of Tredilion Park, Died At Kantara Nov. 28th 1917, Aged 28, Of Wounds Received Nov. 20th In The Advance On Jerusalem. Make Thy Way Plain Before My Face, O Lord.

On the second step -

Also In Memory Of The Other Brave Men Of This Parish Who Gave Up Their Lives In The Great War That Others Might Live In Freedom.

The names of three officers and a company sergeant major follow: Lieutenant-Colonel Robert Hastings Lascelles of the Royal Horse Artillery served throughout the war in France and Belgium, during which time he was awarded the Distinguished Service Order and Chevalier of the French Legion of Honour. He died of pneumonia on 16 February, 1919 and is buried in Charlton Cemetery, Greenwich, London.

Also to serve on the Western Front was Captain Jestyn Llewelyn Mansel, who had fought with his regiment, the 7th Dragoon Guards, in South Africa before going to France in 1914. He was mortally wounded on 20 December, 1914 while leading a charge on an enemy machine-gun position near Festubert.

On the Somme, in August, 1916, Lieutenant Eric George Henry Bates would also lose his life while leading his men in an attack. The objective of his regiment, the Buckinghamshire Battalion of the Oxfordshire and Buckinghamshire Light Infantry, was the German line between Pozières and Thiepval.

The remaining name of the second plaque is that of Company Sergeant Major R. Wall who served with the 8th Battalion, King's Shropshire Light Infantry and was killed on 18 September, 1918 during the attack on Pip Ridge near Salonica.

There are eleven names on the third plaque: Corporal P. Pembridge and Privates A. Powell and W. Morgan of the South Wales Borderers; Private J.A.C. Bedford, Welsh Regiment; Gunners O. Pembridge and A.M. Jones of the Royal Field Artillery; Private A.J. Gibbons who served with the Lancashire Fusiliers; Private R. Radcliffe, Somerset Light Infantry; Sapper G.N. Watkins, Royal Engineers; Artificer P. Sollars, Royal Navy and Trooper J. Laker.

The men on the fourth plaque were all members of the local Territorial Force battalion, the 3rd Monmouthshire Regiment: Sergeant W.H. Pritchard and Privates A.E. Jones, D.S. Morris, A.E. Baldwin, E.V. Jones, R.G. Pritchard, A.G. Evans, T. Jones, G.W. Steen, M.W. Holmes, F. Lewis, H. Taylor and J.J. Worthington.

Three of the men recorded on the war memorial, together with a fourth, are buried in the churchyard. Trooper John Henry Laker served with the 20th Hussars and lived at Mardy. He died, aged thirty-three, on 5 December, 1918. Also from Mardy was Private W. Morgan who was thirty-nine when he died on 14 November,

1918. He is buried alongside Private A. Morgan of the Royal Welsh Fusiliers. Age is given as thirty-eight, date of death - 28 October, 1921. The men share a Commonwealth War Graves Commission double-badged headstone. Artificer 4th Class Percy Sollers served on HMS *Glatton* and was the son of George and Emma Sollers of Mardy. He died on 17 September, 1918. The *Glatton* has been lost in Dover Harbour after a series of explosions on board the previous day.

Within the church, and to the left of the chancel screen, William Thomas is again commemorated. This time on a brass plaque with the inscription -

> *To The Memory Of William Humphrey Thomas Of Tredilion Park. Born August 28th 1889 - Died November 28th 1917 Of Wounds Received In Action Near Jerusalem. Captain 1st Berkshire Yeomanry - Military Cross And Bar. R.I.P. Greater Love Hath No Man Than This, That A Man Lay Down His Life For His Friends.*

The plaque also displays in white enamel, the family Crest, a demi-unicorn, and the motto - 'Virtus invicta gloriosa' (Unconquered virtue is glorious).

LLANTRISANT

St Peter, St Paul, St John's Parish Church
A painted wooden board listing the names of former pupils of Llantrisant and Llanllowell School who served during the First World War hangs in the south porch. This Roll Of Honour previously hung in the school (now closed) and records thirty-

Hand-painted memorial board to former pupils at Llantrisant and Llanllowell School. Now at St Peter, St Paul, St John's Parish Church, Llantrisant.

Parish memorial, St Mary's Church, Llanvair Discoed.

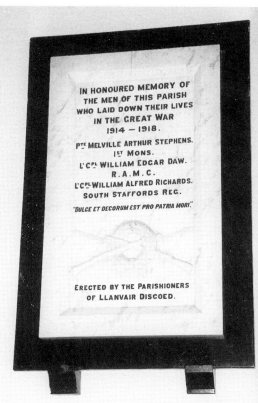

four names (most with regiments) in the following order:

Sidney Jones; Charles Williams, 2nd Monmouthshire Regiment; Charlie Paget, King's Own Yorkshire Light Infantry; Edwin Hunt, Australian Army Service Corps; James Williams, 11th South Wales Borderers; Frederick Williams, 17th Canadian Infantry; William Little, South Wales Borderers; Harold Richards, Royal Field Artillery; Harold Davies, 8th Welsh Regiment; Thomas Davies, South Wales Borderers; Arthur Farr, New Zealand Mounted Rifles; Philip Wilcox, 1/4th Royal Sussex Regiment; Alfonso Morgan, 11th South Wales Borderers; Trevor Morgan, Royal Horse Artillery; Allan Miles, Montgomeryshire Yeomanry; Frederick Hayward, 14th South Wales Borderers; Harry Paget, South Wales Borderers; James Byard; Allan Collins, Royal Field Artillery; Egbert Spary, Royal Field Artillery; Frederick Spary, 2nd Middlesex Regiment; Albert Davies, Royal Welsh Fusiliers; George Davies, South Wales Borderers; William Paget, 3rd Welsh Regiment; John Lewis, 3rd Monmouthshire Regiment; C.A. Dutson, Middlesex Regiment; L. Dutson, Middlesex Regiment; Ernest Farr, New Zealand Royal Field Artillery; George Price, John Jones; William Collins, Canadian Royal Engineers; Percy Birden, Royal Field Artillery; Roger Miles, South Wales Borderers; Ivor Williams, South Wales Borderers.

Inside the church the memorial to those from the parish who were killed takes the form of a brass lectern. There are six names inscribed on the base - Harry and Charley Paget, who were brothers, Charley and James Williams, also brothers Ivor and Percy Williams.

LLANVAIR DISCOED

St Mary's Church
Erected by the parishioners, the memorial on the north wall of the church bears the inscription -

In Honoured Memory Of The Men Of This Parish Who Laid Down Their Lives In The Great War 1914-1918. "Dulce Et Decorum Est Pro Patria Mori."

There are three names recorded: Private Melville Arthur Stephens of the 1st Monmouthshire Regiment, killed in action near Loos on 13 October, 1915 and who has no known grave; Lance-Corporal William Edgar Daw, Royal Army Medical Corps who died in France on 22 July, 1916, and Lance-Corporal William Alfred Richards. He was born in Chepstow and died on 31 August, 1916 while serving with the 1st South Staffordshire Regiment. The memorial is in white marble, mounted on black wood, and includes the device of two crossed rifles passing through a laurel wreath.

LLANWERN

St Mary's Church
There are no memorials or war graves within the church or churchyard. However, a tall stone cross marks the family grave of David Alfred Thomas, 1st Viscount Rhondda of Llanwern who died on 3 July, 1918 and was President of the Local Government Board and Food Controller during the Great War.

MACHEN

Dedicated on 12 February, 1921, the Cornish granite Celtic Cross memorial erected in Commercial Road, Machen bears the inscription in raised letters -

To The Glory Of God And In Honoured Memory Of The Men Of This Parish Who Fell In The Great War 1914-1918.

Below this, twenty-nine names are recorded: J. Banfield, W.E.C.A. Darby, L. Everson, W. Harrington, A. Harris, J.H. Harris, P. Heath, H.J. Hoare, H. Hodges, A. Horton, W.J. Howells, W. Jenkins, T.H. Johnson, R. Jones, J. Kew, F.G. Lewis, A. Matthews, S. Mayberry, W. Morgan, J. Pugh, A. Rees, D.J. Rees, J.H. Richards, A. Rolls, T. Rosser, W. Shute, A. Thomas, T.A. Thomas and H. Whittingham. Those who were killed in the Second World War appear on the right-hand side of the cross.

St John The Baptist Church
Commemorated on the headstone of a family grave in the churchyard at St John's is the name of Private Tom James, who was killed near Festubert on 21 May, 1915 while serving with the Canadian Expeditionary Force.

Close by another family plot records the death of Lieutenant William Edward Cleve Augustus Darby, 1st Battalion, Monmouthshire Regiment, who was killed in action near the Hohenzollern Redoubt on or about the 12 October, 1915. In his memory, his mother erected a stone tablet on the north wall of the church, near to the Altar -

In Loving Memory Of Lieut. W.E.C.A. Darby - 1st Mon. Regt. Son Of The Rev J.C.S. Darby Late Rector Of This Parish - Who Fell In Action In France October 1915.

William Darby has no known grave, his name being recorded on the Loos Memorial. The church is also in possession of an illuminated Roll of Honour, but at the time of writing (December, 2000) this is away being refurbished and framed.

Memorial plaque to William Darby. St John the Baptist   Parish memorial, Machen. Church, Machen.

The churchyard contains one war grave, that of shorthand typist M. Woodruff, Women's Royal Naval Service. A member of a local family who died 18 October, 1918.

MAGOR

The war memorial erected and placed in the Square at Magor in 1924 by Viscountess Rhondda was in memory of her late husband, who died in 1918, and those from Magor and the neighbouring villages who were killed. On one side the inscription -

Praise God For The Men Of Magor And Llandavenny - Undy - Bishton - Redwick - Llandevaud - Penhow And St Brides Who Laid Down Their Lives 1914-1918 - 1939-1945.

The names of those who fell appear on two further sides and have been arranged according to village. There are ten names recorded collectively, under the dates - *1914-18* - for Magor, Undy and Llandavenny: Raymond Walker, Frank G. Wooley, Harry Wooley, Alfred Hanks, William Ford, Sidney W. Williams, Allan H. Berrow, William Attwell, Charles Brice and Thomas S. Chick. Then come the names of eleven men who fell in the Second-World War.

The next panel records three names for Bishton: Francis Williams, George James and Edgar Morgan; two for Llandevaud: Edward Theobald and Walter Davis, and one each for Redwick: Horace L. Cox; Penhow: Trevor W. James (See also Penhow - St John The Baptist Church.), and St Brides: Alban L. Williams.

The forth side of the memorial has, below a cameo portrait in bronze, the inscription -

Remember Also David Alfred Thomas 1st Viscount Rhondda. Born Aberdare 1856 - Died Llanwern 1918 - For He Too Died Serving The Nation As Food Controller.

David Alfred Thomas is buried in St Mary's Church, Llanwern. His Family Arms are set into the top of the memorial, along with the Royal Arms and badges of the Welsh and Monmouthshire Regiments.

Parish Church Of The Blessed Virgin Mary
On the south wall of the nave, a small bronze plaque put up by Thomas William Berrow of Summerleys, Magor in memory of his son, has the following inscription -

In Loving Memory Of Allan H. Berrow - Tank Corps. Born March 3rd 1892 - Died On Active Service Novr. 20th 1918. Buried At St Pol France. He Has Fought The Good Fight.

Private Berrow served with the 7th Battalion, Tank Corps and was twenty-six when he died. He is buried in St. Pol British Cemetery, St Pol-sur-Ternoise. The 7th Battalion had taken part in the storming of the German Hindenburg Line in September-October, 1918, and afterwards withdrawn into Reserve.

Next to this a stained glass window features two saints, and the figure of Christ helping a wounded British officer. An inscription below reads -

Well Done Thou Good And Faithful Servant. Dedicated To God By John And Elizabeth Huggett To The Memory Of Their Son Lieutenant Wyndham Henry

This officer served with the 10th Battalion, South Wales Borderers and was killed on 24 April, 1916 at the Moated Grange, just north of Neuve Chapelle. The Battalion had begun tours of duty in this sector on 14 January, 1916.

On the north wall of the chancel a framed and glazed Roll of Honour headed - *For King And County - Magor - European War 1914-1919* - records the names, each with rank and regiment, of fifty-five men from Magor who served in the forces during the Great War. Those who were - killed in action (+), died (xx), discharged (x) or a prisoner of war (p) are identified. The names appear in two double columns and in the following order:

Left side: Captain H.M. Morris, Manchester Regiment; Lieutenant E. Walker, Royal Field Artillery; (+) Lance-Corporal R. Walker, Grenadier Guards; Staff Sergeant Arnold, Royal Army Medical Corps; Sergeant R.C. Williams, Royal Garrison Artillery; (+) Gunner S.W. Williams, Royal Garrison Artillery; Private E.T. Williams, Welsh Regiment; Lance-Corporal Ford, 3rd Monmouthshire Regiment; (+) Private W. Ford, Grenadier Guards; Private A. Ford, 1st Monmouthshire Regiment; Private T.W. Read, Dorsetshire Regiment; Private J.R. Read, Welsh Regiment; Private F.J. Read, Welsh Regiment; Gunner E.C. Pritchard, Royal Field Artillery; Gunner W.G. Pritchard, Royal Field Artillery; Gunner R. Christopher, Royal Field Artillery; Private T. Christopher, Royal Field Artillery; (+) Private F. Woolley, 2nd Monmouthshire Regiment; (xx) Private E.H. Wolley, 2nd South Wales Borderers; Private H. Rosser, Royal Army Medical Corps; Private J. Higgins, Royal Engineers; Private H.K. James, 1st Welsh Horse; Private J. Pike, Agricultural Labour Corps; Private S.G. Thomas, Royal Engineers; Private S.O. Woods, Royal Field Artillery; Private P.G. Lawrence, 10th South Wales Borderers; Private H. Cox, Royal Field Artillery; Private H. Attewell, Machine Gun Corps; Private C. Rees, South Wales Borderers; Private A. Edwards, Royal Welsh Fusiliers; Driver A. Packer, Royal Field Artillery.

Right side: Sapper Packer, Royal Engineers; Sapper B. Hunt, Royal Engineers; Private R. Hunt, Royal Welsh Fusiliers; Gunner G. Flook, Royal Field Artillery; Private H. Hayes, South Wales Borderers; Private C. Allen, Cheshire Regiment; (p) Private R. Adams, Machine Gun Corps; Lance-Corporal J.R. Jones, Machine Gun Corps; Private H.J. Jones, Cheshire Regiment; Private T.L. Sheppard, Labour Company; Sergeant C. Phillips, 1st Gloucestershire Hussars; Private D. Adams, Royal Marines; Able-Seaman G. Coles, His Majesty's Transport; Private Monks, 1st Monmouthshire Regiment; Private J. Harris, 3rd Welsh Regiment; Private J.S. Davies, Machine Gun Corps; (x) Private O.L. Weare, 3rd South Wales Borderers; Lance-Corporal H.J. Jones, 1st South Wales Borderers; (+) Private A. Hanks, Royal Welsh Fusiliers; Sergeant W.S. Holt, 3rd East Anglian; (xx) Gunner Alan Berrows, Tank Corps; Private Eric Berrows, 1st Cheshire Regiment; (x) Private S. Christopher, Royal Welsh Fusiliers; Private E.E. Duffield, 1st Cambridgeshire Regiment.

Next to the Roll, a wooden plaque with the dedication - *Remember The Men Of This Parish Who Died In The Great Wars* - records the names, along with those who lost their lives in the Second World War, of the seven men shown in the Roll of Honour as killed in action or died: Allan Berrow, William Ford, Alfred Hanks, Raymond Walker, Sidney Williams, Frank Woolley and Harry Woolley.

Memorial to the men of Magor, Llandavenny, Undy, Bishton, Redwick, Llandevaud, Penhow and St Brides. Magor village square.

Panel from the Magor village square memorial, which commemorates Viscount Rhondda.

Memorial window to Wyndham Henry Huggett. Church of the Blessed Virgin Mary, Magor.

REMEMBER ALSO
DAVID ALFRED THOMAS
1ST VISCOUNT RHONDDA
BORN ABERDARE 1856
DIED LLANWERN 1918
FOR HE TOO DIED
SERVING THE NATION
AS FOOD CONTROLLER

Memorial plaque to Allan Berrow. Church of the Blessed Virgin Mary, Magor.

IN LOVING MEMORY OF
ALLAN H. BERROW.
Tank Corps.
Born March 3rd 1892
Died on Active Service Novr 20th 1918.
Buried at St Pol France

He has fought the Good Fight.

Well done thou   good and faith-   ful servant...

MALPAS

Malpas Community Centre

The large memorial board previously displayed in the old Malpas Institute, Malpas Road (now demolished), is now held at the community centre in Pillmawr Road. The dedication reads -

For King And Country - Roll Of Honour - Parishioners Of Malpas Who Served In The Great War 1914-1918. Lest We Forget.

The board is divided into five sections, the centre panel (black with gold letters) being headed - *Killed* - and recording twenty-four names (with regiments) by order of rank:

Captains Edward C. Dimsdale, Rifle Brigade, Gordon P. Steer, Somerset Light Infantry, William E. Dawson, Royal Field Artillery (attached to Royal Air Force); Lieutenants Charles R. Wiseman-Clarke, Royal Garrison Artillery and Edward T.L. Jenkins, Royal Engineers; Sergeants Benjamin Reynolds, Royal Field Artillery, William H. Goodman, John Macrory and Timothy Connors, all of the South Wales Borderers; Leading Seaman Thomas J. Maloney, Royal Naval Division.

The remaining names are shown without rank: Edwin Richards, King's Own Scottish Borderers; Vernon G. Daniels, Yorkshire Regiment; Roland A. Lockwood, Northumberland Fusiliers; Reginald N. Downes, Cheshire Regiment; James J. Brown, Thomas Milward and Charles F. Armitage, all of the South Wales Borderers; Ernest J. Morley, Welsh Regiment; William Blackmore, Monmouthshire Regiment; John O. Tupplin, Master Mariner; George A. Linton, Marine Engineer; David H. Powell, Royal Field Artillery; Tom W.A. Legg, Army Cyclist Corps; and Daniel George, Mercantile Marine.

The four panels headed - *Names With Rank Of Those Who Served* - are placed two either side of that recording the names of those killed.

1st panel: Lieutenant-Colonels Archer G. Prothero, Welsh Regiment and Walter C. Phillips, Royal Field Artillery; Major Aubrey I.R. Butler, Royal Field Artillery; Captains William H. Williams, Cheshire Regiment; Frank E. Dawson, Royal Field

Roll of Honour showing those who were killed and those who served. Maplas Community Centre.

Artillery, Kenneth C. Raikes (awarded Order of the British Empire), Monmouthshire Regiment; Edward P. Steer, Monmouthshire Regiment; Jack F.C. Raikes, Monmouthshire Regiment; William G. Jones, Royal Army Medical Corps; Henry L.S. Griffiths, Royal Army Medical Corps and John R. Jenkins, Cheshire Regiment; Lieutenants Gerald R. Moxon, Royal Garrison Artillery; Geoffrey B. Dawson (awarded Military Cross), Royal Field Artillery, John R. Pickford, Royal Field Artillery; Walter L.C. Phillips, Royal Field Artillery; Robert Williamson, Gordon Highlanders and Fred H. Carter, Welsh Regiment; Sergeant Major George H. Barnes, Royal Welsh Fusiliers; Sergeants Sidney J. Elsgood, South Wales Borderers; Henry G. Foster, Rifle Brigade and Frederick Coles, Royal Fusiliers; Frederick G. Legg, Donald Gregory, Albert Hardy, Henry Skillern and George H. Evans, all of the Royal Navy; Percy Sharpe, Walter C. Deverell and David Price, listed as serving with the 'Dragoon Guards;' Charles Evans, William H. Power, Jesse Gillard, Herbert H. Jarvis, Sidney H. Lewis, Peter Maguire, Thomas H. Jarvis, Reginald P. Carter, William Blackwell and Frederick Blackwell, all of whom served with the Royal Field Artillery.

2nd panel: Frederick Hardy, Royal Field Artillery; Thomas H. Osmund, Lancashire Fusiliers; Robert J. Ashby, Thomas H. Power, Edward J. Gillard, George H.J. Attwell and Ernest H. Baker, Royal Garrison Artillery; James Seal, Wallace P. Knowle and Thomas D. Price, Royal Fusiliers; John Williams and William Williams, both Grenadier Guards; Henry Birch, Welsh Guards; John H. Taylor, Warwickshire Regiment; Wilfred Bishop, King's Liverpool Regiment; George Evans and Robert Williams of the Cheshire Regiment; William Evans, Oliver F. Williams, Thomas V. Cocker, Frank L. Lewis, Herbert Workman, Edgar J. Hill, Arthur J. Hill, George E. Byard, Ivor C. Lewis, Charles H. Nevison and Walter C. Williams of the South Wales Borderers; David J. Moulder, Gloucestershire Regiment; Alfred H. Gillard, Robert G. Brookes, Matthew Bayliss and George A. Moulder, Welsh Regiment; William Godwin, Thomas C. Jarvis and John Morgan, Royal Welsh Fusiliers; Lewis Evans, Nottinghamshire and Derbyshire Regiment; Sidney L. Page, Staffordshire Regiment; Albert E. Barton, Loyal North Lancashire Regiment.

3rd panel: Alfred Cotterill, King's Own Yorkshire Light Infantry; Frederick J. Price, William Power, Edward Palfrey, Leonard Palfrey, George Davies, Harold Lockwood, William Brooks, Albert Brooks and Leonard Baker, all of the Army Service Corps; William H. Powell, Edward J. Ashby, Thomas H. Farr and Norman Lockwood, Machine Gun Corps; Harold H. Jarvis, Army Cyclist Corps; Arthur H. Milne, Australian Imperial Forces; David R. Milne, William T. Hill, Alexander Phillips and Alfred Palfrey, Royal Army Medical Corps; William Dowdle, Army Veterinary Corps; Cecil Elston, Labour Corps; Edward Hewer, Auxiliary SC; William T. Richards, Alan W. Robinson, Trevor Morley, Charles A. Pearson, Isaac Cocker, William A. Mogford and Harold H. Morley of the Monmouthshire Regiment; Ernest Nicholls and William H. Parsons, Canadian Forces; Trevor E. Lewis, William A. Baker, Henry H. Blackwell and Charles Darley, Royal Air Force; Nathaniel Harvey, Charles V.N. Nott and Ernest G. Moulder who served with the Mercantile Marine.

4th panel: Edgar C. Workman, 12th East Surrey Regiment; William J. Daniels, 15th Divisional Royal Engineers; Robert Atkins, 1st Monmouthshire Regiment; Stanley James, Royal Field Artillery.

St Mary's Parish Church

St Mary's Church is located on the Malpas Road (A4051), Newport (corner of Llanover Close) and close to Junction 26 of the M4 Motorway. Inside the church, on the north wall, there is a memorial inscribed -

To The Glory Of God And In Memory Of The Men Of Malpas Who Fell In The Great War 1914-1919.

The bronze tablet was erected by the parishioners and bears twenty-one names - Captain Edward Charles Dimsdale of the Rifle Brigade was serving as Adjutant to the 1st Monmouthshire Regiment when he was killed at Frezenberg, Belgium on 8 May, 1915. He has no known grave and is commemorated on the Menin Gate. Returning from India, Captain Gordon Pemberton Steer of the Somerset Light Infantry was sent to France in September, 1915. There he was attached to the 2nd Wiltshire Regiment and was mortally wounded near Givenchy on 26 December, 1915. Lieutenant Edward Tuberville Llewellin Jenkins of 59th Field Company, Royal Engineers also died of his wounds. On this occasion after the Somme fighting of July, 1916. The names of two other officers appear on the St Mary's memorial - Lieutenant Charles Francis Ralph Wiseman-Clarke, who is commemorated elsewhere in the church, and Captain William Ernest Dawson. His body is buried in the churchyard.

The remaining names are: Sergeant Benjamin Reynolds, Royal Field Artillery; Sergeants William Henry Goodman and John Macrory, both of the 6th Battalion, South Wales Borderers; Sergeant Timothy Connors, 7th South Wales Borderers; Thomas Joseph Molony, Royal Naval Division; Edward Richards of the 1st Battalion, King's Own Royal Lancasters; Roland Alfred Lockwood, 1st Northumberland Fusiliers; Vernon George Daniels, 1st Green Howards; Reginald Noel Downs of the 6th Cheshires; James John Brown and Thomas Milward, both of the 2nd South Wales Borderers; Charles Frederick Armitage, 1st South Wales Borderers; Ernest John Morley, 6th Welsh Regiment; William Blackmore, 1st Monmouthshire Regiment; John Oxenham Tuplin, who is buried in the churchyard, and George Albert Linton, a marine engineer.

On the south wall, and on a marble tablet displaying the badge of the Royal Artillery, Lieutenant Ralph Wiseman Clarke is commemorated -

Memorial tablet to Ralph Wiseman Clarke. St Mary's Parish Church, Malpas.

To The Brave & Dear Memory Of Ralph Wiseman-Clarke. Lieutenant Royal Garrison Artillery Who Fell At Ypres In The Great War On February 20th, 1916 Aged 19 Years. 'He For England Died'.

He served with 108th Battery and was buried in Railway Château Cemetery, Vlamertinghe, Belgium.

Also buried in Belgium (Westhof Farm Cemetery, Neuve Eglise) is Sergeant William Henry Goodman of the 6th Battalion, South Wales Borderers, who was awarded the Military Medal and killed, aged twenty-eight, on 15 June, 1917 at Messines. He was the son of George and Emma Goodman of Ealing Cottage, Malpas and his name is commemorated on a family grave within the churchyard.

Buried in the churchyard are four servicemen from the First World War. All, except Gunner Powell who has a Commonwealth War Grave Commission headstone, occupy private graves:

Corporal Albert Thomas Bailey, Royal Engineers (Postal Section) was married to Nellie Bailey of 22 Goodrich Crescent, Newport. He was forty-six when he died of malaria at Lord Derby Hospital, Warrington on 17 September, 1919.

Captain William Ernest Dawson, Royal Field Artillery was attached to Royal Air Force (Artillery and Infantry Co-operation School) when he was killed in a flying accident at Winchester on 16 September, 1918. He was twenty-four and the second son of William Frederick and Margaret Ada Dawson of Llantarnam Hall, Newport.

Gunner David Horace Powell served with the 48th Battery, 36th Brigade, Royal Field Artillery and was the son of Thomas and Margaret Julia Powell of 1 West View, Malpas. He died, aged twenty-two, on 3 November, 1919 from wounds received in France.

Master John Oxenham Tuplin, Mercantile Marine served on the SS *Gibel-Hamam*. He is buried in a private grave (with his wife who died in 1956). The kerb and headstone are inscribed -

In Loving Memory Of John Oxenham Tuplin (Master Mariner) Who Lost His Life By Enemy Action On The High Seas Sep. 14th, 1918 - Aged 49 Years.

The *Gibel-Hamam* (Bland & Co.) was torpedoed and sunk by a German submarine (*UB 103*) off Abbotsbury, Dorset on 14 September, 1918 while carrying coal from Swansea to France. The *UB 103* was itself sunk two days later in the English Channel.

MARSHFIELD

Parish Church Of St Mary The Virgin
On the north wall of the nave a white marble memorial mounted on black displays within a laurel wreath the inscription -

To The Glory Of God And In Affectionate Memory Of The Following Men Of This Parish Who, In The Great War 1914-1918, Died That We Might Live.

Fourteen names, together with regiments, are recorded: Private J.W. Baker, 18th (Queen Mary's Own) Hussars; Private W.M. Baker, Royal Gloucestershire Hussars; Second-Lieutenant F. Cawley, Royal Air Force; Lance-Corporal E. Davidge, Wiltshire Regiment; 3rd Engineer E.L. Davies, Merchant Service; Sergeant A.H.

Evans, Welsh Guards (awarded the Distinguished Conduct Medal); Private Kite, 6th Inniskilling Dragoons; Guardsman T.J. Kite, Grenadier Guards; Able Seaman F.J. Kyte, Royal Naval Division; Private R.F. Mayne, Welsh Regiment; Private G. Pembridge, Royal Fusiliers; Private C.C.C. Thomas, King's Liverpool Regiment; Second-Lieutenant T.H.B. Webb, Welsh Guards and Private F. Taylor, South Wales Borderers. The wreath is surmounted by a crown and two crossed-flags - the Union Jack and White Ensign of the Royal Navy. Private Mayne was a change ringer at St Mary's.

Lance-Corporal Davidge, of the 1st Wiltshire Regiment, was killed quite early in the war. 'D' Company's trenches at Hooge, records the battalion war diary, being overrun by the enemy on 17 November, 1914 and later regained by a bayonet charge. Of Albert Henry Evans, DCM, Major C.H. Dudley Ward, DSO, MC, writes how while in trenches near Lagnicourt, near the Hindenburg Line, on 16 September, 1918, the shelling was very severe and the sergeant was mortally wounded. 'His acts of courage and coolness while tending the wounded are beyond number - a quiet, smiling, smart man of medium height, with clear blue eyes and square jaw, with a cheery word for every stricken man, never weary, never flustered - he was a great loss.'

Albert Evans is also commemorated a short distance away on the kerbstone of a family grave in the churchyard at Castleton Baptist Church.

The other Welsh Guardsman, Second-Lieutenant Thomas Webb, is mentioned on a family memorial elsewhere in the church, and Second-Lieutenant Frederick Cawley is buried in the churchyard.

Also on the north wall, a brass plaque commemorates an officer related to a former vicar of St Mary's -

To The Glory Of God + And In Proud And Loving Memory Of Sidney Herbert Morgan - Second Lieut. East Surrey Regiment - Who Was Killed In France Whilst Leading His Men On The 4th April, 1917. Aged 30. Grandson Of The Late Rev. S. Evans - Vicar Of This Parish. I Thank My God Upon Every Remembrance Of You.

The plaque has the badge of the East Surrey Regiment etched into the top left-hand corner. Sidney Morgan served with the 12th Battalion and was killed in trenches at St Eloi, Belgium.

A fine white and brown marble family memorial, located on the south wall of the nave, shows in the centre between two columns the figures in gold of the Virgin Mary and an angel. Below this - *Mors • Janua • Vitæ.* Recorded on the left side of the memorial -

In Ever Loving And Tender Memory Of Ellen - Beloved Wife Of Lt. Col. Sir Henry Webb Bart. Who Passed Over At Oswestry The 4th Of Jan. 1919 And Of Betty His Only Daughter Who Passed Over At Eastbourne The 10th Of Dec. 1900. They Both Lie At Rest At Tunbridge Wells. On the right side - *And In Proud And Loving Memory Of His Only Son Thomas Harry Basil 2nd Lt. Welsh Guards Who Was Killed In Action At Gouzeaucourt France The 1st Of Dec. 1917 - He Lies At Rest Near The Battlefield. And Also Of Engr. Capt. Walter Kent Williams, R.N. M.V.O. Uncle Of Basil Webb Who Went Down In H.M.S. Bulwark The 26th Of Nov. 1914.*

Of Thomas Webb's death, regimental historian C.H. Dudley Ward records, 'All the wounded were brought in by midday and only the line of dead remained to speak for the valour of the men. In front of the men was Webb, well ahead on the right...'.

A plain wooden cross erected by the Marshfield Royal British Legion in the churchyard commemorates the fallen of both world wars. It bears the simple inscription -

To The Glory Of God And In Memory Of The Fallen. Lest We Forget.

Set into the stone base of the old village cross, the new memorial was dedicated on 19 November, 1991.

The churchyard also contains the grave of Second-Lieutenant Frederick Cawley of the 35th Training Depot Station, Royal Air Force. He was the son of Alfred and Agnus Cawley of Cae Garw, St Mellons and died, aged twenty, in a flying accident on 13 October, 1918.

Parish memorial, St Mary's, Marshfield.

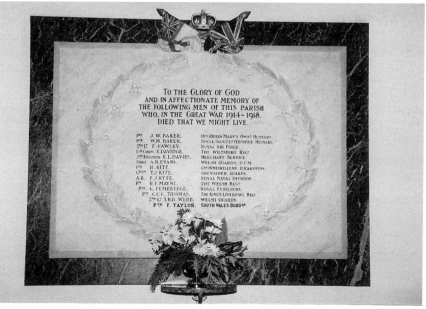

Webb family memorial, St Mary's, Marshfield.

Cross erected by the Royal British Legion in 1991, St Mary's Churchyard, Marshfield.

MATHERN

The stone cross on the corner of Chapel Lane, Mathern has the inscription around the base -

To The Glory Of God And In Memory Of Those Of Mathern Parish Who Fell In The Great War 1914-1918. Their Name Liveth For Evermore.

Carved into the base, which has eight sides, there are the names of ten men from the Great War, each appearing in order of date of death.

Private Albert Warlow of the Royal Engineers was killed on 26 August, 1914, and during the retreat from Mons. Less than a month later, Robert Arnold, a private in the Royal Marine Light Infantry, would die in the North Sea when his ship, the cruiser *Aboukir*, was sunk by a torpedo.

One of the many local men who died in Belgium during the fighting at Frezenberg Ridge on 8 May, 1915, was Captain Claude W. Stanton of the 1st Battalion, Monmouthshire Regiment. Part of a letter written by this officer not long before his death was recorded in Les Hughes and John Dixon's book - *Surrender Be Damned* - 'If during the next few days I have the misfortune to get hit you must always remember it is not more than has happened to thousands as it is being done in a great cause.' In Mesopotamia on 9 April, 1916, Private Samuel Closs of the 6th East Lancashire Regiment, having laid out all night in readiness for the attack near Sannaiyat, charged forward with his company at 4.20 am. When still two hundred and fifty yards from the enemy's trenches, records the battalion war diary, the sky was lit up by flares and immediately the advancing East Lancashires were cut down by shell, machine-gun and rifle fire.

Just over a month later, on the Somme, Private Reginald Davis suffered a similar fate when with the 5th South Wales Borderers he took part in the attack on the Intermediate Line near High Wood. Private Christopher John Luckett also died on

Mathern village memorial.

the Somme, having joined the 12th Welsh Regiment and transferring later to the 2nd Battalion.

Exactly a year later, on 9 October, 1917, Private Sydney Jones of the 9th Manchester Regiment also fell in France and in the last year of the war Private C. Prickett of the 12th Manchesters was killed on 24 April. Private Daniel Gibson, shown on the memorial as having served with the 8th Welsh Regiment, fell on 20 September, 1918 and Private Walter Gill died a few weeks later on 26 October. He served with the 18th Battalion, Machine Gun Corps and was killed at the Battle of the Selle during the final advance in Picardy.

MICHAELSTON-Y-FEDW

St Michael's Church
On the north wall of the nave, a marble memorial is inscribed -

> *Sacred To The Memory Of The Following Men Of This Parish Who Made The Supreme Sacrifice In The Great War -*

records five names. Two men, Corporals Wilfrid Charles Emerson and William John Morgan, served with the Royal Gloucestershire Hussars. The former was killed during an attack on the Regiment's positions at Qatia and Oghratina on 23 April, 1916, the latter falling on 27 September, 1918 in Palestine. Bombardier Benjamin Organ of the Royal Field Artillery died on 3 September, 1917, from wounds received in France. The last two men were also killed on the Western Front - Lance-Corporal Arthur John Phelps of the 2nd Buffs, at the Hohenzollern Redoubt on 28 September, 1915, and Private Walter George Davies of the 11th Cheshire Regiment during the Battle of the Aisne in May, 1918. The memorial ends with the inscription -

> *'Greater Love Hath No Man Than This, That A Man Lay Down His Life For His Friends'. This Tablet Was*

Parish memorial, St Michael's Church, Michaelston-y-Fedw.

SACRED TO THE MEMORY OF THE FOLLOWING MEN OF THIS PARISH WHO MADE THE SUPREME SACRIFICE IN THE GREAT WAR

CPL. WILFRID CHARLES EMERSON
ROYAL GLOUCESTER HUSSARS.
CPL. WILLIAM JOHN MORGAN,
ROYAL GLOUCESTER HUSSARS.
BOM DR BENJAMIN ORGAN,
ROYAL FIELD ARTILLERY.
L. CPL. ARTHUR JOHN PHELPS,
EAST KENT REGIMENT.
PTE. WALTER GEORGE DAVIES,
11TH CHESHIRE REGIMENT.

"GREATER LOVE HATH NO MAN THAN THIS, THAT A MAN LAY DOWN HIS LIFE FOR HIS FRIENDS"

THIS TABLET WAS ERECTED BY PARISHIONERS AS A TOKEN OF THEIR UNDYING GRATITUDE TO THE FALLEN.

MITCHEL TROY

St Michael and All Angels Church

On the north wall of the nave there are twelve names recorded on a white marble tablet mounted on wood: Albert C. Baldwin, Alfred Croudace, William Heath, William Hope, George J. Howells, John James, William Roberts, Ivor Rowland, Charles Stockholm, James G. Wallen, William Watkins, George Williams - *'Their Name Liveth For Evermore'*. Above this, the inscription -

To The Glory Of God And In Honoured And Grateful Memory Of The Men Of This Parish Who Fell In The Great War 1914-1918.

MONMOUTH

Located in St James Square, the Monmouth town memorial, a single soldier standing on a pedestal, was designed by Reginald Harding and unveiled in 1921. It bears the inscription - *To The Memory Of The Monmouth Men Who Fell In The Wars 1914-1918, 1939-1945.*

There is also one plaque commemorating a soldier from the Korean War. The First World War section, which consists of two bronze plaques of forty-one names each, is recorded in alphabetical order and with ranks and regiment:

1st plaque: Petty Officer F.E. Adamson, HMS *Fisgard*; Lieutenant A.K. Armstrong, Royal Army Medical Corps; Second-Lieutenant E.E. Arnott, Welsh Regiment; Corporal S.T. Ayers, King's Shropshire Light Infantry; Sappers F. Ballingham, W. Barrett and J. Bastock, all of the Royal Monmouthshire, Royal Engineers (Militia); Sergeant F. Baynham, Cheshire Regiment; Rifleman R.J. Bean, King's Royal Rifle Corps; Lance-Corporal W. Bennett, 1st Royal Fusiliers; Private F. Bevington, King's Liverpool Regiment; Private G. Bishop, South Wales Borderers; Trooper G.V. Brooks, 6th Dragoon Guards; Second-Lieutenant E.T.S. Bricknell, South Wales Borderers; Private A. Butcher, King's Shropshire Light Infantry; Corporal D. Bye, Royal Welsh Fusiliers; Sergeant F. Collins, 2nd Monmouthshire Regiment; Private A.W. Cook, South Wales Borderers; Trooper T. Clements, 2nd Life Guards; Private G. Groudace, 3rd Welsh Regiment; Private S. Croudace, South Wales Borderers; Lieutenant E.O. Davies, 2nd Monmouthshire Regiment; Sapper J.M. Davies, Royal Engineers; Private S. Davies, King's Shropshire Light Infantry; Captain D. Dudley, 91st Punjabis, Indian Army; Private S.J. Elias, 2nd Welsh Regiment; Sergeant J.E. Farmer, Royal Field Artillery; Quartermaster Sergeant L. Farror, Royal Engineers; Sapper L. Fasson, Royal Engineers; Sapper C.L. Fletcher, Royal Monmouthshire, Royal Engineers (Militia); Bombardier T.C.F. Fuller, Royal Field Artillery; Sapper L. Gagg, Royal Monmouthshire, Royal Engineers (Militia); Sergeant J. Gardiner, South Wales Borderers; Gunner R. Gill, Royal Garrison Artillery; Corporal A. Griffiths, South Lancashire Regiment; Private A.T. Guy, Welsh Guards; Private G. Hawkins, South Wales Borderers; Lance-Corporal H. Holman, Royal Monmouthshire, Royal Engineers (Militia); Lance-Corporal J.

Howells, 2nd South Lancashire Regiment; Private J. Hoskins, Royal Welsh Fusiliers; Trooper E. Hunt, 4th Hussars.

2nd plaque: Private R.T.H. Hutton, Machine Gun Corps; Trooper V. Ivins, 6th Dragoon Guards; Sapper W. Jenkins, Royal Engineers; Sapper F. Jones, Royal Enginners; Private G. Jones, South Wales Borderers; Private R. Jones, 2nd Monmouthshire Regiment; Private W. Jones, Cheshire Regiment; Private G. Kings, 2nd Monmouthshire Regiment; Sapper C. Kyte, Royal Monmouthshire, Royal Engineers (Militia); Private A. Lewis, South Wales Borderers; Private W.G. Leddington, 2nd Monmouthshire Regiment; Private T. Lockwood, Hampshire Regiment; Lieutenant A. Lowe, South Wales Borderers; Sergeants J. Llwyarch and G. Meadmore, both of the 2nd Monmouthshire Regiment; Private S.A. Moore, 3rd Monmouthshire Regiment; Trooper A. Morris, 19th Hussars; Sapper B.E. Morris, Royal Monmouthshire, Royal Engineers (Militia); Second-Lieutenant R.S. Macgeough-Bond, Royal Field Artillery; Private C.A. Page, Welsh Guards; Sapper L. Pendre, Royal Engineers; Private W.O. Phipps, 2nd Monmouthshire Regiment; Private J. Powell, King's Shropshire Light Infantry; Rifleman W. Powell, King's Royal Rifle Corps; Corporal G. Pyner, 6th Labour Battalion, Royal Engineers; Sapper B.E. Reed, Royal Monmouthshire, Royal Engineers (Militia); Gunner S. Rees, Royal Field Artillery; Private T. Richards, Labour Corps; Corporal G. Roberts, 2nd Monmouthshire Regiment; Private W.C. Roberts, 11th Hussars; Petty Officer G.E. Rowberry, HMS *Pegasus*; Sergeant S. Ruck, 2nd Monmouthshire Regiment; Company Sergeant Major W. Sartin, Royal Engineers; Private C.H. Stroud, Royal Welsh Fusiliers; Private G. Tyndall, 2nd Monmouthshire Regiment; Private T. Vedmore, Royal Army Medical Corps; Private W. Vedmore, South Wales Borderers; Private A. Watkins, South Wales Borderers; Private A. Watkins, 3rd Monmouthshire

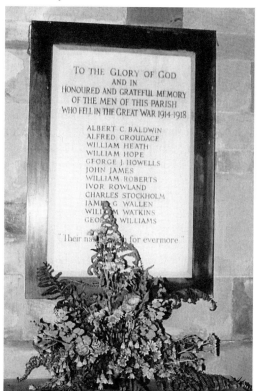

Parish memorial, St Michael and All Angels Church, Mitchel Troy.

Monmouth town memorial.

Regiment; Private F. Watkins, Labour Corps; Corporal G. Woodfield, 2nd Monmouthshire Regiment.

Monmouth School

The stone cross situated in the School grounds bears the inscription - *In Memory Of Old Boys Of Monmouth Grammar School Who Gave Their Lives In The Great War 1914-1919.* There are seventy-three names recorded by year of death, without rank or regiment, around the four-sided base to the cross:

1914: H.H. Watkins, H.F. Herd.

1915: V.L. Matthews, W.N. Breakwell, V.H. Watkins, B.W. Evans, C.G.C. Payne, E.O. Davies, W.L.M. Webb, G.E. Weatherhead, D. Dudley, T.H. Clements, C.D.W. Rooke, F.T. Harris, S.J. Evans, A.C.R. Davies, F.B. Farran.

1916: A.J. Latham, C. Page, L.A. Phillips, A. Weatherhead, E.S. Teague, H.G.S. Rees, H.T. Redler, W.J. Rea, I. Jones, R. Hughes, J.E. Davies, H.R.G. Davies, S.R. Hockaday, H.W. Thomas, E.E. Arnott, E.T. Bricknell, H.J. Richards.

1917: J.L. Evans, A.J.H. Bowen, R. Rawlins, T.D. Broughton, D.J.B. Busher, V.G. Ursell, P.G. Heyworth, F. Adamson, E. Thomas, C. Freeman, E.S. Saunders, S.T. Ayers, W. Bennett, C.E. Baumgarte, R.S. MaG. Bond, S.A. Davis, F. Bailey, J.R. Williams, J. Bolton, W.H. Banchini, H.S. Dowdeswell, A. Lowe.

1918: G.J. Howells, C.H.M. Chapman, T.H. Aston, A.C. Phipps, F. Edwards, P.J. Guest, L.J. Horne, G. Wosborne, J.W. Bastock, A.B. Foott, R.L. Bolton, M.H. Watkins, J. Sayes.

1919: H. Reilly, E.N. Cunliffe, R.T. Parry, J.M.D. Mills.

The cross and its base sit on three steps, the uppermost of which has an additional three names: F.E. Greenland, R.G.L. Cumbley and G. Bateson.

In 1996, the School Chapel of Remembrance, which was created after the Second World War, was moved from its original position at the east end of the main Chapel. Now at the west end, the Chapel has on the north side a marble tablet inscribed -

To The Glory Of God This Shrine Is Dedicated To The Memory Of The Old Boys Of This School Who Gave Their Lives For Their Country.

Housed within the area are the Memorial Books for both world wars.

Parish Church Of St Mary The Virgin

On the north wall, and within the Good Shepherd Chapel, are sixty-four names painted on wood panels. An inscription reads - *In Memory Of The Monmouth Men Who Fell In The Great War 1914-1919* - and the names recorded are: F. Adamson, A.K. Armstrong, E.E. Arnott, S.T. Ayers, W. Ayres, F. Ballinger, W. Barrett, J.W. Bastock, F. Baynham, R.J. Bean, W. Bennett, W. Betteridge, H. Bevan, F. Bevington, E.T.S. Bricknell, G. Brooks, D. Dudley, V.P. Elias, J.A. Evans, J. Evans, J. Farmer, L. Farror, C. Fletcher, T.C. Fuller, L. Gagg, R. Gill, A.T. Guy, A. Griffiths, B. Harvey, G. Hawkins, H.F. Holman, J. Howells, J. Hoskins, E. Hunt, H. Hussey, R.T. Hutton, V. Ivins, W. Jenkins, G. Jones, R.S. Jones, W. Jones, H.G. Kings, C. Kyte, W.G. Leddington, A. Lewis, T. Lockwood, A. Lowe, J. Llywarch, R.S. MacGeouch-Bond, J. Marr, A.S. Manns, G.M. Meadmore, S.A. Moore, A.S. Morris, C. Page, C.G.C. Payne, L. Pendre, M. Phillips, W. Phipp, C.H. Powell, J. Powell, W. Powell, D. Pritchard and G. Pyner. The cost of this, records *Kelly's Directory of Monmouthshire*

Monmouth School memorial.

& South Wales for 1926, being met by Alderman G.R. Edwards. Placed above the Roll of Honour, and part of the war memorial, is a stained glass window by C.E. Kempe. The figures represented being King David and Joshua, with St Alban, holding the palm of martyrdom, and St Oswald.

On the south wall of the nave a small brass plaque has the inscription -

In Honour And Remembrance This Tablet Is Erected By The Staff Of The General Post Office Monmouth As A Tribute To The Memory Of Their Brave Comrades Who Lost Their Lives In The Great War For Civilisation 1914-1918.

There are six names recorded: Henry W.F. Collins, John M. Davies, Alfred J. Davies, Frederick Jones, John Lly. Warch and Horace Warren. The memorial, which ends with the words - *'Their Name Liveth For Evermore'* - was originally located in the Main Post Office in Priory Street and removed to St Mary's when recent modifications to the building were carried out.

The south wall also has a number of brass tablets erected by officers of the Royal Monmouthshire Royal Engineers (Militia) in remembrance of their 'Brother Officers'. Seven of these are in commemoration of First World War officers who lost their lives - Captain William Geoffrey Walford, 4 November, 1918, aged twenty-three; Lieutenant Michael Anthony Waterer, 11 October, 1918, aged twenty-five;

Good Shepherd Chapel memorial, St Mary's, Monmouth.

Lieutenant Archibald Thurston Thomas Lindsay, 26 March, 1918, aged twenty-one;
Lieutenant Ralph Mortimer Wrigley, 6 November, 1918, aged twenty-one;
Lieutenant John Evelyn Malcolm, 19 February, 1919, aged twenty-six; Second-
Lieutenant Percy Latham Beck, 6 March, 1915, aged twenty-three, and Second-
Lieutenant Aubrey Farfield Dunn who was twenty-eight when he died on 21 May,

Memorial screen dedicated to the crew of HMS Monmouth, *St Mary's, Monmouth.*

1916. Aubrey Dunn was drowned at Pwlholm and is buried in St John The Baptist Churchyard, Llanblethian. Also on the south wall is a memorial to Lieutenant Arthur Keith Armstrong, Royal Army Medical Corps, who was killed on the Aisne in France on 14 September, 1914. He was thirty-three.

An oak and glass panelled screen can be found at the entrance to the tower. This bears the inscription -

Dedicated To The 690 Men Of HMS Monmouth Lost With Their Ship At The Battle Of Coronel On The 1st November, 1914. There Were No Survivors.

This, the only memorial to HMS *Monmouth,* was erected in 1996 by relatives of those lost, members of the Monmouth Royal Naval Association and the officers and crew of HMS *Monmouth.* Having joined its squadron in the North American Station, the armoured cruiser *Monmouth* was one of the ships searching along the South American coast for the German vessels - *Karlsruhe* and *Dresden.* On 1 November, the enemy were engaged and soon the British flagship, HMS *Good Hope,* was sunk. Then came the *Monmouth* which, according to HMS *Glasgow,* was lost with all hands about 9.25 pm.

Royal Monmouthshire Royal Engineers (Militia) Headquarters
The Memorial Cross is located in the car park outside the Regimental Museum and Headquarters at Monmouth Castle. On the base of the cross, and below the regimental badge, the following inscription -

To The Glory Of God And In Memory Of The Officers And Other Ranks Of The Royal Monmouthshire Royal Engineers Who Gave Their Lives In The Great War 1914-1918.

There are one hundred and eleven names arranged in three columns by order of rank:

1st column: Captains W.G. Walford and R.M. Wrigley; Lieutenants A.T.T. Lindsay, P.L. Beck, H.A. Dunn and M.A. Waterer; Sergeants C. Butler, J. Foley, H. Hawkins, W. Morgan, G. Oliver, W.H. Sayle and J. Welsh; Corporals J. Cain, T.A. Lewis, J. Rope, C. Willetts and C. Williams; Acting-Corporal E. Jenking; Second-Corporals E. Morgan and A. Stubbles; Lance-Corporals J. Davaney, F. Keats, L.D. McKinnon, B. Mincher, J. Shiplin, S. Smith and C. Tristram; Sappers W. Ashmore, A. Ayres, F. Ballingham, J. Bastock, W. Booth, J.W. Braden, J.W. Brayne, J. Brew and J.T. Campbell.

2nd column: J. Chebsey, D. Christie, H. Church, A. Coles, T. Cottam, E. Cronin, C.S. Drowley, C. Fletcher, W. Goodwin, E. Grant, A. Griffiths, J. Hall, F. Hankins, R.J. Harris, W. Harrison, W. Haynes, F. Hayward, F. Hill, E. Hinch, H. Hiscocks, R. Hobbs, H. Hold, T.J. Hughes, J.W. James, C.S. Jones, J. Jones, W. Jones, T.C. Kelly, F. Keates, C. Kyte, L. Lambre, O. Lees, W. Llewellyn, T. Lomer, J. Mahan, S.C. Major and W. McRobbie.

3rd column: J. Meadowcroft, E. Mounter, J. Murphy, L. Oliver, H. Osbourne, E. Parkin, P.W. Perry, H. Price, H. Ramsbottom, W. Reading, J. Robins, W. Saunders, F. Sheppard, F. Shimmin, H. Smith, A. Stirling, D. Sullivan, J. Sullivan, T. Sullivan, R. Swain, H. Taylor, J. Taylor, A. Thomas, T. Toorney, T. Trowen, J. Ward, H. Warren, G. Watson, M. Welsh, H. Wenman, J. Wheeler, E. Williams and R. Williams; Drivers O. Alexander, W. Barr, H. Hawkins and L. Pendre.

NASH

Parish Church Of St Mary The Virgin

To the right of the chancel arch there is a marble plaque bearing the design of a wreath of laurels encircling a crossed rifle and sword. Below this is the inscription -

To The Glory Of God And In Honoured Memory Of The Men Of The Parish Who Gave Their Lives In The Great War 1914-1919.

There are three names recorded: Sergeant Henry Charles Adams, of the Royal Garrison Artillery; Private Trevor Tom Jones, a South Wales Borderer, and Private William R. James, also of the South Wales Borderers. William Robert James was a member of the 2nd Battalion and died at sea on 14 August, 1915 during the Gallipoli campaign. He was the son of William and Caroline James of Holly Cottage, Nash. Below the names - *Greater Love Hath No Man Than This That A Man Lay Down His Life For His Friends.*

To the right of the plaque, and on the south wall of the church, there is a framed Roll of Honour begining with the words - *For King And Country.* The Roll records the names of those parish members who served in the Great War. Inscribed by hand, there are thirty-six names, each with rank and regiment:

Left side: The three men who fell head the list Sergeant Henry Charles Adams, Royal Garrison Artillery (killed in action 27 September, 1915); Private Trevor Tom Jones, South Wales Borderers (killed 31 July, 1917); Private William R. James, South Wales Borderers (drowned 14 August, 1915); then - Private H.E. Adams, King`s Liverpool Regiment; Private R. Adams, South Wales Borderers; Private W. Adams, Machine Gun Corps; Private S. Adams, 8th Somerset Light Infantry; Gunner R. Ashfield, Royal Field Artillery; Rifleman E.J. Bassett, 1st Monmouthshire Regiment; Private F. W. Bassett, South Wales Borderers (awarded Distinguished Conduct Medal); Private A.S. Bassett, 3rd West Yorkshire Regiment; Private A.F. Bennett, Army Service Corps; Private N. Barton, South Wales Borderers; Gunner J. Ball, Royal Marine Artillery; Sapper G. Davies, Royal Engineers; Private W. England, Royal Welsh Fusiliers; Private T. Green, South Wales Borderers.

Right side: Private D. Jones, South Wales Borderers; Sapper W. Jones, Royal Engineers; Corporal L.S. Jones, King`s Liverpool Regiment (awarded Meritorious Service Medal); Private J. Jones, 17th Army EE; Gunner W.N. Jones, South Wales Borderers; Sapper D.S. Preece, Royal Engineers; Private W. Pollard, 17th Cheshire Regiment; Sergeant Edward Ryall, South Wales Borderers (awarded Military Medal); Private E. Ryall, South Wales Borderers; Driver J. Ryall, Royal Field Artillery; Sapper W. Slade, Royal Engineers; Corporal A.R. Sewell, 3rd Welsh Regiment; Private L.H. Webb, Welsh Regiment; Sapper F. Williams, Royal Engineers; Private T. Whittaker, South Wales Borderers (awarded Military Medal); Corporal W. Whittaker, South Wales Borderers; Private E.L. Whittaker, South Wales Borderers; Private M.M. Whittaker, 1st Welsh Regiment; H.L. Hale, Queen Mary`s Army Auxiliary Corps.

Private Trevor Tom Jones` name can also be found on the north wall of the chancel. He is commemorated on this occasion by a brass plaque (mounted on slate) -

To The Glory Of God And In Loving Memory Of Pte. Trevor Tom Jones - 11th Batt.

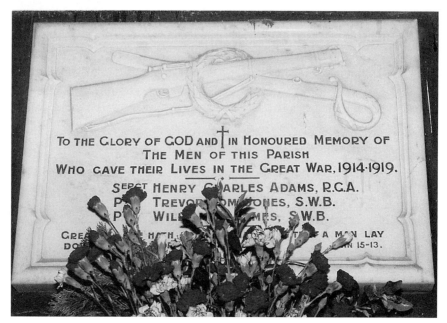

Parish memorial, St Mary's, Nash.

S.W.B. Fourth Dearly Beloved Son Of Wyndham And M.A. Jones - Common House, Nash. Born Octr. 25th 1892 - Killed In Action July 31st 1917 - Buried At Langemark, Belgium. Not Left To Lie Like Fallen Tree. Not Dead But Living Unto Thee.

The churchyard contains one war grave, that of Private Reginald Waters, 11th Battalion, South Wales Borderers, who was born in Usk. He enlisted into the army at Newport, resided in Goldcliffe and died, aged eighteen, on 20 January, 1917. Private Waters is buried in a family grave. His Commonwealth War Graves Commission headstone lies horizontal within the kerbstone and is made from Welsh slate.

NEW TREDEGAR

The figures of two soldiers, one man standing over his wounded comrade, surmount the town's war memorial in James Street. Etched into the front side of the red marble pedestal is the inscription -

Lest We Forget. Erected By Public Subscription To The Glorious And Imperishable Memory Of The Men Of New Tredegar And District Who, By Their Courage And Devotion Helped To Save Europe And Civilisation. August 1914 - November 1918. Yours The Glorious Price To Pay, Ours To Record With Grateful Pride That Freedom Lives On Earth Today Because You Died.

Also inscribed, in both English and Welsh - *Their Name Liveth For Evermore* (Eu Henw A Bery Byth).

The remaining three sides of the pedestal bear the names, without rank or regiment, of one hundred and sixty-five men who were killed:

1st side: G. Adams, W.J. Addison, H. Allaway, E. Akers, J. Bassett, W. Bath, W.I. Batten, D.J. Beynon, H.H. Boon, W.J. Bowen, F. Brooks, J. Brooks, E. J. Button, O.

Charles, T.H. Clarke, F. Codrington, D.S. Cook, I. Cooper, J.V. Craig, W.C. Cutler, D.E. Davies, E. Davies, I.T. Davies, T. Davies, T. Davies, W. Davies, J.W. Davis, R.J. Elliot, J. English, A. Evans, A.A. Evans, I. Evans, E. Evans, E. Evans, J.M. Evans, J.H. Evans, I. Evans, W.I.D. Evans, G.J. Fitzhenry, W. Graves, L. Green, C. Greenman, E. Griffiths, R. Griffiths, W. Grimes, T. Gunner, B. Holt, D. Hughes, R.H. Humphreys, G.H. Humphries, W.J. Humphries, W.J. Hunt. A. Gausun has been added to the bottom of the list.

2nd side: I. James, D.J. James, G.A. James, W.A. James, W.J. James, H.F. Janes, J.E. Jenkins, J.E. Jenkins, M. Jenkins, M. Jenkins, E. Jones, E. Jones, D.L. Jones, D.J. Jones, H. Jones, J.D. Jones, J.R. Jones, J. Jones, R.E. Jones, R. Jones, L. Jones, R.R. Jones, W.T. Jones, T.D. Jones, W.H. Jones, T.A. Kenealy, J.R. Kendall, T. Kift, W. King, E. Kirkham, E. Knight, G. Lacey, A.T. Lancett, E. Lancett, J.J. Langford, B. Lewis, J. Lewis, R. Lewis, L. Lewis, J. Lloyd, J. Lloyd, J. Lloyd, G.E. Lloyd, W.J. Lloyd, W.T. Lodwick, Dr. E.W.S. Martin, L.F. Macneill, R. Mansfield, H.E. Mapp, H. McLean, J.I. Mills, W. Mills, L. Mitchell, C.B. Mitchell. W.C. Andrews and W. Stenson have been added.

3rd side: O. Mitchell, W.H. Morgan, J. Moore, J.M. Norris, G. Otten, L. Otten, W. Panes, H.T. Parfitt, J. Perryman, A. Pink, B.T. Phillips, W. Pocock, G.W. Powell, J. Price, J. Price, D.G. Price, P.L. Price, W.R. Pritchard, H. Pulsford, W. Rees, W. Richard, F. Richards, G. Roberts, J. Roach, I. Simms, W. Stenson, T. Stephens, D.J. Taylor, E. Thomas, E.J. Thomas, G.H. Tomlin, T. Trigg, T.W. Voss, G. Wall, J. Walsh, G. Walters, F.S.

New Tredegar memorial.

Ware, R. Ware, B.G. Watkins, J. Watkins, W.H. Watts, J. Wells, J. Wells, H. Wells, C.H. Westgarth, C. Williams, G. Williams, D. Williams, D. Williams, H. Williams, J. Williams, L. Williams, T.J. Williams, F. White, T. Willis, W. Woods. G. Williams has been added.

St Dingat`s Church

On the wall to the right of the chancel entrance, a marble tablet begins with the inscription -

In Loving Memory Of The Following Gallant Churchmen Of New Tredegar Who Made The Supreme Sacrifice In The Great War 1914-1918 - and ends with - *'Greater Love Have No Man Than This'*.

There are seventy-six names recorded in two columns according to rank:

Left column: Sergeants W. Batten, C. Lacey, C. Wall; Corporals E.P. Kirkham, J. Price, W.H. Watts, J.J. Wells; Lance-Corporals T. Trico, C.H. Humphries; Privates T. Adams, E. Akers, J. Bassett, H.H. Boon, A.E. Causon, S. Cook, J. Craig, C. Cutler, E.R. Daniels, I.T. Davies, T. Davies, D. Donovan, R. Elliot, E. Evans, L. Green, E. Griffiths, W.C. Grimes, D. Hughes, W.J. Hunt, A. James, A.I. James, G.A. James, W.J. James, M. Jenkins, D.J. Jones, D.Ll. Jones, W.Ll. Jones, W.T. Jones, W. Jones.

Right column: Privates T. Kift, W. King, E. Knight, E. Lancet, T. Lancet, L.

Lewis, G.E. Lloyd, W.J. Lloyd, E. Mack, R. Mansfield, C. Mayo, C.B. Mitchell, L.W. Mitchell, O.S. Mitchell, J. Moore, W.H. Morgan, J. Norris, W. Pains, N.T. Parfitt, J. Perryman, A. Pink, Jno. Price, J. Price, P.L. Price, W. Sims, J. Southall, G. Stallard, J. Stallard, E.J. Thomas, J. Thomas, T.W. Voss, F.S. Ware, J. Watkins, G.H. Westgarth, D. Williams. The last three names are - Lance-Corporal F. Richards and Privates J. Lloyd and W.J. Davies.

NEWBRIDGE

The original Newbridge war memorial, a cenotaph bearing the names of seventy-nine servicemen who were killed during the Great War, was unveiled in 1936 and situated in Caetwmpyn Park overlooking the town. On the front of the memorial the dates - *1914-1918* - and the inscription - '*At The Going Down Of The Sun And In The Morning We Will Remember Them*'. The names, some recorded with regiments, appeared in two columns on a bronze panel:

Left column: T. Abraham and C. Beresford, both of the South Wales Borderers; H. Birt, 2nd Monmouthshire Regiment; J. Bryant (no regiment given); H. Carter, Royal Welsh Fusiliers; V. Carter and S. Cleaver (no regiments given); C. Coles, T. Coombes, J. Dallow, D. Bowen-Dart, A. Davies and J. Davies, all of the South Wales Borderers; J.E. Davies, Royal Navy; W.E. Davies, Gloucestershire Regiment; A.I. Durbin, South Wales Borderers; L.H. Edge, Royal Navy; J.W. Edwards and F. Ellway (no regiments given); J. Evans, South Wales Borderers; E. German, Welsh Regiment; M.G. Gough, Royal Marines; A.W. Grimes and A. Hillier, South Wales Borderers; F. Hillier, 2nd Monmouthshire Regiment; E. Humphries, South Wales Borderers; J. Jackson, 2nd Monmouthshire Regiment; H.C. James, 'R.R.B.', R. James and R. Jenkins, South Wales Borderers; T. Jenkins (no regiment given); W.M. Jenks and C.S.F. Jones, South Wales Borderers; R. Jones and T. Jones, Royal Welsh Fusiliers; W. Jones, 2nd Monmouthshire Regiment; W. Jones and W.E. Lander (no regiments given). W.G. Carnock (no regiment given) and A.S. Coulton, South Wales Borderers have been added to this column.

2nd column: F. Lewis, 1st Welsh Regiment; H.J. Lewis, South Wales Borderers; J.H. Lewis, Royal Marines; J.A. Maiden and D. Meredith, South Wales Borderers; P.O.B. Morris, Royal Naval Division; D. Murphy, Royal Field Artillery; A. Newman, South Wales Borderers; J. Newman, Welsh Regiment; H.G. Noble and J. Owen, South Wales Borderers; J. Parker, 2nd Monmouthshire Regiment; S. Peacock, J.J. Pearne, E.S. Price, G. Price, S. Price, J.M. Pryce and E. Reynolds, all South Wales Borderers; J.A. Richards, Dorsetshire Regiment; W. Roberts, 2nd Monmouthshire Regiment; W. Rowlands, A.C. Salmon and R. Sheppard, South Wales Borderers; C. Taylor, Royal Field Artillery; J.J. Tilley, South Wales Borderers; G.E.V. Tyler, Royal Field Artillery; A. Venner, Royal Engineers, Tunnelling Companies; A. Ward and B. Watson, South Wales Borderers; H. Whitcombe, 2nd Monmouthshire Regiment; G.S. Williams and S.G. Williams, Royal Field Artillery; T. Williams (no regiment given); T.J. Williams, A Workman and E. Workman, South Wales Borderers. B.M. Evans and A. Harvey (no regiments given) have been added to this column.

In 1995 the memorial, now including the dates 1939-1945 and names of those who fell during the Second World War, was donated to the Museum Of Welsh Life at St Fagans near Cardiff, and in the following year re-dedicated by His Grace the

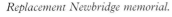

Original Newbridge memorial. Now at the Museum of Welsh Life, St Fagans.

Replacement Newbridge memorial.

Most Reverend Alwyn Rice Jones, Archbishop of Wales.

To replace the Caetwmpyn Park cenotaph, two bronze panels bearing the same detail as before were set into the wall of a small car park behind the police station in Meredith Terrace, Newbridge. That for B.M. Evans, however, now appears as E.M. Evans. The same inscription and dates appear above, and the panels are divided by a plain cross.

NEWPORT

The main town war memorial, a forty-foot portland stone cenotaph mounted on two Cornish granite steps, was unveiled by Major-General the Right Hon. Lord Treowen, Lord Lieutenant of Monmouthshire on 2 June, 1923. The architects were C.F. Bates, ARIBA and C.L. Jones, MSA. Located in Clarence Place, at the junction of Caerleon road and Chepstow road, the laying of the foundation stone was by the Mayor, Councillor Edward Davies, JP, on the previous 11 April. It was originally planned to unveil the memorial on the 8 May. This being the eighth anniversary of the Battle of Frezenberg Ridge in which the 1st Battalion, Monmouthshire Regiment (headquarters in Newport) took part and suffered over four hundred and fifty casualties. However, the work was not completed in time.

Three sides of the memorial have been inscribed - *1914-1918 - 1939-1945 Their Memory Endureth For Ever* - on one - *1914-1918 - 1939-1945 To Our Heroic Dead* - on another, and - *In Dewrion Eu Hen Waun Perarogli Sydd* - on the third.

The memorial also includes an illuminated Roll of Honour which is held in Newport Library, John Frost Square. Bound in red leather, and dated 1923, the book was designed by Fred Richards, who was also responsible for the opening page. The illumination of the other pages was completed by J.H. Rowe, and the hand-written entries were by Eva Caroline Bates. Measuring fourteen by eighteen inches, the Roll of Honour has the Arms of Newport embossed in gold on the front cover, and on the first page the inscription - *Greater Love Hath No Man Than This That A Man Lay Down His Life For His Friends.* This is followed by a dedication page, which has below the Royal Arms -

In This Book Are Written The Names Of Four Women And One Thousand Four Hundred And Seventy Two Men Who In The Great War Laid Down Their Lives For Their King And Country. 1914-1918.

The four women referred to appear on the first page of the book: Worker Gertrude Winifred Allam Dyer, Woman's Army Auxiliary Corps; Nursing Sister Alice Annie Guy, Scottish Women's Hospital; Driver Dulcie Llewellyn-Jones, Women's Royal Air Force, and Telegraphist Beatrice Olivette White, Signals.

The sections that follow are - 'Royal Navy And Mercantile Marine', which has two hundred and nine names, together with ranks and names of ships etc; 'Army,' covering one thousand two hundred and eighty-six servicemen, together with their ranks and regiments, and 'Royal Air Force,' which has twelve names with ranks. Total - one thousand five hundred and seven.

All Saints Community Church

The war memorial in the original All Saints Church, Newport recorded the names, without rank or regiment, of one hundred and forty-nine men from the area who were killed -

To The Glory Of God And In Honoured Memory Of The Men Of This Parish Who Gave Their Lives In The Great War 1914-1918. This Tablet Was Erected By Parishioners And Friends.

When the church was demolished in 1994, plans were immediately set up to erect a new building on the original site in Brynglas Road. This was opened in September, 1998, and at the same time the old memorial was placed in a new position within *Parish memorial, All Saints Community Church, Newport.*

the car park. The plaque is now in a surround of local stone with a base matching the brickwork of the new church. The white marble tablet has the names arranged in six columns:

1st column: Thomas R. Ackland, Arthur H. Adams, Frederick E. Andrews, Alfred C. Baggs, James Baggs, Albert T. Bailey, James Baker, Frederick R. Ball, Henry E. Baldwin, Daniel G. Barton, Albert L. Batten, William H. Belcher, Benjamin Bennett, Fred Bennett, Bernard F. Bistrom, John F. Brewis, Joseph N.S. Brewis, William T. Brewis, James Brown, William B. Brute, Stanley A. Burgess, Graham S. Burley, Alfred Burrup, Albert E. Bush, Charles Chamberlain.

2nd column: Arthur S. Chappell, Frederick S. Chard, Reginald Charles, Robert E. Charles, William A. Charles, William Christopher, Thomas H. Coffy, Alfred Collier, Stanley C. Collier, Charles Cook, Henry G. Coombs, Frederick J. Cork, Ernest Cowling, Gilbert W. Davies, George F. Dix, John A. Durbin, Thomas E. Edwards, Charles Emmett, William Evans, William C. Evans, Richard J. Finighan, George H. Fortey, Harold J. Francis, Carl O. Friberg, William Garbutt.

3rd column: James H. Goulding, Samuel C. Grace, Thomas Grace, Walter Griffiths, David J. Heirene, Dennis Heirene, William Hickery, Francis J. Higgs, Edgar Hopkins, Charles Howells, Ernest Howells, Thomas C. Hudman, Rosser W. Hunton, Albert T. James, John James, William James, Thomas Jennings, Percy Johnson, Clifford D. Jones, Walter Kelly, Alfred L. Kendall, Arthur King, Isidore B. King, Joseph King, William T. Lacey.

4th column: William J. Larcombe, Tom W.A. Legge, William R. Lewison, Frank Limbrick, George A. Linton, Thomas E. Lloyd, Alfred R. Lockwood, Robert C. Lovell, William E. Lurvey, Alfred E. Martin, Ernest Martin, William Martin, Thomas E.J. Max, Rowland C. Mayell, John McPherson, Frederick C. Meadows, Thomas Millward, Edward T. Moran, George Morgan, Thomas Morgan, Ernest J. Morley, Harry E. Morrish, Richard B. Nicholas, George E. Parker, Walter Parkins.

5th column: Alfred Pearson, Alfred Perry, William Perry, William H. Poole, George B. Pope, Wilfred Pope, William G. Prosser, Albert E. Pumford, William E. Rawlinson, Albert E. Rocke, William E.H. Rogers, William W. Rowsell, Ernest J. Russell, William H. Saysell, Ernest Seeley, Albert A. Senior, Reginald J. Sheedy, William Small, Egbert J. Smith, John Snow, William J. Stanton, William Sullivan, Samuel Sweet, William E. Taylor, Francis H. Thomas.

6th column: George E. Thomas, Percival W. Thompson, Thomas Upton, Benjamin Uzzell, Arthur Vaughan, Henry C. Vaughan, William Vickery, Samuel Wainwright, John Watts, William Watkins, Albert Whittaker, Alfred J. White, Victor R. White, Charles Whiting, George Williams, Rosser Williams, Timothy Williams, Charles Wilkins, Clifford Wilkins, John Windsor, William F. Worthy, Joseph Wren, Richard H. Young, Thomas H. Young.

Bridge Street Post Office

The Post Office Workers' memorial is situated in the far right-hand corner of the main Post Office in Bridge Street, Newport and comprises a Sicilian white marble slab mounted on Belgian black marble. It bears the inscription -

Erected By The Post Office Workers Of Newport And District In Memory Of Their Colleagues Who Lost Their Lives In The Great War, 1914-1919.

ERECTED BY THE POST OFFICE WORKERS
OF NEWPORT AND DISTRICT
IN MEMORY OF THEIR COLLEAGUES WHO LOST THEIR LIVES
IN THE GREAT WAR, 1914-1919.

BAILEY. A. T.	GINELLO. I.	PARRY. A.G.
BAULCH. P.	GOMERY. C.	PEARSON. A.
BEIGHTON. A.W.	GRAY. J.A.	PHILLIPS. I., M.M.
CAMBRAY. G.	HARRIS. R. J.	REES. E.
CHURCH. H.S.	HAWKINS. H.E.	ROWSELL. W.W.
CLISSOLD. E.V.	HAWYES. S.	SHAKESHEFF. G.M.
COOK. C.	HOPKINS. A.E.	STICKLER. H.J.
CUTLER. E.G.	HOWELL. W. J.	STOKER. E.
DAVIS. E. J.	HURLEY. J.	SULLIVAN. W.
DOWDING. A. J.	JENKINS. E.E.	THOMAS. C.
ELLIOTT. C.C.	KNIGHT. W.	WILTON. E.
FINN. D.	McPHILLIPS. J.	WRIGHT. G.R.
GIBBON. J. H.	MOORE. A.R.	
GIBBS. C.G.	NORVILLE. H.E.	

Post Office Workers' memorial, Bridge Street Post Office, Newport.

There are forty names listed alphabetically in three columns:

1st column: A.T. Bailey, P.Baulch, A.W. Beighton, G. Cambray, H.S. Church, E.V. Clissold, C. Cook, E.G. Cutler, E.J. Davis, A.J. Dowding, C.C. Elliott, D. Finn, J.H. Gibbon, C.G. Gibbs.

2nd column: I. Ginello, C. Gomery, J.A. Gray, R.J. Harris, H.E. Hawkins, S. Hawyes, A.E. Hopkins, W.J. Howell, J. Hurley, E.E. Jenkins, W. Knight, J. McPhillips, A.R. Moore, H.E. Northville.

3rd column: A.G. Parry, A. Pearson, I.M.M. Phillips, E. Rees, W.W. Rowsell, G.M. Shakesheff, H.J. Stickler, E. Stoker, W. Sullivan, C. Thomas, E. Wilton, G.R. Wright. Lance Corporal Ienan Phillips, Royal Army Medical Corps, won the Military Medal. He was from Abertillery and died of wounds in France on 1 September, 1918.

The names and inscription are surrounded by a border of laurel leaves, and incorporated into the memorial, in their proper heraldic colours, are the Arms of Newport, Monmouthshire and Brecknockshire. The Newport postal area included at one time part of the latter county. The tablet was unveiled by Post Office Surveyor (South Wales District), Mr. G.L. Harding, on 16 October, 1921 and was originally displayed in the old Post Office building in High Street. Additional names for the Second World War have been added.

In ever grateful
memory of the
Officers and Old Boys
of the Newport Battalion
of the Boys' Brigade
who gave their lives
in the great war
A.D. 1914-1919.

Civic Centre

Originally located on the stairway of the old Town Hall, the Newport Boys' Brigade memorial is now held in store at the Newport Borough Council Civic Centre. The

*Boys' Brigade memorial,
Civic Centre, Newport.*

inscription reads -

In Ever Grateful Memory Of The Officers And Old Boys Of The Newport Battalion Of The Boys Brigade Who Gave Their Lives In The Great War. A.D. 1914-1919.

This is within a wreath of laurels and surmounted by the Boys' Brigade badge. The Newport Battalion raised enough money during the war to purchase and equip two motor ambulances at a cost of nearly £700. A Roll of Honour consisting of sixty-one names listed by their former companies was compiled and read out by Captain Herbert W. Lewis, Officer Commanding Newport Boys' Brigade upon the unveiling of the memorial on 5 April, 1921.

Duckpool Road Baptist Church memorial, Newport.

Duckpool Road Baptist Church

The white marble tablet to the right of the pulpit, and below the gallery, is inscribed -

Duckpool Road Baptist Church - In Ever Grateful Memory Of - H.W. Beanland, C. Bevan, W. Bevan, B. Camfield, A.L. Ford, H. Jones, G.P. Lamb, A.B. Lavers, F. Marsh, F.E. Price, V. Proud, T. Redmore, F. Redmore, R.E. Smale, G.V. Smith, B. Stevens, W.E. Stevens, J.S. Taylor, W.A. Wagstaff, O. White, H.G. Williams, A. Wilks -

Worshippers At This Church Who Fell In The Great War, 1914-1919. And To Mark The Church's Appreciation Of All Those Who So Nobly Served Their Country In Her Time Of Need. 'Thy Will Be Done'.

Two of the names recorded are also commemorated by their own stained glass windows: John Stanley Taylor, who served with the 18th Welsh Regiment and was killed in France on 17 October, 1916, and Arthur Llewellyn Ford who fell on 15 April, 1918 while serving with 6th Battalion, South Wales Borderers.

Emmanuel Chapel

The old Alma Street Baptist Church was closed down in April, 1976 and in its place, a new church, the Emmanuel Chapel, was built in Rutland Place. Opened on 12 November, 1977, the building contains the war memorial that previously hung in Alma Street, a brass plate is inscribed -

To The Glory Of God And In Loving Memory Of Our Gallant Men Who Fell In The Great War 1914-1918. They Also Served.

The names, regiments and dates of death recorded are: Chief Engine Room Artificer R.A. Percy Hayward Jenkins, HM Submarine *D6*, 24 June 1918; Chief Engine Room Artificer Frederick William Jones, SS *Sharon*, November 1914; Sergeant Godfrey Percival Harding, 2/1st Monmouthshire Regiment, 11 May 1918; Rifleman Harold Theopilus Jones, 1st Monmouthshire Regiment, 6 July 1916; Private Albert Edward Clutton, Army Service Corps, 19 July 1915; Private Reginald Williams,

Cheshire Regiment, 1 November 1918.

Chief Percy Hayward Jenkins lost his life off the north coast of Ireland on 24 June, 1918. The *D6* was sunk four days later by the German submarine *UB73*. Godfrey Percival Harding was taken prisoner in France and would die in a German Prisoner of War Camp on 11 May, 1918. He is buried in the Berlin South-Western Cemetery, Stahnsdorf. Private Alfred Edward Clutton died during the East Africa Campaign, and Private Reginald Thomas Williams was killed in France while serving with the 10th Cheshire Regiment.

Havelock Street Presbyterian Church

To the left of the pulpit, a white marble tablet has the following inscription -

> *In Honoured Memory Of The Following Members Of This Church And Congregation Who Laid Down Their Lives In The Great War. 'Greater Love Hath No Man Than This, That A Man Lay Down His Life For His Friends'.*

Twelve names are recorded: William Charles Dally, Ernest Frank Davies, George France Davies, Ralph Davies, Archie Evans, Arthur W. Harris, William Hughes, Ivor Meredith, Wilfrid Miller, Stanley Howard Stevens, George Watkins and Owen Trevor Watkins. The tablet is surmounted by a mantel, a Cross and the words - *To The Glory Of God* carved into the centre between the dates *1914 - 1919*.

The memorial belonging to the old Great Central Hall Presbyterian Church in Commercial Road, is now located on the wall to the right of the pulpit at Havelock Street. Set in a wood frame, a bronze plaque has in raised letters - *In Honoured Memory Of Those Who Fell In The Great War* - Thomas S. Adams, James H. Alexander, William J. Attewell, Charles Cox, George Davies, Arthur J. Doran, Albert Greenslade, Thomas Jacobsen, Ernest E. Jenkins, William Martin, George H. Meredith, Walter Perkins, Harry D. Row, George T. Stevens, William C. Tanner, Jonas Travers. The wood surround is surmounted by a carved mantel displaying a laurel wreath between the dates - *1914* and *1918*.

Havelock Street Presbyterian Church memorial, Newport.

Great Central Hall Presbyterian Church memorial. Now at Havelock Street Presbyterian Church, Neweport.

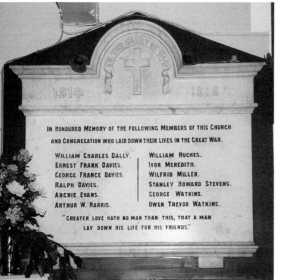

Mount Zion Church memorial, Newport.

Mount Zion Church

The metal tablet mounted in a wood frame to the left of the pulpit has the following inscription in Welsh - *'Eu Haberth Nid A Heibo' - Coffa Hiraeth Am - Edward Jones - John Henry Davies B.A. - Aelodau O'r Eglwys Hon A Roddasant Eu Bywydau Yn Aberth Dros Gartref A Chyflawnder Yn Y Rhyfel Mawr 1914-1918* - (Their Sacrifice Not In Vain - Loving Memory For - Edward Jones - John Henry Davies BA - Members Of This Church Who Gave Their Lives In Sacrifice For Their Home And Justice 1914-1918). Mount Zion Church is in Hill Street, Newport.

National Westminster Bank

The NatWest branch on the corner of High Street and Bridge Street has a small bronze plaque with the inscription -

A Tribute To The 2681 Members Of The Staff Of This Bank Who Served In The Great War 1914-1918 And In Honoured Memory Of The 415 Who Gave Their Lives For Their Country.

The wording is enclosed within a frame of laurel leaves with, above, the shield from the Arms of Newport, and the letters - *NP & UBE*. The National Provincial Bank had merged with the Union of London and Smiths Bank, under the title of - 'National Provincial and Union Bank Of England' in 1918 and the figures represent the total number of employees throughout the country. Similar memorial plaques to that in Newport were erected in NP&UBE branches elsewhere.

Three men from the Newport branch lost their lives in the First World War: Lieutenant John Guy Frampton, of the 1st Monmouthshire Regiment, killed in France on 11 October, 1918; Sergeant Kirk Hearder, who fell at Frazerburgh Ridge on 8 May, 1915, and Selwyn Harry Pike, originally from Bath, Somerset, who was killed while serving with the 6th Dragoons on 18 July, 1918.

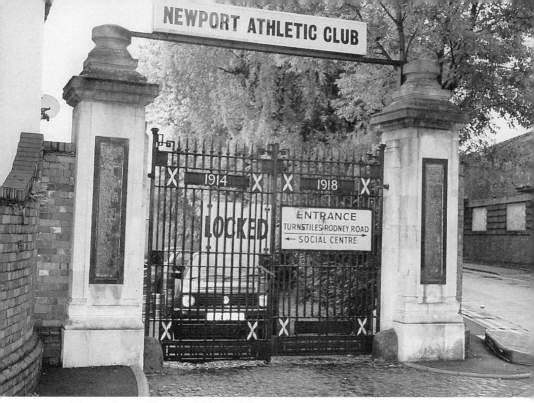

Memorial gates, Newport Athletic Club.

Newport Athletic Club

The memorial takes the form of a set of gates at the old entrance to the club grounds in Rodney Road, Newport. Unveiled by Lord Tredegar on 6 September, 1923 and commemorates the eighty-six members of the club who lost their lives in the Great War. Club members, who included a number of Welsh international rugby players, served with several regiments and provided personnel for the 'Newport Athletic Club Platoon' of the 8th Battalion, South Wales Borderers. These are the five names listed under the heading - *N.A.C. Platoon.* The names are inscribed on two copper tablets set into the stone pillars:

Left pillar: T. Arthur, J. Bartlett, C.R.J. Campbell, C.R. Carter, R.E. Charles, G. Cheesman, W.R. Cooper, W. Curran, N.T. Daniel, M.S. Duckham, S. Duncanson, H.T. Edwards, W. Emerson, C. Fisher, W.P. Geen, T. Gibbs, F. Greenland, F.N. Groves, C.M. Harrington, K. Hearder, E.C. Holloway, G. Hulme, W.S. Jeffreys, M. Jenkins, H.T. Jones, I.S. Jones, T.A. Jones, J. Kew, A. King, B. King, S. Langmaid, E.F. Lawlor, S. Lawrie, C.E. Lewis, R.C. Lovell, C.V. Lyne, D.D. Monaghan, A.R. Moore, J.H.L. Moore, N.C. Newland, W.B. Nightingale, W. Onions, C.H. Owen, C.C. Phillips.

Right pillar: E.S. Phillips, L. Phillips, L.A. Phillips, W.J. Phillips, W. Price, C.M. Pritchard, O. Pumphrey, A.J. Redmod, W.G. Redshaw, H.J. Richards, S.E. Richards, C.L. Robinson, W.J. Robinson, W. Saycell, H.V.K. Soloman, D. Spanswick, F.L. Spencer, T.S. Spittle, G.P. Steer, R.B. Stokes, R. Summers, R. Taylor, T. Thomas, R.W. Thompson, J.H. Tucker, E.J. Trew, B. Uzzell, P.D. Waller, M.H. Watkins, S.

Watkins, V.H. Watkins, W.E. Wernet, E.H. Williams, E.S. Williams, J.H. Williams, J.L. Williams, O.M. Williams, *N.A.C. Platoon*: A.G. Cook, J.T. Haley, F. Hill, A.F. Hunt, G.F. Seary.

Of the internationals associated with the Club, and whose names appear on the memorial gates, details of six men are recorded in *Newport Rugby Football Club 1874-1950* by Steve Lewis. Charles Meyrick Pritchard first played for the Newport Rugby Club in 1902 and was capped for Wales fourteen times. Serving with the 12th Battalion, South Wales Borderers, Captain Pritchard led a raiding party on enemy trenches near Loos during the night of 12/13 August, 1916. He was wounded several times and as a result died.

Capped six times for Wales, Phillip Dudley Waller was a member of the British Isles team that toured South Africa in 1910. He remained in the country and when war broke out joined the South African Forces in Johannesburg. Second-Lieutenant Waller, 71st Siege Battery, South African Heavy Artillery, was twenty-eight when he was killed by shellfire near Arras on 14 December, 1917. He is buried in Red Cross Corner Cemetery, Beagny.

Killed during the German 'Liquid Fire' attack at Hooge on 31 July, 1915, Second-Lieutenant William Purdon Geen of 'B' Company, 9th King's Royal Rifle Corps, was one of some three hundred and fifty casualties suffered by his battalion that day. He played three times for Wales and also represented Oxford University. Will Geen has no known grave, his name being recorded on the Menin Gate Memorial to the missing in Flanders.

On 25 September, 1915, during the operations at the Hohenzollern Redoubt, Command of the 12th Battalion, Royal Fusiliers was handed over to Major Richard Davie Garnons-Williams. This old regular soldier had retired from the army in 1890, but, aged fifty-eight, had re-joined at the outbreak of war. Moving forward to relieve the Black Watch, the Fusiliers, records the Battalion war diary, '...had no time for preliminary reconnaissance.' Major Garnons-Williams and his men held out for some time under constant shell-fire and infantry attacks by the enemy - 'The Battalion had no rations, no water, no sleep. They arrived without bombs, yet they beat off every enemy attack.' Richard Garnons-Williams had represented Wales in both rugby and football.

Sergeant Louis Augustus Phillips of the Royal Fusiliers, notes Steve Lewis, first played rugby while at Monmouth School. He later joined the Newport club and subsequently played four times for Wales. Joining the Public Schools Brigade, he was killed on 14 March, 1916. The war diary of the 20th Battalion, Royal Fusiliers recording that a small attack was made by the enemy that day.

Buried at Corbie Communal Cemetery in France, Captain John Lewis Williams of 'C' Company, 16th Battalion, Welsh Regiment died from his wounds on 12 July, 1916. The 16th had just been relieved from the fighting at Mametz Wood. This international, records Steve Lewis, played for Newport, Cardiff and was capped seventeen times for Wales.

Orb Works

The John Lysaght Ltd Orb Steel Rolling Works memorial lies within the works grounds (now Orb Electrical Steels Ltd) in Corporation Road. The monument bears a copper plaque inscribed between the dates - *1914* and *1919* - *Employees At The*

Orb Works memorial, Newport.

Newport Works Who Died For Their Country In The Great War. The plaque records one hundred and twenty-one names in three columns, listed according to the various departments in which each man worked:

Mills: D. Adams, S. Aston, T.E. Aston, F. Barker, J. Barlow, W. Beddington, O. Beddows, A.G. Bennet, S. Berry, L.S. Brewster, E. Brothwood, J. Cadman, J. Cain, T. Cain, S. Clarke, T. Coombs, T. Counsell, J. Cousins, P. Coyle, J. Doughty, J.W. Edmundson, A. Edwards, J. Edwards, W. Edwards, L. Fallon, J.T. Fellows, C.A. Furnace, T.A. Geary, J. Gibbs, G. Green, J. Head, C. Hiscox, G. Hughes, J. Johnson, R. Johnson, P.H. Lyons, R. Martin, F. Morris, W. Mort, H.A. Moss, C. Nash, J.T. Newell, H. Overend, W. Phillips, S. Pitts, F. Richards, J. Robinson, W. Robinson, A. Royster, B. Tonks, I. Tonks, H. Turner, E. Shaw, W.J. Smith, H.G. Spicer, G. Summer, T. Swatman, A. Waller, J. Watkins, T. Whilde, W.H. Wilkinson, G. Williams, J. Williams, R. Williams, W.G. Williams.

Staff: A.D. Addams-Williams, A.G. Kimber, R. Stewart.

Bar Bank: F.B. Adams, E.C. Hooper, J. Pope, B. Price, T. Shea, R. Taylor, E. Underwood.

Brass Shop: J. Henry, I. Russell, A. Shutt, H. Whittington.

Close Annealing: C. Baker, R. Boswell, J. Fitzpatrick, J.H. Pumford, J. Salter, W. Terry.

Cold Rolling: E. Bennett, W. Clarke, G.H. Hyde, H. Price, D. Ward, A.G. Williams.

Sheetweighing: S.T. Chilcott, A. Doughty, J.J. Goodridge, T.H. Gorman, A.E. Hales, W.J. Innes, H.A. Law, J. Pleace, W. Shotton, F. Slade, H.W. Snell, H. Stretter, R.W. Thwaites, A. Wagstaff, F. Wheeler.

Miscellaneous: R. Anderson, J.H. Bebb, C. Caines, A.E. Carey, T. Chapman, H.

Clay, C.H. Clissold, W.H. Crayford, W. Hall, T. Johns, B. Marshall, T.H. Mulcahy, A. Peter, W. Plummer, A.T. Williams.

Below the names is the inscription - *Erected By Their Proud And Grateful Employers.*

A similar dedication also appears on a cast-iron tablet held (until a new location can be found within the works) in store. Headed - *Employees At The Wolverhampton Works* - the memorial records three names within a laurel wreath: J.R. Gladstone, A.E. Townsend and Matthew Ralph. Captain John Ravenhill Gladstone was from West Hill, Llandaff near Cardiff and was killed during the Battle of Albert, on 23 August, 1918, while serving with the 6th Battalion, Leicestershire Regiment. He was twenty-three, and is buried in Serre Road Cemetery No.1. Also killed on the Somme was Private Ralph Matthew. Born in Wolverhampton, he joined the 10th Worcestershire Regiment and was killed on 31 October, 1916.

St Andrew's School

The memorial brass plaque recently put up in the Junior School Hall by the local Royal British Legion is inscribed -

In Grateful Remembrance Of All Members Of This School Who Gave Their Lives In The World Wars 1914-1919 - 1939-1945. R.I.P.

Shortly after the end of the First World War, a cherry tree was planted in the playground to commemorate those who had lost their lives. Each year in November, wreaths and wooden crosses are placed there by the pupils and *The Last Post* sounded by a local bugler. The school is situated in Milner Street, off Corporation Road.

St John The Baptist Parish Church

Located in the centre of consecrated ground at the Oakfield Road side of the church is a limestone Calvary Cross inscribed -

To The Glory Of God In Memory Of The Men Of This Parish Who Gave Their Lives For Freedom & Honour In The Great War 1914-1919. R.I.P.

This inscription is set around the middle of three steps, the lower having - *This Cross Is Placed Here By George Rawlings Martyn And Ellen His Wife.*

Inside the church, the second window in the south aisle was dedicated on 23 June, 1920 as a memorial to the men of the parish who had been killed. Designed by Kempe, the window is described in the church records as follows: 'Christ crucified worshipped by a Roman soldier, traditionally St Longinus, at the foot of the Cross. In the centre light, St Alban, the first English martyr, stands behind the kneeling St Nicholas, patron saint of sailors. The third light shows St. Martin, patron saint of soldiers, and a beggar wearing half of the saint's cloak.'

Accompanying the window, and just below, an attractive tablet comprising brass panels set into painted stone bears the following inscription in Old English script -

The Above Window Is Placed Here In Ever Grateful Memory Of The Men Of This Parish And Congregation Who At The Call Of King And Country In The Great War Of 1914-1919 Left All That Was Dear To Them Endured Hardness Faced Danger & Finally Passed Out Of The Sight Of Men By The Path Of Duty & Self Sacrifice Giving Up Their Own Lives That Others Might Live In Freedom.

Parish memorial, St John The Baptist Parish Church.

This dedication appears in the two upper sections of the tablet. Below this, three more, the centre section being headed by the Royal Arms, record those who were killed:

Left section: Captain Wilfred Beckett Birt, 9th East Surrey Regiment; Private Arthur Brown, South Wales Borderers; Corporal James Capel, 5th South Wales Borderers; Rifleman Charles George Cox, 1st Monmouthshire Regiment; Bombardier Donald Clifford Cox, Royal Field Artillery; Private Tom Cousins, 11th South Wales Borderers; Captain Donald Saunders Currey, 1st Monmouthshire Regiment; Captain Smart Cullimore, 11th South Wales Borderers; Driver Frederick Charles Cornford, 331st Brigade, Royal Field Artillery; Lance-Corporal Walter Evans, 1/4th Oxfordshire And Buckinghamshire Light Infantry; Lance-Corporal Cyril Arthur Fisher, MM, 2nd South Wales Borderers; Rifleman Bertram Walter Gill, 1st Monmouthshire Regiment; Company Sergeant Major Harold I. Gardner, 1st Monmouthshire Regiment; Private Frederick T. Hutchins, 9th Royal Welsh Fusiliers; Corporal Joseph Hutchins, 5th Brigade, Australian Imperial Forces; Second-Lieutenant George William Hastings, 3rd Monmouthshire Regiment.

Centre section: Sergeant George Herbert James, 2nd South Wales Borderers; Private T.B. Spencer Jones, 9th Wellington Regiment, New Zealand Expeditionary Force; Captain Herbert Tapson Jones, MC, Royal Field Artillery; Captain Charles Vyvyan Lyne, 17th Welsh Regiment; Private Frederick Leeson, 1/5th Loyal North Lancashire Regiment; Second-Lieutenant Douglas C. Earle Marsh, 6th Dragoon Guards; Rifleman Gerald Percy Sims Meares, 1st Monmouthshire Regiment; Private William S. Morgan, 47th Field Ambulance, Royal Army Medical Corps; Able Seaman Edwin F. Morgan, Nelson Battalion, Royal Naval Division; Corporal Sidney Ivor Mayo, Royal Engineers; Private Frederick Frank Parsons, 1st Monmouthshire

Regiment; Rifleman Charles Arthur Pitt, 1st Monmouthshire Regiment; Rifleman Frank James Pitt, 1st Monmouthshire Regiment.

Right section: Rifleman Victor Gordon Pearce, 1st Monmouthshire Regiment; Captain C. Meyrick Pritchard, 12th South Wales Borderers; Private William Musgrave Ross, Royal Munster Fusiliers; Private Frank Seymour Rowland, Royal Fusiliers; Private Walter James Robinson, East Kent Regiment; Rifleman William Henry Saysell, 1st Monmouthshire Regiment; Captain Francis Leslie Spencer, 2nd Monmouthshire Regiment; Driver William Henry Sefton, Royal Army Medical Corps; Private Ralph Summers, 2nd Battalion, Australian Imperial Forces; Second-Lieutenant Percy Eldin Tyson, 3rd Welsh Regiment; Sergeant Wyndham W. Waters, 1st Monmouthshire Regiment; Rifleman W. Noel Wilkinson, 16th Royal Irish Rifles; Private Leonard W. Wilkinson, 5th Gordon Highlanders; Sapper George Percival White, Royal Engineers; Rifleman Edward G. Winter, 11th King's Royal Rifle Corps; Second-Lieutenant Robert H. Winter, 10th South Staffordshire Regiment; Sergeant Kirk Hearder.

Private Arthur Brown of the 1st South Wales Borderers was from Pillgwenlly, Newport and the first to meet his death. His battalion took over positions near Zillebeke in Belgium on 9 November, 1914 and repulsed a strong enemy attack two days later. Another Borderer, Sergeant George Herbert James, was killed 28 May, 1915 at Gallipoli. The 2nd Battalion war diary recorded that two were killed and nineteen wounded, mostly from spent bullets, at that time while in the Gurkha Bluff and Gully Ravine areas. The church possesses a silver-gilt chalice, made by G&S Co. Ltd. and dated 1922, dedicated to Sergeant James.

The first officer to fall was Second-Lieutenant Robert Harold Winter of the 7th South Staffordshire Regiment, succumbing to his wounds on 17 December, 1915, the day before his battalion evacuated the Gallipoli Peninsular. Robert Winter is recorded as having been buried at sea. Another officer with no known grave, his name being recorded on the Thiepval Memorial to the missing on the Somme, is Second-Lieutenant Percy Eldin Tyson. Killed while serving with the 2nd Welsh Regiment on 8 December, 1916, aged twenty-six, and was the son of John and Annie Tyson of 26 Risca Road, Newport.

Next door to the Tysons, Hubert and Anne Currey at 28 Risca Road would also lose their son. Captain Donald Saunders Currey, a 1st Monmouthshire officer, attached to the 7th Royal Berkshire Regiment, being killed on 24 April, 1917 at Salonica during the attack on Pip Ridge, south-west of Doiran. The memorial ends with the inscription - *These Men Were Very Good To Us And We Were Not Hurt. They Were A Wall Unto Us By Night And By Day.*

The Kempe window in the north aisle was given by Mr T. Summers in memory of his brother and two sons, one of whom was killed while serving with the 2nd Australian Imperial Forces. The window, notes the church records, illustrates the text - 'Be thou faithful until death and I will give you a Crown of Life', and features the figures of St Stephen, St Paul and St John. A brass dedication plaque set into brown marble records in Old English lettering -

A.M.D.G. And In Loving Memory Of Edwin John Summers Who Died December 13th 1923, Also Of His Two Sons, Owen Who Died November 7th 1904, And Ralph (A.I.F.) Who Was Killed In Action At Gallipoli May 1915, This Window Is Dedicated. R.I.P.

A large brass sanctuary gong has the inscription -

In Loving Memory Of Captain Francis Leslie Spencer, 2nd Monmouthshire Regiment, A Former Server Of This Church Who Was Killed In Action Near Cambrai France December 2nd 1917.

Captain G.A. Brett, DSO, MC, records in his history of the 2nd Monmouthshire Regiment, how Captain Spencer, with two platoons of 'A' Company, held trenches against several enemy attacks throughout the day - 'Daylight found them in inadequate cover with the Germans barely a hundred yards distant. Lieutenant Hopkins was wounded by a grenade thrown by an enterprising German who crawled within range, but a worse blow befell the Battalion a few hours later when Captain (Monty) Spencer, a keen, popular and stout-hearted officer, was shot through the head.'

St John The Evangelist Parish Church

There are four Newport soldiers commemorated in the church at St John's Road, Maindee. At the west end of the south aisle there are three brass plaques, all to the memory of men from Newport's local Territorial Force battalion, the 1st Monmouthshire Regiment. With the regimental badge etched into the top left-hand corner, the first plaque bears the inscription -

In Proud And Loving Memory Of Lt. Col. Charles Lawson Robinson, V.D. Commanding 1st Battn. Monmouthshire Regt. Killed In Action Near Ypres May 8th 1915 - Aged 45 Years - 'Greater Love Hath No Man Than This, That A Man Lay Down His Life For His Friends'.

Charles Robinson had been a member of the Monmouthshires for many years and held the Volunteer Decoration. Killed during the fighting at Frezenberg Ridge, near Ypres, he has no known grave and his name is recorded on the Menin Gate.

The next plaque has two cap badges engraved, and the following inscription -

In Loving Memory Of George Davey Howells - 2nd Lieut. 1st Battn. Monmouthshire Regt - Attached 15th Battn Cheshire Regt. - Killed In Action Near Ypres Whilst In Charge Of A Raid 28th February 1918. Aged 22 Years. The Window Above And This Tablet Were Erected By His Parents.

The window referred to was destroyed by a fire on 12 November, 1949. Also lost in *Memorials to Charles Lawson Robinson, George Davey Howells and Ronald William Thompson. St John The Evangelist Parish Church, Newport.*

the disaster was the memorial window unveiled by the Right Hon. Lord Tredegar on 11 December, 1920, two bronze tablets bearing the names of three hundred and eighty-four men and women who gave their lives in the Great War, and the reredos erected by Mr Edward Phillips in memory of his two sons.

Lieutenant Howells, as the inscription suggests, was killed in action while attached to the 15th Cheshire Regiment. The raid was on an enemy position at Memling Farm near Poelcapelle. H.M. Davson recalls the incident in his history of the 34th Division - 'An unfortunate accident marred the start as 2nd Lieutenant Howells, together with his servant and another man who were standing thirty or forty yards behind the point of assembly, were killed by one of the first shells of the barrage.' The firing was from British guns.

Another 1st Monmouthshire Regiment officer, who lived at Glen Bank, Newport, is commemorated on the third tablet -

In Loving Memory Of Ronald William Thompson - 2nd Lieutenant 1st Battn The Monmouthshire Regt - Killed In Action Near Festubert - April 11th 1918 - Aged 24 Years. Pro Patria.

Once again, the memorial displays the Dragon badge of the Monmouthshires. Ronald Thompson has no known grave, his name being recorded on the Arras Memorial in France.

At the other end of the church, and on the south wall of the chancel, a brass tablet records the following -

Dulce Et Decorum Est Pro Patria Mori - In Loving Memory Of Walter James Furzer - A Chorister Of This Church - Lance Corporal Royal Gloucestershire Hussars (Yeom). Mortally Wounded In The Battle Of Raffa Egypt - January 9th - And Died January 21st 1917 Aged 24 Years. Until The Day Breaks And The Shadows Flee Away.

The inscription is headed by the cap badge of the Royal Gloucestershire Hussars Yeomanry. The Regimental records of the Royal Gloucestershire Hussars note how in the fighting at Raffa on 9 January, 1917, they led the advance under machine-gun fire and snipers firing from the sand dunes along the coast. Unable to place the wounded in any sheltered spot, the stretcher-bearers carried out their duty under fire throughout the day.

St Mark's Church
On the south wall of the Chancel in St Mark's Church, Gold Tops, Newport, a marble tablet bears the inscription -

A.M.D.G. (Ad Maior Dei Gloriam = To The Greater Glory Of God) *The Choir Stalls In This Chancel Are Placed To The Honoured Memory Of The Following Sons Of The Parish Of St. Mark's Newport Who Gave Their Lives For Their King And Country In The Great War 1914-1918.*

The memorial was erected by the parishioners in 1922 and records twenty-six names without rank or regiment: R.E. Charles, M. Duckham, S. Duckham, A. Gabb, W. Geen, A. Hill, G. Hendy, C. Howells, A.T. Jones, H. Jones, T.A. Jones, W.E. Jones, F.A. Llewellyn, T. Llewellyn, D.E. Marsh, A.H. Mills, N. Milne, A. Morris, J. Morris, C.M. Pritchard, C.N. Reed, W.E. Rolf, F.C. Single, C.S. Stallard, R. Taylor,

Original grave marker belonging to Douglas Charles Earle Marsh. Now at St Mark's Church, Newport.

T. Weight. The memorial also notes the name of the vicar in 1922, I. Roberts, MA, and two church wardens - A.C. Mitchell and T.M. Prosser.

To the left of the tablet a stained glass widow commemorates the death of a young officer -

To The Glory Of God And The Dearly Loved Memory Of Douglas Charles Earle Marsh, 2nd Lieut. 6th Dragoon Guards (The Carabiners) Who Died At Rouen, April 8th 1918, Of Wounds Received In Action At The Successful Defence Of Amiens, Aged 19 Years. Erected By His Father And Mother As A Memorial To Their Dearly Loved Only Son. 'Leaving To Us Who Pass Where He Passed An Undying Example Of Willing And Faithful Service'.

The window shows the figures of two saints, Rouen Cathedral (*Mors 1918* written below), and Winchester College (*Vita 1911-1916*), where Douglas attended during the years 1911-1916. Also held in the church is a wooden cross, a small brass plate at the bottom of which bears the inscription -

From His Grave In France - St. Saver Cemetery, Rouen. Another plate on the arms of the cross reads - *To The Dearly Loved Memory Of Douglas Charles Earle Marsh, 2nd Lieut. 6th Dragoon Guards (The Carabiners) Who Died, April 8th 1918 Of Wounds Received In Action Aged 19 Years.*

The inscription is headed by a regimental cap badge.

The chancel screen was a gift from a former warden of St Mark's. A brass plate on the north side bears the inscription -

To The Glory Of God This Chancel Screen, The Gift Of Arthur Mawson Of Greencourt, (Formally A Warden Of This Church), Was Presented As A Thank Offering For The Safe Keeping Of His Three Sons-In-Law - John William Reid, William Reid Brown And Stanley Horatio Williams, Who Faithfully Served Their King And Country For Upwards Of Three Years In France During The Great War, 1914-1918.

Another family is remembered within the church. This time in the form of an oak litany desk bearing a small brass plate inscribed -

In Loving Memory Of Lt. Arthur Davies, Lt. Henry Davies, Sub-Lt. John Davies Who Died In The Service Of Their Country 1915.

All that remained of the original Newport High School for Boys memorial after a fire at the school in December, 1944, were two bronze plaques bearing the names of eighty Old Boys who were killed. These were placed in St Mark's and remained there after a new memorial was dedicated at the School in 1952. In November, 1954, two new plaques, one each for the First and Second World Wars, were also installed. These too are now in the possession of St Mark's (see Bettws High School).

St Mary Street Baptist Church

In an oak frame, a memorial to four members of the church is located to the right of the pulpit. The dedication reads -

St. Mary Street Baptist Church, Newport. Sunday School Peace Memorial. In Loving Memory Of - Private A.J. Doran - Driver W.E. Doran - Private W. Watkins - Private R.J. Stockwell - Who Gave Their Lives For Their Country In The Great War 1914-1918.

Each name appears below a portrait photograph. Reginald John Stockwell served with the 9th Battalion, Loyal North Lancashire Regiment and was killed during a counter-attack near the village of Croiz du Bac on 10 April, 1918. Arthur John Doran of the 9th Welsh was also killed in France, losing his life just six days before the Armistice, while William Edward Doran died in Egypt on 6 January, 1918. He served with 390th Battery, Royal Field Artillery and is buried in Cairo War Memorial Cemetery. William Watkins served with the 2nd South Wales Borderers and was killed on 4 February, 1917 during an operation on the Somme at Le Transloy.

The same four names, together with six from the Second World War, appear on a steel plate mounted on wood -

To The Glory Of God This Tablet Is Dedicated To Those Who Gave Their Lives In The Great World Wars. Their Name Liveth For Evermore.

The memorial is also located to the right of the pulpit.

St Mary Street Baptist Church, Newport memorial.

St Patrick's Memorial Chapel, St Mary's Catholic Church, Newport.

St Mary's Catholic Church

A metal plaque in St Patrick's Chapel, St. Mary's, Stow Hill bears the inscription -

As A Perpetual Record Of The Heroism Of The Catholic Men Of This Parish Who Sacrificed Their Lives In The Great War 1914 To 1918 These Memorial Tablets Were Inscribed With Their Names. The Sanctuary Of This Church Was Enclosed With The New Altar Rails And Decorated, And The Altar Of Saint Patrick Was Erected.

The two tablets referred to are in marble and record one hundred and ninety-seven names, alphabetically and with regiments in six (three per tablet) columns:

1st column: W. Ahearn, Royal Engineers; W. Allison, Mercantile Marine; J. Attwood, King's Own Royal Lancaster Regiment; J.F. Avery, 3rd Welsh Regiment; T. Banks, 2nd Welsh Regiment; F. Bennett, 1st Monmouthshire Regiment; Jas. Bickerstaff, Mercantile Marine; Jno. Bickerstaff, Mercantile Marine; C. Blake, Mercantile Marine; J. Brady, Royal Navy; J. Brickley, South Wales Borderers; F. Broad, 2nd Welsh Regiment; A.J. Burke, 1st Monmouthshire Regiment; C. Burke, Welsh Guards; F. Burke, South Wales Borderers; J. Cain, South Wales Borderers; T. Cain, South Wales Borderers; J. Callaghan, South Wales Borderers; C.R. Campbell, East Kent Regiment; W.J. Casey, Royal Welsh Fusiliers; J.A. Cashman, South Wales Borderers; C.R. Clark, 1st Monmouthshire Regiment; E. Clark, East Yorkshire Regiment; A. Coleman, Mercantile Marine; J. Collins, South Wales Borderers; T. Collins, Royal Irish Regiment; J.F. Connolly, Essex Regiment; T. Connors, South Wales Borderers; P. Coyle, South Wales Borderers; J.P. Crean, South Wales Borderers; J. Crowley, Royal Munster Fusiliers; L. Crowley, Royal Welsh Fusiliers; W. Curran, Royal Engineers.

2nd column: M. Curtis, Royal Field Artillery; T. Curtis, 1st Monmouthshire Regiment; J. Dahill, 7th Gloucestershire Regiment; W. Daley, Welsh Regiment; B. Danaher, South Wales Borderers; J.C. Dart, 1st Monmouthshire Regiment; W. Davies, South Wales Borderers; W.A. Davies, Royal Field Artillery; P. Deighton, Royal Irish Rifles; R.H. Delahay, 1st Monmouthshire Regiment; W.C. Dermody, Royal Navy; E.T. Donovan, South Wales Borderers; R.P. Donovan, Royal Army Medical Corps; W.J. Donovan; Royal Munster Fusiliers; J.P. Downey, South Wales Borderers; J.P. Drayton, South Wales Borderers; J. Driscoll, Royal Navy; J. Driscoll, South Wales Borderers; J. Duggan, I.R.; M. Duggan, Mercantile Marine; W.H. Edwards, South Wales Borderers; T. Evans, 1st Monmouthshire Regiment; R. Fitzmorris, South Wales Borderers; J. Fitzpatrick, South Wales Borderers; J. Foley, 1st Monmouthshire Regiment; A.V. Fox, Royal Irish Fusiliers; C. Franklin, Royal Welsh Fusiliers; J. Gallivan, Royal Dublin Fusiliers; D.J. Geary, Royal Field Artillery; C. Golledge, Welsh Regiment; J.H. Goulding, Machine Gun Corps; P. Grenville, 1st Monmouthshire Regiment; J. Griffiths, Royal Engineers.

3rd column: W. Gwyer, Royal Navy; J. Haggerty, Irish Guards; J.C. Haley, South Wales Borderers; M. Hard, Welsh Regiment; J.J. Harrington, Royal Flying Corps; C.V. Harvey, 1st Monmouthshire Regiment; P.M. Healy, South Lancashire Regiment; D.J. Heirene, East Lancashire Regiment; D. Heirene, 1st Monmouthshire Regiment; D.M. Heirene, Army Service Corps; T.E. Hillman, 1st Monmouthshire Regiment; W. Holland, 1st Monmouthshire Regiment; W. Holland, South Wales Borderers; T. Horrigan, Royal Welsh Fusiliers; W. Hoskins, South Wales Borderers; A.V. Haurahine, South Wales Borderers; T. Haurahine, Royal Army Medical Corps; A. Haurahine, 1st Monmouthshire Regiment; P. Hughes, 1st Monmouthshire Regiment; G. Huish, 1st Monmouthshire Regiment; D. Hurley, Royal Welsh Fusiliers; J. Hurley, Royal Engineers; W.J. Inns, Royal Horse Artillery; A.C. Jenkins, 1st Monmouthshire Regiment; V.J. Jenner, Welsh Guards; J.W. Jennings, Mercantile Marine; C. Jones, Grenadier Guards; E.J. Jones, South Wales Borderers; H.J. Jones, 1st Monmouthshire Regiment; W.H. Jones, King's Shropshire Light Infantry; J.J. Kearns, Royal Navy; J. Kelly, South Wales Borderers; R. Kelly, South Wales Borderers.

4th column: T.W. Kelly, 1st Monmouthshire Regiment; M. Landers, South Wales Borderers, E.F. Lawlor, 2nd Monmouthshire Regiment; J.F. Lawlor, Royal Naval Reserve; C.P. Leyson, South Wales Borderers; A.V. Logan, 1st Monmouthshire Regiment; C.D. Lomas, King's Liverpool Regiment; W.J. Mahoney, Gloucestershire Regiment; J.M. Mansfield, South Wales Borderers; T. Martin, South Wales Borderers; J.P. McCarthy, Worcestershire Regiment; W. McHale, Grenadier Guards; W. Miles, South Wales Borderers; T.J. Moloney, Royal Navy; E.T. Moran, 1st Monmouthshire Regiment; T.H. Mulcahy, South Wales Borderers; J. Mullins, Royal Welsh Fusiliers; C.P. Murphy, Royal Garrison Artillery; J. Murphy, 1st Monmouthshire Regiment; J. Murray, Royal Welsh Fusiliers; J.N. Murray, Royal Army Medical Corps; F.T. Myles, Mercantile Marine; J.T. Newell, South Wales Borderers; C.D. O'Brien, Durham Light Infantry; D.J. O'Brien, King's Liverpool Regiment; W. O'Brien, South Wales Borderers; W.B. O'Brien, Grenadier Guards; M. O'Callaghan, South Wales Borderers; D. O'Connell, Royal Gloucestershire Hussars; J. O'Connell, South Wales Borderers; P. O'Connor, Royal Navy; A.J. O'Keeffe, Royal Naval Division; C. O'Keefe, South Wales Borderers.

5th column: C. O'Keefe, Royal Navy; D.A. O'Keefe, King's Liverpool Regiment;

145

J.F. O'Keefe, Leinster Regiment; T.J. O'Leary, 1st Monmouthshire Regiment; P. Olsen, South Wales Borderers; J. O'Neill, Royal Welsh Fusiliers; T. O'Neill, Royal Engineers; R. O'Shea, Mercantile Marine; J. O'Sullivan, South Wales Borderers; W.C. Parry, Royal Welsh Fusiliers; A. Peters, Welsh Regiment; F.R. Pocock, Mercantile Marine; J. Power, South Wales Borderers; P. Power, Mercantile Marine; J. Price, South Wales Borderers; F. Probert, Royal Field Artillery; H.J. Reynolds, South Wales Borderers; I. Richards, South Wales Borderers; W. Robinson, Royal Naval Division; A.G. Rossiter, Manchester Regiment; A. Russell, 1st Monmouthshire Regiment; M. Ryan, South Wales Borderers; R. Ryan, South Wales Borderers; T.P. Ryan, Welsh Regiment; C.M. Saunders, Lincolnshire Regiment; J. Scott, Welsh Regiment; F. Shea, South Wales Borderers; R.J. Sheedy, Mercantile Marine; E.J. Shergold, King's Shropshire Light Infantry; W.G. Simmons, Welsh Regiment; C.H. Sinclair, Mercantile Marine; A. Slattery, South Wales Borderers; M. Slattery, South Wales Borderers.

6th column: L.C. Southam, 1st Monmouthshire Regiment; T. Stanton, South Wales Borderers; J. Stokes, Royal Field Artillery; J. Sullivan (10195), South Wales Borderers; J. Sullivan (13446), South Wales Borderers; J. Sullivan (14892), South Wales Borderers; W.E. Sullivan, Royal Navy; J. Sweeney, Mercantile Marine; T.J. Symonds, South Wales Borderers; H. Tapson-Jones, Royal Field Artillery; F. Thomas, 1st Monmouthshire Regiment; G.E. Thomas, Royal Army Medical Corps; J. Thomas, 1st Monmouthshire Regiment; J. Thomas, Mercantile Marine; T. Tugby, South Wales Borderers; J.J. Tyrrell, South Wales Borderers; T.R. Upton, South Wales Borderers; D. Wallace, South Wales Borderers; J. Watts, South Wales Borderers; W. Welsh, South Wales Borderers; W.E. Wernet, South Wales Borderers; B.W. Williams, 1st Monmouthshire Regiment; W.A. Williams, Royal Highlanders of Canada; F.J. Williams, Welsh Regiment; J. Williams, Royal Munster Fusiliers; L. Williams, South Wales Borderers; O.M. Williams, 1st Monmouthshire Regiment; F.H. Wilmott, South Wales Borderers; T. Woore, Royal Field Artillery; G. Workman, East Yorkshire Regiment; M. Wright, Royal Welsh Fusiliers; A.V. Whitfield, Royal Naval Division.

The left-hand tablet has the Latin inscription - *Hi Dei Regis Patriae Splendide Memores* between the dates - *1914 - 1918*, at the top, and *Requhem Æternam Dons Fis Domine* at the bottom. On the right-hand tablet - *Sui Obliti Famam Meruere Perennem*, between - *1914-1918* - at the top, and - *Et Lux Perpetua Luceat Eis* - below. The altar of Caen stone and Irish marble, records *The Newport Christmas Annual* for 1925, was designed by Messrs. F.R. Bates, & Son, of Newport.

St Matthew's Church

St Matthew's in Church Road, Newport has an east window set into eight sections, each featuring the figure of a Saint, and the inscription -

To The Glory Of God And As A Thanks Offering In Memory Of The Members Of This Congregation Who Served In The Great War Of 1914-1918.

St Philip's Church

The following, taken from *II King's* (Chapter 18, Verse 19), appears below an oil painting on the west wall of St Philip's in Jenkins Street, Newport - *And Rabshakeh Said Unto Them, Speak Ye Now To Hezekiah. Thus Saith The Great King, The King Of*

Assyria:- What Confidence Is This Wherein Thou Trustest? This is followed by the inscription - *In Memory Of E.F. Killed In Action At Dèmuin Near Amiens On Good Friday March 29th 1918.*

The painting, which depicts a scene based on the quotation, was donated by a former vicar of St Philip's, The Revd Charles Feetham, in memory of his brother Major-General Edward Feetham, CB, CMG. The General, who had served in both the Sudan Expedition of 1885 and the South African War, 1901-1902, was appointed to the command of the 39th Division in France on 20 August, 1917. He was killed, records the General Staff diary of the 39th Division, whilst walking along the main street of Dèmuin. An enemy shell exploded on a house close by, and the General was hit in the neck by a fragment.

St Stephen And Holy Trinity Church
On the south side of the church in Alexandria Road, near the entrance to the vestry, a Roll of Honour in a dark wood frame depicts the figure of Christ entering a church with a flock of sheep. The illustration, a pen and ink drawing by George R.W. Phillis, has the caption - *The Door Of The Fold. 'I Am The Resurrection And The Life'.* To the left of the picture, the inscription - *'Greater Love Hath No Man Than This That A Man Lay Down His Life For His Friends'* - and to the right - *'Rest Eternal Grant Unto Them. O Lord, And Let Light Perpetual Shine Upon Them'.* Below the picture, the dedication -

To The Glory Of God And In Sacred Memory Of The Men Of St. Stephens Church And Congregation Who Fell In The Great War.

Twenty-four names, with regiments, follow: G. Williams, W.G. Rice, E. Jones and J. Betts, of the Royal Navy; G.G. Betts, Merchant Navy; E. Betts, Australian Imperial Forces; B.H. England, Royal Engineers; W. Swift, Welsh Regiment; T. Niell and E. Mapstone, Royal Field Artillery; W. Miller, Royal Garrison Artillery; C.H. Seer, Royal Field Artillery; E. James, T. Buck, T. Morgan, A. Hoods and C.H. Hoods, all of the South Wales Borderers; E. Hoods, Welsh Regiment; W.J. Upton, South Wales Borderers; W. Dix, W. Thayer and A.H. Morgan, of the 1st Monmouthshire Regiment; T. Roberts, Army Ordnance Corps, and F.N. Hansen of the Welsh Guards.

In 1975 Holy Trinity Church in Potter Street was closed down and demolished two years later in 1977. The church hall was in Trinity Street and had, until 1900, been the premises of the Temple Street Voluntary School. On the wall of the Holy Trinity Church Hall a brass plate bore the inscription -

Lest We Forget. This Memorial Is An Affectionate Tribute From Mr. W. Richards, The Last Headmaster, In Grateful Remembrance Of All Old Temple Street Boys Who Served In The Great War, 1914-1918 Of Whom The Following Are Known To Have Died For Their Country -

Walter Oakey, Robert Brown, William R. Jones, John Morgan, Wilfred Miller, Arthur Dart, Samuel Dart, William Hale, Thomas Hale, Jonas Travers, William Pring, Thomas John, William Jacobson, John Tolcher, George Cambray, Zechariah Sims, William Perry, Sameul French, Thomas Lewis, Job Salter, Frank Hathaway, William Upton, Thomas Buck, Daniel James, John Westacott, Albert Hood. When the hall was closed down the memorial was brought to St Stephen's and is now (May, 2000) held in store.

St Thomas's Church, Maesglas

The brass lectern at St Thomas' in Old Cardiff Road previously belonged to St Luke's Church, Bridge Street, Newport which was demolished in 1994. The following inscription appears at the base -

To The Greater Glory Of God And In Loving Memory Of Sergeant Alfred John White 1/5th Gloucestershire Regiment. Died In France From Wounds Received In Action On 9th Day Of October 1918. Beloved Second Son Of William And Jane A. White, 4 Fields Road, Newport. Also In Grateful Acknowledgement Of The Safe Return Of Their Two Sons & Son-In-Law.

On the 5 October, 1918, the 1/5th Gloucestershire Regiment took part in the attack on the French village of Beaurevoir. The Battalion assaulting the south side of the village. The war diary of the 1/5th Gloucesters records how, when nearing the embankment which skirted the west of Beaurevoir, casualties occurred from our own guns. The village was later taken and a line established along the eastern side. There were additional casualties throughout the 6th and again on the 9th when a further advance was made towards the village of Maretz.

St Woolos Cathedral

The memorial to the dead of Newport's own battalion is situated at the west end of the nave on either side of the Norman arch -

To The Glory Of God And To The Undying Memory Of The Officers, Warrant Officers, Non Commissioned Officers And Riflemen Of The 1st Battalion, Monmouthshire Regiment (T.F.) Who Gave Their Lives In The Great War 1914-1919.

The names, there are five hundred and ninety-seven, are inscribed on two Nailsworth stone panels (four columns each) in rank order. These are headed by a

selection of Regimental Battle Honours - *South Africa - Neuve Chapelle - Ypres* and *Loos* on the south side - *Somme - Arras - Lens* and *Canal Du Nord* on the north side.

The memorial was unveiled by Major-General The Hon. E.J. Montagu-Stuart-Wortley, CB, CMG, DSO, MCO on Saturday 7 May, 1921. The General being GOC 46th (North Midland) Division (with which the 1st Monmouthshire served as Pioneer Battalion) between June, 1914 and July, 1916.

1st column: *Lieutenant-Colonels:* J. Jenkins (King's Royal Rifle Corps attached. Awarded Military Cross), C.L. Robinson (holder of the Territorial Decoration), F.J. Trump (attached to the 1/6th South Staffordshire Regiment); *Majors:* E.S. Williams, O.M. Williams; *Captains:* D.S. Currey (attached

One of two memorial tablets commemorating members of the 1st Monmouthshire Regiment. St Woolos Cathedral.

7th Royal Berkshire Regiment), E.C. Dimsdale (Rifle Brigade attached), H.T. Edwards, W.M. James, J.C. Lewis (attached 6th King's Shropshire Light Infantry); B.L. Perry, T.S. Spittle, C.W. Stanton; *Lieutenants:* W.E.C.A. Darby, D.M.W. Evans, J.R. Evans, J.G. Frampton, E.S. Phillips; *Second-Lieutenants:* H.A. Birrell-Anthony, H.C. Archer, H.J. Ballinger, A.P. Duncan, S.R. Duncanson (attached 11th Cheshire Regiment), C.S. Hall, G.D. Howells (attached 15th Cheshire Regiment), L.G.W.S. Jones, R. King (attached 1st South Wales Borderers), A.G. Lewis (South Wales Borderers attached), A.L. Meredith, N.C. Newland, A. Richards, S.E. Richards, L.H.C. Smith, W.V. Stewart, R.W. Thompson (attached 4th South Lancashire Regiment), G. Widowfield, D.J. Williams (attached 6th King's Shropshire Light Infantry); *Regimental Sergeant Major:* H.J. Humphries; *Company Sergeant Majors:* C. Firr, H.J. Gardner, W. Parkinson, W.G. Winston; *Company Quartermaster Sergeant:* A.J. Dix; *Sergeants:* J.W. Crump, T.C. Davies, W.H. Day, A.W. Garbutt, G. Harding, C.V. Harvey, K. Hearder, J. Marshfield, W. Miles, E.T. Moran, F. Morgan, J.A. Robinson, J.H. Spencer, A.A. Sullivan, H.M. Underwood.

2nd column: *Lance-Sergeants:* H. Catterall, W.J. Haskell, T. Jones, E. Payne; *Corporals:* J. Bland, W.E. Briscoe, R.W. Brown, G. Cambray, T. Counsell, T.C. Curtis, A. Edwards, W.T. John, R. Keogh, W.E. Lock, H. Morgan, T.H. Roberts, A. Russell, S. Turley, G. Wall, T. Webb (awarded Military Medal), J. Wells, W.H. Westbury; *Lance-Corporals:* A.P. Bosworth, C. Bowen, T. Coombs, A.J. Dowding, A.E. Fisher, A.V. Fishlock, H.F. Golding, T.H. Griffiths, H. Hall, E. Hambley, F. Hammond, A. Hiley, C.W. Hobbs, R.G. Holbrook, T. Howells, H. Hughes, R. Hughes, H.G. Humphries, S. Hunt, A.J. James, T. John, E.W. Jones, C. Kingerlie, J.M. Lavis, R. Law, W. Morgan, E.H. Morris, P.C. Morris, W. Morris, J.G. Nudd, A.C. Oxenbury, F.E. Seary, F. Thomas, J.T. Thomas, D. Ward, W. Waters, E. Welch, J. Williams; *Riflemen:* L. Adams, W. Alban, E. Andrews, W.G. Andrews, W.G. Ardren, J. Arkinstall, M. Ashcroft, P. Ashman, J. Aspinall, C. Austin, W.H. Avery, N.G. Ayliffe, A. Bailey, E.J. Bailey.

3rd column: *Riflemen:* H. Bailey, J. Bailey, J.L. Bailey, V.S. Bailey, B.R. Baiss, F. Baiss, R. Barker, T. Barton, J. Baxendale, V. Beare, B. Beasley, L. Beatty, R.J. Beckett, J. Bellingham, I. Bennett, S.L. Bennett, W. Bennett, H. Bentley, C. Bestwick, R. Blacker, W. Blackmore, A. Blight, C. Blown, A.J. Boast, A. Booth, E. Bowden, O. Bowen, L. Bray, T.M. Bray, W. Briarly, I. Briddon, E.G. Brown, J. Brown, F.C. Browning, A. Burke, H.S. Burroughs, T. Byfield, H. Carey, W. Carter, W.J. Carter, W. Case, J.J. Casey, J.P. Chapman, W.A. Charles, J. Charlsworthy, E. Charlton, E. Cheek, S.J. Chubb, W.G. Church, R. Clark, C.R. Clarke, J. Clements, S.T. Cloud, R.M. Cole, W.G. Cole, W. Collier, B.W. Collins, J. Comer, J. Commer, A.J. Coombes, D. Cooper, E.N. Cooper, F. Cooper, H. Cooper, H. Coops, C.J.G. Cox, W.H. Crayford, H. Crickmore, J. Crossley, J. Dade, W.G. Daer, T. Dance, J.C. Dart, D.J. Davies, G. Davies, H. Davies, J. Davies.

4th column: *Riflemen:* K.J. Davies, M. Davies, R. Davies, W.G. Davies, W.A.J. Dawes, R.G. Dawson, J.W. Deakin, C.G. Dean, H.H. Delahay, R.G.D. Dempster, J. Dennett, W.J. Dick, W. Dixbury, F. Doggett, J. Donovan, C. Drower, S.M. Duckham, P. Dudley, J. Dyer, S. Earnshall, J. East, F. Eburn, H.A. Edmunds, J. Edwards, R.P. Edwards, T. Edwards, W.R. Edwards, W.H. Elleway, C.A. Ellis, H. Ellison, H. Entwhistle, A.A. Evans, D.B. Evans, F. Evans, G. Evans, S.M. Evans, T. Evans, F. Farrest, D. Field, H. Flook, J. Foley, A.J. Foskett, E.C. Francis, T. Francis, E.S.

Frankham, I. Froy, B.H. Gale, A.H. Gallop, A. Gardner, J. Garnett, F. Gaytside, H.S. Gigney, A.W. Gilbery, B. Gill, J. Gilligan, J.H. Goodyear, F. Gough, C. Gray, J.A. Gray, J. Greenhalgh, C. Greenham, J. Greenslade, P. Grenville, F. Grey, W. Gribble, A. Griffiths, A.G. Griffiths, N.C. Grimes, D.J. Gunstone, J. Hall, T.G. Hancock, V. Hanson, J.F. Harding, A.J. Harris, E. Harris, W. Harry, R.B. Hart.

5th column: *Riflemen:* W. Hartley, R. Hassell, G.A. Hastie, L. Headlam, A.L. Heathfield, F. Hellingworth, E. Hickman, F. Hicks, G. Higginston, S. Hill, J. Hillman, T.J. Hillman, F.G. Hodder, E. Holland, W. Holland, A. Holmes, G.A. Holt, J. Hongus, A.L. Hooper, H. Hord, B. Hornby, A. Hourihane, A. Howell, C. Howells, J.M. Howells, W. Howells, A. Hughes, B. Hughes, J.R. Hughes, P. Hughes, G. Huish, E. Humphries, T. Humphries, W. Hunt, G.H. Hyde, W. Jackson, H. James, W.M. James, J. Jarrett, W.R. Jefferies, J.E. Jeffrey, A. Jenkins, A.C. Jenkins, W.J. Jenkins, E.H. Jennings, N. Johnson, P. Johnson, A.J. Jones, A.P. Jones, A.T. Jones, A.W. Jones, D. Jones, D.T. Jones, E. Jones (2215), E. Jones (4879), F. Jones, H.B. Jones, H.G. Jones, H.S. Jones, H.T. Jones, P. Jones, P.E. Jones, S. Jones (227535), S. Jones (263133), T.T. Jones, W. Jones (1147), W. Jones (3555), W.J. Jones, J. Kelly, T.W. Kelly, J. Kendell, T. Kift, A.G. Kimber, A. Kinsey, J. Knott, I. Lake, C. Lambert, S. Langmaid.

6th column: *Riflemen:* J. Lawson, T.C. Lee, E.P. Leech, A.J. Lewis, G. Lewis, J.R. Lewis, R. Lewis, W.H. Lewis, W.R. Lewison, W.J. Lloyd, A. Logan, W.A. Lucas, A. Madge, H.G. Mapp, W. Marchant, F.H. Martin, W. Mason, A. Matthews, H. Mayne, W. McCann, M.L. McLaughtan, E.G. Mead, G.P.S. Meares, I. Meredith, T.G. Meredith, A.S. Miles, J. Millership, A. Miskell, I.W. Mitchell, A.R. Moore, J.M. Moore, W.H. Moore, A.H. Morgan, C.E. Morgan, D. Morgan, E. Morgan, M. Morgan, W. Morgan, A. Moriton, J. Morrall, C.C. Morris, C.H. Morris, J. Morris, T. Morris, G. Morse, F. Moseley, F. Mosely, G. Mousdell, F. Murphy, J. Murphy, A. Newport, A. Newton, J. Newton, A.N. Nibbs, J.H. Norris, T. O'Leary, T.J. O'Leary, W.J. Onions, W.S. Orpwood, G.J. Owens, J. Palmer, A. Panter, W.B. Parkinson, E.J. Parry, H.A. Parry, P.S. Parry, F. Parsons, H.T. Peacock, P. Peacock, N.G. Pearce, E. Pendlebury, J. Petheram, A.B. Phillips, C.J. Phillips, D. Phillips, J. Philpin, C.A. Pitt, F.J. Pitt.

7th column: *Riflemen:* W. Pilkington, A.C. Plank, S. Pomeroy, C.T. Pook, A.J. Pope, J. Pope, R.H. Porter, R.W. Porter, F.R. Portnell, W. Powell, F.R. Powles, A. Price, E. Price (1826), E. Price (226630), H. Price, J.H. Price, W. Price, E.G. Prickett, C. Priest, H. Pritchard, N.L. Pritchard, J.M. Probert, J. Pye, G. Quenton, J. Radcliffe, S. Rainstick, E. Rattee, J. Reardon, A.H. Rees, J.D. Rees, J.J. Rees, P. Rees, W.C. Richards, C. Riley, C.J. Roberts, H.P. Roberts, W. Robertson, F. Robinson, G. Robinson, J. Robinson, J. Rosevere, R. Ross, A.J. Rouse, V. Rowe, H. Rowland, W.F. Rowson, T. Salmon, R.H. Sansom, F. Saunders, W.H. Saysell, P.J. Scannell, J. Scott, A. Seamer, H.T.C. Seddon, C.W. Selley, B.C. Shaw, J.H. Shepherd, J. Sherman, P. Sibthorpe, W. Simmonds, Z. Sims, W.R. Skinner, J. Skyrme, W. Small, E.C. Smart, R.S. Smart, A. Smith, A.H. Smith, H. Smith, J. Smith (1628), J. Smith (229002), R.J. Smith, T. Smith, W.G. Snelgrove, J.C. Speck, J. Spencer, W. Spencer, H.C. Stephens.

8th column: *Riflemen:* M. Stephens, W. Stephens, C.G. Stevens, E.B. Stevens, J. Stewart, S.J. Stone, E.G. Strong, F.W. Strong, R.C. Surlock, G.A. Sutton, F.C. Taylor, H. Teague, W. Thayer, C. Thomas, E.J. Thomas, F. Thomas, G. Thomas, J.

Thomas, P. Thomas, T. Thomas, T.J. Thomas, T. Thompson, W. Tilley, J. Tindall, J.A. Tiplin, W. Torry, R.W. Travers, E.L.H. Trew, A. Trow, D. Tudor, P.H. Turner, T. Vaughan, S.S. Verity, J. Vernall, H. Vince, A. Waller, C. Walker, J. Walker, D.T. Walters, G. Ward, F. Warman, S. Warwick, S. Watkins, S.J. Watkins, E.J. Webb, H. West, J. Whalley, A. Wheeler, A. White (3037), A. White (290465), J. White, J.W. White, L.M. Whitney, G. Whitlock, A.R. Whittle, A.E. Wilkes, J. Wilkinson, A. Williams, A.G. Williams, A.W. Williams, B.W. Williams, C.H. Williams, E. Williams, J. Williams, J.E. Williams, J.R. Williams, O. Williams, P.A. Williams, R.J. Williams, T.H. Williams, W.J. Williams, W.C. Windsor, D. Winkworth, E.E. Winter, A.H. Woosnam, W. Workman, W.C. Young.

St Woolos Cemetery

Just inside the main entrance to the cemetery in Bassaleg Road stands a Cross of Sacrifice. The base of which bears the inscription -

To The Honoured Memory Of One Hundred And Ninety Seven Sailors And Soldiers Who Gave Their Lives For Their Country During The Great War 1914-1918 Of Whom One Hundred And Forty Nine Lie Here And Forty-Eight In Christchurch Cemetery Both In The County Borough Of Newport Mon. This Cross Of Sacrifice Is One In Design And Intention With Those Which Have Been Set Up In France And Belgium And Other Places Throughout The World Where Our Dead Of The Great War Are Laid To Rest. Their Name Liveth For Evermore.

The burials recorded by the Commonwealth War Graves Commission (CWGC) for the two cemeteries are in fact - forty-nine in Christchurch and one hundred and sixty-seven at St Woolos. A small group of approximately forty CWGC headstones can be found close to the Risca Road entrance (section 25), but the majority of war graves, many of which have private family headstones, are scattered over this vast cemetery. Of those buried at St Woolos, many are local men and women. However, servicemen from all parts of the British Isles, and overseas, having been wounded in action, were sent to the Royal Gwent, and other war hospitals in the Newport area.

Private W. Abraham, 3rd Battalion, Welsh Regiment. Died 4 December, 1918. (See Able Seaman Walter Henry Abraham below).

Able Seaman Walter Henry Abraham, Royal Naval Volunteer Reserve, of HMS *Vivid* died, aged twenty-two, on 29 November, 1920. He was the son of Henry and Louis Abraham of 60 Alexandra Road, Newport. He is buried with his brother, Private W. Abraham (see above) in a family grave. They share the same CWGC headstone (double-size) bearing the badges of both men's units.

Gunner Robert Anderson, No. 2 Depot, Royal Garrison Artillery, was born in Motherwell, Lanarkshire. He lived with his wife Edith Kate Anderson at 13 Albert Avenue, Newport and died, aged thirty-one, on 14 January, 1915.

Private Albert Arnold, 1st Battalion, Bedfordshire Regiment, was from Tylers Causeway, Hertfordshire. He died from wounds received in France on 2 December, 1916.

Private William Robert Austen, Labour Companies, King's (Liverpool Regiment), was married to Emily Austen of 12 Sidney Street, Newport. He enlisted into the army at Southport, Lancashire and died, aged thirty-eight, on 23 February, 1917.

Lance-Corporal H.C. Baker, 'C' Company, 1st Battalion, Monmouthshire

Grave markers to French seamen. St Woolos Cemetery, Newport.

Regiment, was the son of Mark and Emily Baker and married to Claudean Amelia Baker of 7 Aderlaide Street, Crindau, Newport. He died, aged thirty-four, of nephritis on 24 May, 1921.

Private John Clifford Baker, Royal Defence Corps, was the son of William and Mary Ann Baker of St Giles-in-the-Wold, Great Torrington. He lived in Griffithstown, previously served with the Monmouthshire Regiment, and died, aged fifty-four, on 17 March, 1917.

Private H. Bannister, 1st Battalion, Devonshire Regiment. He later transferred to the Labour Corps and died 16 January, 1921.

Driver William Barber, Royal Field Artillery, was from Birmingham. He died 18 June, 1917.

Private T. Barry, 32nd Company, Royal Army Ordnance Corps, was the son of

Grave of a Belgian soldier. St Woolos Cemetery, Newport.

Three soldiers commemorated by a single Commonwealth War Graves Commission headstone. St Woolos Cemetery, Newport.

Richard and Margaret Barry of Chapel Street, Cloyne, Co. Cork, Ireland. He died, aged thirty, on 3 July, 1921.

Able Seaman Herbert Ivor Bateman, HMS *Serene*, Royal Navy, was the son of John Edward and Mary Bateman of 57 Durham Road, Newport. He died, aged twenty-three, on 17 May, 1920.

Private George Richard Beagen, King's (Liverpool Regiment), was born in London and married to Rachael Elizabeth Beagen of 19 Marshfield Street, Newport. He transferred to 784th Company, Labour Corps and died, aged forty-three, on 9 October, 1918.

Corporal Herbert Watkin Beanland, 2nd (City of London) Battalion, London Regiment, was the son of George Watkin and Martha Beanland of Newport. He enlisted into the army in Westminster, London and died, aged twenty-two, on 26 December, 1917.

Private Frank William George Beesley, 4th (City of London) Battalion, London Regiment, was from Hackney in London and the son of Florence Beesley of 3 Markhouse Avenue, Walthamstow, Essex. He died, aged twenty-seven, from wounds received in France on 6 July, 1916.

Lance-Corporal D. Bowen, Welsh Regiment, died 27 May, 1916 and is buried with M.J. Collins and J. Power (see below). The soldiers have a single CWGC headstone approximately three times the size of the normal pattern.

Sapper Arthur Boyle, Inland Water Transport, Royal Engineers, was born in Shankill, County Antrim, Ireland. He died 17 July, 1918.

Sub-Lieutenant (Paymaster) William Percy Brace, HMS *Pembroke*, Royal Naval Reserve. Died of influenza at Gosport on 25 October, 1918.

Private Percy Reginald Bransfield, 'C' Company, 3rd Battalion, South Wales Borderers. He died, aged seventeen, of meningitis on 8 August, 1915 and lived at 5 Mansel Street, Newport.

Private Patrick Brett, 2nd Battalion, Royal Irish Regiment, was from Tramore, Co. Waterford, Ireland. He died on 25 January, 1916.

Private Frederick Broad, 2nd Battalion, Welsh Regiment, was married to Eleanor Broad of 6 South Market Street, Newport. He died, aged thirty-nine, on 10 January, 1915 from wounds received in France.

Private Albert Brooks, 494th MT Company, Royal Army Service Corps, was twenty-seven when he died of pneumonia on 9 February, 1919.

Private William Benjamin Brute, 3rd Battalion, South Wales Borderers, was the son of Peter and Mrs M.A. Brute of 35 Albany Street, Newport. He died, aged thirty-one, on 17 October, 1918.

Pioneer George William Budden, Royal Engineers, served with the Inland Waterways and Docks section of the RE. He was twenty-one when he died on 21 October, 1918 and the son of George William and Alice Maud Budden of 1 Mountjoy Road, Newport. George Budden has a CWGC headstone within a family plot. He is buried with his parents.

Lance-Corporal G.R. Carter, 52nd Company, Royal Army Ordnance Corps, died 24 June, 1919.

Private Albert Daniel Clargo, 3rd Battalion, South Wales Borderers, died 27 October, 1917.

Private Peter Clements, 1st Battalion, Duke of Cornwall's Light Infantry, was from Cardiff. He was wounded in France and died 20 February, 1917.

Driver Stanley Charles Collier, 4th Welsh Brigade, Royal Field Artillery, was the son of Mr C.C. Collier of 104 Barrack Hill, Newport. He died, aged nineteen, on 13 February, 1917.

Private M.J. Collins, 18th Battalion, Middlesex Regiment, was from Clonakilty, County Cork, Ireland and was the son of Michael and Elizabeth Collins. He died, aged thirty-eight, on 7 March, 1916 and occupies a grave with two other soldiers (see Lance-Corporal D. Bowen above).

Private Jeremaih Cremen, 4th Battalion, Monmouthshire Regiment, was born in Cardiff and married to Alice Rebecca Cremen. He died 17 February, 1917.

Private M. Crowley, 2nd Battalion, Monmouthshire Regiment, died 25 May, 1920.

Lance-Corporal William Curran, 96th Field Company, Royal Engineers. Died from wounds received on 22 January, 1918.

Pioneer William Edward Dallimore, Royal Engineers, died at Lydney Red Cross Hospital, Gloucestershire on 2 March, 1918. He was twenty-six and lived at 18 Lewis Street, Newport.

Pioneer John Henry Dawson, Royal Engineers, served with the Railway Construction Troops Depot. He was the son of John and Mrs S. Dawson of 2 Edwards Terrace, Abertridwr, Cardiff and died, aged twenty-five, on 5 November, 1918.

Private T. Dixon, 50th Canadian Infantry (Alberta Regiment), died 19 December, 1916.

Private Albert Jeremaih Dowsell, 11th Battalion, South Wales Borderers, was married to Winifred Mary Ann Dowsell of 21 Bristol Street, Newport. He died, aged forty-one, on 10 October, 1919. Albert Dowsell is buried with his wife who died in July, 1955.

Trimmer J. Driscoll, Royal Naval Reserve of HMS *Vivid*, died 4 March, 1916.

Private Thomas Driscoll, Royal Defence Corps, was married to Ada Driscoll of 55 Alma Street, Newport. He died, aged sixty-four, on 23 June, 1919.

Pioneer B. Dunn, Royal Engineers, died 26 November, 1919. He served in the army under the name of W. Thorney.

Rifleman William Henry Ellaway, 1st Battalion, Monmouthshire Regiment, was the son of William and Harriet Ellaway of 33 Corporation Road, Newport. He died, aged twenty, on 8 May, 1915.

Private Edward Evans, 5th Battalion, South Wales Borderers, was from Maindee and was the son of Benjamin and Lilian Evans. He transferred to 613th Company, Labour Corps and died, aged thirty-three, on 11 November, 1918.

Corporal Evan Evans, Royal Welsh Fusiliers, was the son of Evan and Sarah Evans and married to Grace Evans of 23 The Green, Denbigh. He died, aged thirty-two, from phthisis on 9 June, 1917.

Private G.S. Faben, 570th Agricultural Company, Labour Corps, died 3 January, 1919.

Private David Fergus, Royal Scots Fusiliers, was born in Riccarton, Ayrshire, the son of Alexander and Angus Fergus of 21 Portland Street, Kilmarnock. He transferred to No. 12 Company, Labour Corps and died, aged twenty-one, on 26 February, 1918.

Private W.H. Fidler, 52nd Canadian Infantry, died 6 September, 1918.

Sapper Thomas Foley, Royal Engineers, died 24 July, 1917.

Private Henry John Forsyth, 1st (City of London) Battalion, London Regiment, lived in Clerkenwell, London. He died on 30 October, 1916 from wounds received in France.

Private George Frankilin, 1st Battalion, Royal Welsh Fusiliers, won the Military Medal in France and died, aged thirty-eight, of wounds received on 29 November, 1917. He was married to Alice Franklin of 22 Frederick Street, Newport.

Cadet Frederick Donald Frost, Cadet Distributing Depot, Royal Air Force, was born in Newport and is recorded as being married to Kathleen Maud Frost of 26 Rapson Road, Durban, Natal, South Africa. He died from pneumonia, aged twenty-nine, on 18 October, 1918.

Signalman John Evelyn Garrett, Royal Naval Volunteer Reserve, served on the decoy ship HMS *Penshurst (Q7)* and died, aged twenty-one, on 14 January, 1917. He was the son of John E. Garrett of 12 Carlisle Street, Newport.

Private Arthur Henry Gibbon, 4th Battalion, Royal Welsh Fusiliers, was the son of T. and W. Hannah Gibbon of 31 Power Street, Newport. He transferred to 548th Agricultural Company, Labour Corps and died, aged nineteen, of phthisis on 23 February, 1919. Arthur Gibbon is buried in a private family grave.

Rifleman G. Gough, 5th Battalion, King's (Liverpool Regiment), was the son of Albert and Annie Gough of 42 Lewis Street, Newport. He transferred to 564th Agricultural Company, Labour Corps and died, aged twenty, on 20 December, 1918.

Private James Henry Goulding, 'G' Training Company, Machine Gun Corps (Infantry), was the son of James and Bessy Goulding of 14 Victoria Square, Newport. He was married to Catherine Goulding of 5 Agincourt Street, Newport and died, aged twenty-eight, of influenza on 21 November, 1918.

Second-Lieutenant George Harry Gratton, Royal Flying Corps, died 4th March, 1918.

Pioneer James Henry Green, Royal Engineers, died 13th April, 1919.

Sapper John Griffiths, 262nd Railway Troops Company, Royal Engineers, was married to Margaret Griffiths of 25 Dean Street, Newport. He died, aged thirty-four, on 12 May, 1917.

Private Walter H. Groom, Royal Defence Corps, was born in Dunstable, Bedfordshire. He lived in Watford, enlisted into the army in Finsbury, London and died on 16 June, 1917.

Sapper Charles William Harris, Royal Engineers, was born at Whatstandwell, Derbyshire. He lived at Rowsley, enlisted into the army in Derby (originally North Staffordshire Regiment) and died 14 July, 1918.

Able Seaman Henry Hayes, HMS *Lowestoft*, Royal Naval Volunteer Reserve, died on 24 February, 1917. He was aged forty.

Private William Hector, Royal Defence Corps, was born in Taunton, Somerset, the son of John and Harriet Hector, and married to Ann Hector of 11 West Street, Baneswell, Newport. He died, aged fifty-two, on 9 July, 1917. Private Hector had previously served with the Monmouthshire Regiment.

Second Engineer Alfred Frederick Heusser was a member of the Merchant Marine Reserve and served on the tug *Woonda*. He was married to Martha A. Heusser of 14 Prince George Road, Stoke Newington, London and died, aged fifty-three, on 9 November, 1918.

Private John Hewlett, 17th Lancers, was born in Oxford and the adopted son of Margaret H. Elton of 11 Winnifred Terrace, Cwmtillery. He enlisted into the army at Newport and died, aged thirty-one, on 20 March, 1915.

Able Seaman Ernest James Hobbs, Royal Naval Volunteer Reserve, was the son of John Charles and Emily Hobbs of 39 Alma Street, Newport. He died, aged twenty-two, on 29 July, 1918.

Private Albert Hood, 1st Battalion, South Wales Borderers, died from wounds received in France on 7 January, 1915. He was twenty-four and the son of Joseph William and Margaret Hood of 56 Wolseley Street, Newport. Private Hood has a CWGC headstone placed within a family plot. His brothers, Charles and Ernest, were both killed in the First World War, and they are commemorated on the kerbstone, along with their parents.

Private Thomas Hudman, Worcestershire Regiment, was from Newport and married to Daisy Ellen Hudman. He died, aged thirty-four, on 27 February, 1919.

Sergeant William George Jackson, 1st Battalion, Monmouthshire Regiment, was married to Sarah Jane Jackson of 428 Corporation Road, Newport. He died, aged twenty-eight, on 27 June, 1918.

Master Gunner 3rd Class E. Jenkins, No. 20 Fire Command, Royal Garrison Artillery, died 7 July, 1919.

Sergeant Stanley Holland Johns, 10th Battalion, Welsh Regiment, is recorded by the CWGC as having been a journalist from Cardiff. He died, aged forty-one, on 3 February, 1916.

Lance-Corporal Thomas Johns, 1st Battalion, Monmouthshire Regiment, was born in Cwmbran the son of John and Emma Johns. He died, aged thirty-seven, on 19 June, 1917.

Private D.C. Jones, Royal Welsh Fusiliers, was married to Ethel Jones of 3 Waters Lane, Newport. He died from appendicitis, aged twenty-seven, on 2 February, 1920.

Private Frank Douglas Jones, 15th Battalion, Loyal North Lancashire Regiment, resided at 18 Courtybella Terrace, Newport. He died, aged twenty, on 19 July, 1919.

Able Seaman Harold David Jones, HMS *President III*, Royal Naval Volunteer Reserve, died 19 October, 1916.

Private Harold Theophilus Jones, 1st Battalion, Monmouthshire Regiment, died from wounds received in France on 7 July, 1916. He was twenty-eight and the son of William Jones of 9 Rutland Place, Newport.

Private Henry John Jones, Monmouthshire Regiment, was accidently drowned on 1 January, 1916. He was fifty-six and married to Kate Jones of Albion Street, Newport.

Nurse Lilian Kate Jones, Volunteer Aid Detachment, died 6 June, 1916.

Telegraphist T.D. Jones, Royal Naval Volunteer Reserve, died, aged twenty-six, on 27 August, 1918. His parents lived at 34 Capel Crescent, Newport.

Private Richard Kelly, 1st Battalion, South Wales Borderers, was sent home from France suffering from frost-bite. He died, aged forty-eight, on 17 January, 1915 and was the son of Mrs Margaret Kelly of 40 Baldwin Street, Newport.

Private Alfred Llewellin Kendall, 456th Protection Company, Royal Defence Corps, was married to Alice Sarah Kendall. He died, aged fifty-three, on 25 March, 1919.

Private W.J. Lacey, 2/8th Battalion, Worcestershire Regiment, died on 12 October, 1916 from wounds received in France.

Private Charles Langtry, Royal Defence Corps (previously Gloucestershire Regiment), was born in Yeovil, Somerset and lived in Fishponds, Bristol. He was the son of Mrs Harriet Langtry and died, aged forty-eight, on 15 May, 1918.

Bombardier F.J. Limbrick, 5th Brigade, Royal Field Artillery, was the son of George and Harriet Limbrick of 15 Pugsley Street, Newport. He died, aged twenty-four, from wounds received in France on 5 February, 1919.

Sergeant C. Linton, South Wales Borderers, was the son of Charles and Susan Linton and married to F.K.M. Linton of 61 Hewerton Street, Newport. He served on the Western Front, where he was Mentioned In Despatches, and died, aged twenty-nine, on 9 November, 1920.

Driver T. Llewellyn, Royal Field Artillery, served with the 2nd Division Ammunition Column and died 21 March, 1918.

Able Seaman Thomas Lloyd, 4th Reserve Battalion, Royal Naval Volunteer Reserve, was the son of Thomas and Sarah Ann Lloyd of 96 Alexandra Terrace, Newport. He died of pneumonia, aged twenty, on 28 February, 1917.

Pioneer P. Lynch, Royal Engineers, was the son of Peter and Mary Lynch and married to Rose Lynch of 59 Lower Dominick Street, Dublin. He was born at Carnaross, Kells, County Meath and died, aged forty-eight, on 6 May, 1918. Private Lynch is buried in the same grave as Bandsman J. Sciberras (see below).

Private W.W. McAvera, 3rd Battalion, Devonshire Regiment, died 6 July, 1919.

Driver T. McCarthy, Royal Field Artillery, lived at 167 Shaftesbury Street, Newport. He died, aged twenty-five, on 11 January, 1921.

Lance-Sergeant John MacDonald, Royal Defence Corps, died, aged fifty-one, on 10 January, 1919.

Sailor G. Macleod, Mercantile Marine, died, aged thirty-one, on 11 January, 1919 from injuries received while serving on SS *Grorud*. He was the son of Lachlan and Jemima Macleod and married to Flora Macleod of Castlebay, Isle of Barra, Outer Hebrides.

Private James McMahon, 1st Battalion, Royal Irish Regiment, was from Clonmel, County Tipperary, Ireland. He died from wounds received in France on 29 April, 1915.

Sapper J. McPhillips, 3rd Signal Construction Company, Royal Engineers, died, aged twenty-three, on 28 February, 1919.

Rifleman Gerald Percy Sims Meares, 'B' Company, 3/1st Battalion, Monmouthshire Regiment, resided at 26 Brynghyn Road, Newport. He died of pneumonia, aged twenty-two, on 16 March, 1916.

Gunner James Meredith, Royal Garrison Artillery, was born at Llanfoist the son of Henry and Margaret Meredith. He died, aged thirty-five, on 2 September, 1917.

Private Samuel Minford Millar, 110th Field Ambulance, Royal Army Medical Corps, was from Ballymacarret, Co. Down. He died on 4 April, 1916.

Air Mechanic 3rd Class F.A. Mogford, Recruits Depot (Blandford), Royal Flying Corps, was the son of Benjamin and Matilda Mogford of 25 East Usk Road, Newport. He died, aged thirty-six, on 13 March, 1918.

Private Patrick Molyneux, Welsh Regiment, was born in Duagh, County Kerry, Ireland the son of Thomas and Johanna Molyneux. He had served in the Boer War and died, aged forty-one, on 21 April, 1917.

Pioneer Enoch Morgan, 81st Labour Battalion, Royal Engineers, was from Tipton, Staffordshire. He enlisted into the army in London and died on 26 April, 1916. Enoch Morgan is buried in a family grave.

Private Eric Fennell Trevor Morgan, 9th Battalion, Manchester Regiment, was wounded at Ypres and died, aged nineteen, on 23 August, 1917. He was the son of the Revd Henry Morgan of Holy Trinity Rectory, Cardiff Road, Newport.

Sergeant Archibald Cyril Moore, No. 2 Stores Distributing Park (Newcastle), Royal Air Force, died, aged twenty-seven, on 28 November, 1918.

Sergeant Harry Edward Morrish, 1/4th Welsh Brigade Ammunition Column, Royal Field Artillery, was from Eton Road, Newport. He died, aged thirty-six, on 3 January, 1917.

Private T. Mortimer, 1st Battalion, Royal Welsh Fusiliers, died, aged twenty, at Devonport Military Hospital on 4 December, 1915. He is buried with his parents, Thomas and Ann Mortimer, in a family plot.

Private Edward Naylon, Royal Defence Corps. Previously served with the Monmouthshire Regiment and died, aged fifty-two, on 24 July, 1917. He resided at 58 Gordon Street, Maindee.

Rifleman Albert Henry Neate, 1st Battalion, Monmouthshire Regiment, died 5 September, 1915. He was born in Bristol and married to Emily Neate of Barn House, Carrow Hill near Penhow.

Private M. O'Brien, 1/1st Welsh Horse Yeomanry, died 5 March, 1921. He had transferred from the Yeomanry to 802nd Area Employment Company, Labour Corps.

Private D. O'Leary, South Wales Borderers, died 30 December, 1917.

Company Sergeant Major G. Osborne, Welsh Regiment, was attached to the Regimental Depot in Cardiff. He was married to Mrs. J. Osborne of 4 Alfred Street, St. Philips, Bristol and died, aged forty-six, on 13 February, 1920.

Private Charles Herbert Owen, 8th Battalion, York and Lancaster Regiment, was wounded at Ypres. He died, aged thirty-five, on 14 May, 1918.

Private A. Pearson, No. 20 Company (Tidworth), Royal Army Medical Corps, was married to Mary Ann Pearson of 7 Ross Street, Newport. He died, aged thirty-nine, on 13 March, 1919.

Private W. Perry, South Wales Borderers, was the son of William and Mary Perry and married to Elizabeth Kate Perry of 52 Hewertson Street, Newport. He died, aged thirty-five, on 30 December, 1920.

Worker V. Phillips, Queen Mary's Army Auxiliary Corps, was the daughter of Mrs C.M. Phillips of 32 Barrack Hill, Newport. She died, aged twenty, on 8 March, 1919.

Private Joseph Philpin, 2nd Battalion, Monmouthshire Regiment, was the son of Margaret Philpin. He was from Newport and died, aged twenty, on 28 March, 1915.

Private Neville Arthur Pilgrim, 13th Field Bakery, Army Service Corps, was born in Southsea, Hampshire. He lived in Cambridge, enlisted into the army at Coventry, and died 9 June, 1918.

Private J. Power, Irish Guards, died 7 August, 1916. He is buried in a grave with two other soldiers (see D. Bowen and M.J. Collins).

Rifleman Frederick Reginald Powles, 1st Battalion, Monmouthshire Regiment, was the son of Frederick William and Rosina Powles. He died, aged twenty-seven, at the 3rd Western General Military Hospital in Newport on 13 April, 1918. His

CWGC headstone is placed within a family plot.

Lance-Corporal William Prosser, 'C' Company, 2/8th Battalion, Lancashire Fusiliers, was thirty-one when he died from wounds received on 22 July, 1917. He was married to Gertrude Prosser of 122 Shaftesbury Street, Newport.

Private Thomas William Pullin, 6th Battalion, Welsh Regiment, records the CWGC, served in China and was formerly with the Royal Engineers. He died, aged forty-four, on 22 October, 1917.

Private Albert Pumford, 6th Battalion, Yorkshire Regiment, was born in Wolverhampton and lived in Newport. He died from wounds received in France on 23 June, 1916.

Captain Arthur Rich, Special List, worked on recruiting. He died on 29 February, 1916.

Stoker Frank Richards, HMS *Indefatigible*, Royal Naval Reserve, died 9 August, 1915.

Private Albert Edward Richings, 5th Battalion, South Wales Borderers, was the son of William Randle Richings and married to Florence Gwendoline Richings of Pier Villa, Black Rock, Portskewett. He died, aged twenty-six, on 6 November, 1920 from wounds received in France.

Private Gilbert Ridout, 2nd Battalion, Grenadier Guards, was born in Shepton Mallet, Somerset. He enlisted into the army in Cardiff and died from wounds received in France on 9 December, 1916.

Sapper William Rogers, Royal Engineers, was married to Margaret Ann Rogers of 56 Price Street, Newport. He died, aged thirty-one, on 27 July, 1916.

Trimmer John McStewart Ross, HMS *Victory*, Royal Naval Reserve, was the son of Richard and Emily Ross of 4 Albion Street, Newport and married to Ruth Ellen Ross. He died at Gosport Hospital, aged thirty, on 13 January, 1919. John Ross is buried in a family grave.

Rifleman C. Rowan, 1st Battalion Monmouthshire Regiment, died on 7 March, 1919.

Sergeant Hector Hoskin Rule, 29th Battalion (British Columbia Regiment), Canadian Expeditionary Force, died from wounds received in France on 10 October, 1918. He was thirty years old, the son of Joseph and Sarah Rule, and married to Mabel Rule of 728 King's Road, Victoria, British Columbia.

Private A. Rumble, 16th Battalion, South Lancashire Regiment, was the son of Mrs H. Rumble of 10 High Street, Newport. He died, aged twenty-four, on 26 November, 1918.

Private Charles James Rysdale, 1st Battalion, Monmouthshire Regiment, died, aged thirty-five, on 12 January, 1917.

Private George Edward Salter, 9th Battalion, South Wales Borderers, was married to L.J. Salter of 12 Temple Street, Newport. He died, aged thirty-four, on 25 July, 1918.

Lance-Sergeant Edward Robertson Macfarlane Saunders, 1st Battalion, Rifle Brigade, was born in Dundee, Perthshire and won the Military Medal in France on 2 April, 1918. Wounded, he was sent to hospital in Newport and subsequently died on 27 September. He was forty-three, the son of John Saunders and married to Elizabeth Saunders of 27 Tranton Road, Bermondsey, London.

Able Seaman L. Scherland, SS *Foy*, Mercantile Marine, died on 11 December, 1919.

Bandsman Joseph Sciberras, HMS *Vivid*, Royal Navy, was from Malta and a regular sailor. He held the Long Service and Good Conduct Medal and died, aged forty-three, from phthisis on 27 August, 1918. His wife, Rosaria, lived at 48 Str. Vescovo, Valletta, Malta and his parents were John and Margarita Sciberras. Joseph Sciberras is buried with Pioneer P. Lynch (see above), the grave being marked by a single double-size CWGC headstone.

Private R. Shaddock, 'D' Company, 12th Battalion, South Wales Borderers, was the son of William and Sarah Ann Shaddock of Newport. He died, aged twenty, on 30 March, 1919.

Private Z. Sims, 1st Battalion, South Wales Borderers, was the son of Robert James and Fanny Dorcas Sims of 16 Wingate Street, Newport. He died, aged twenty-six, on 7 February, 1919.

Private John Soden, 3rd Battalion, Welsh Regiment, was born in Northampton. He lived in Cardiff, enlisted into the army at Newport and died on 18 July, 1918.

Gunner Joseph William Stanton, Royal Garrison Artillery, was from Newport. He died 25 February, 1918.

Private Alfred Suller, 53rd (Young Soldiers) Battalion, South Wales Borderers, was the son of Margaret Suller of 3 Broad Street, Newport. He died, aged eighteen, on 10 October, 1918.

Sapper John Sullivan, No.1 Siege Company, Royal Monmouthshire Royal Engineers Militia, lived in Newport and died on 19 May, 1916.

Ordinary-Seaman William Edward Sullivan, Royal Naval Volunteer Reserve, served at HMS *Pembroke*. He was the son of Mary Elizabeth Sullivan of 1 Aston Crescent, Newport and died, aged eighteen, on 4 September, 1917.

Corporal G.F. Swallow, Royal Engineers, was forty when he died on 17 February, 1920. He was married to Gladys Violet Swallow of 15 Richmond Road, Newport.

Captain Herbert Tapson-Jones, 4th Welsh Brigade, Royal Field Artillery, died on 12 November, 1918 from wounds received. He was twenty-five and married to Gladys Tapson-Jones of 26 Chepstow Road, Newport.

Driver Reginald Edwin Taylor, 7th Reserve Battery, Royal Field Artillery, died, aged eighteen, on 5 April, 1916. He was the son of John William and Rose Taylor of 13 Charlesville, Pontnewynydd, Pontypool. Reginald Taylor has a CWGC headstone placed into a family plot. He is buried with his parents.

Private Abraham Thomas, 3/7th Battalion, Royal Welsh Fusiliers, died, aged thirty-four, from enteric on 15 September, 1916.

Private Arthur Charles Thomas, South Wales Borderers, was the son of Charles and Harriet Thomas of 93 Malpas Road, Newport. He died, aged twenty-six, on 11 August, 1919.

Air Mechanic 2nd Class Bertie D. Thomas, Royal Air Force, was married to Agnes Thomas of 23 Colne Street, Newport. He died, aged thirty-four, on 6 July, 1920.

Private Charles William Thomas, 2nd Battalion, South Wales Borderers, was the son of Danie and Charlotte Thomas of 37 Robert Street, Newport. He died, aged twenty-five, on 8 March, 1917.

Private H. Thomas, 14th Battalion, Hampshire Regiment, died on 21 November, 1918 from wounds received on the Western Front. He had previously served with the Essex Regiment.

Petty Officer 1st Class John Thomas, HMS *Defiance*, Royal Navy, died 19 January, 1916. He was forty-seven.

Deck Hand Lewis Edward Thomas, HMS *Idaho*, Royal Naval Reserve, has a CWGC headstone within a family plot. He died, aged forty-seven, on 13 May, 1917 and is buried with his wife, Alice and son Stephen. The family lived at 48 Wolseley Street, Newport.

Rifleman William Thomas, 1st Battalion, Monmouthshire Regiment, is buried in a private family grave. He died on 23 February, 1917.

Private William Toms, 21st Protection Company, Royal Defence Corps, was born at Sopworth, Wiltshire. He lived in Cwmbran, where he joined the Monmouthshire Regiment, and died on 16 May, 1916.

Private J. Toshkoff, 72nd Battalion (British Columbia Regiment), Canadian Expeditionary Force, died 28 November, 1917.

Pioneer E.R. Townsend, Royal Engineers, served with the Inland Waterways and Docks section of the RE and died on 3 August, 1918.

Rifleman G. Wallace, 1st Battalion, Monmouthshire Regiment, died on 13 February, 1919.

Private W.H. Wallington, "C" Company, 4th Battalion, Royal Welsh Fusiliers, lived at 7 Emlyn Street, Newport. He died, aged eighteen, on 13 February, 1919.

Rifleman Bernard Charles Walsh, 3/1st Battalion, Monmouthshire Regiment, was the son of James Patrick and Helena Walsh of 'Rockleigh', Marson Road, Clevedon, Somerset. He died, aged thirty, on 1 February, 1920.

Lance-Corporal O.T. Watkins, 124th Field Company, Royal Engineers, died 17th February, 1919.

Private John Watts, 3rd Battalion, South Wales Borderers, was born in Cork, Ireland and married to Mary Ann Watts of 19 Mellon Street, Newport. He died, aged thirty-four, on 27 July, 1916.

Petty Officer Stoker Robert William Weetch, Royal Navy, served on HMS *Oriole*. He was the son of James Oliver and Elizabeth Weetch and died, aged twenty-eight, on 5 November, 1918.

Seaman Robert West, HMS *Albermarle*, Royal Naval Reserve, was nineteen when he died on 31 March, 1916. He was the son of Robert and Elizabeth West of 6 Beacon Terrace, Ferryden, Montrose.

Sapper John Joseph Westacott, No. 2 Home Service Operating Company, Royal Engineers, lived in Newport. He enlisted into the army at Sandwich, Kent and died 17 February, 1917. John Westacott's CWGC headstone is placed within a family plot.

Lance-Corporal Charles Whiting, Royal Defence Corps, died, aged fifty-three, on 29 May, 1919. He was married to Helena Whiting of 3 Fair Oak Terrace, Chepstow Road, Newport.

Company Sergeant Major E. Williams, 19th (Labour) Battalion, Cheshire Regiment, died 28 August, 1916.

Driver John Thomas Williams, 'D' Battery, 306th Brigade, Royal Field Artillery, died 14 May, 1918.

Deck Hand Lewis Williams, HMS *Pembroke*, Royal Naval Reserve, died, aged fifty-three, on 10 September, 1917.

Leading Deck Hand William John Williams, HMS *Vivid*, Royal Naval Reserve, was the son of William Williams and married to Annie Maria Williams of Newport. He died, aged forty-two, on 2 September, 1918.

Private Reginald John Wiltshire, 24th Battalion, Welsh Regiment, was the son of Mr and Mrs J. Wiltshire of 16 Graham Street, Newport. He was twenty-five when he died from wounds received in France on 23 October, 1918.

Private John Henry Woodbury, 4th Battalion, Royal Welsh Fusiliers, was the son of Charles Henry Woodbury of 26 East Usk Road, Newport. He died, aged eighteen, on 8 December, 1918. John Woodbury is buried in a private family grave.

Sergeant Richard Henry Young, 14th Area Command, Military Foot Police, had previously served with the Welsh Horse Yeomanry (No. 110), enlisting in August, 1914 and going with the regiment to Gallipoli. He was the son of George and Emma Young, married to Ethel Blodwin Young of 14 Station Street, Newport and died, aged twenty-seven, on 8 November, 1918.

Also buried in St Woolos Cemetery, and recorded in the CWGC Register for Monmouthshire, are nine men listed under the heading of 'Foreign National 1914-1918.' The headstone of Soldier Antonio Da Silva Amorim of the Portuguese Army, which is similar in design to the usual CWGC Portland stone marker, bears the inscription - *Portugal 1917-1918 - Transporte Gunene - Falecido Em 14.5.1921* - while that for Ernest Seraphin Alfred Marie Partfoot, a soldier of the Belgian Army, includes place and date of birth among other detail - *4e Régiment De Ligne - Né A Bruges Le 6 Septembre 1892 - Mort Pour La Blgique Le 17 April 1915* - below a circle made up of the Belgian colours - viz: black, yellow and red. A cross is superimposed into the central yellow section.

The remaining seven men are listed as 'French Navy,' and have short crosses made from Portland stone, each recording rank, name of ship, date of death and the inscription - *Mort Pour La France*. Matelot Jean Baptiste Barbinziza, of the *Imerina*, who died on 7 July, 1915 and Canonnier Emile Gerbier of the *Radium*, died 26 September, 1918, are buried in the same grave and share a single marker. Matelot Marcel Jean Marie Boursicaut, *Garonne*, 24 July, 1918; Matelot Louis Joseph Marie Droal, *Irma*, 28 February, 1915; Matelot Jean Marie Valentin Lintanf, *Ouessant*, 5 November, 1917; Matelot Francois Louis Marie, *Radium*, 10 September, 1915, and Henrie Joseph Eugene Lippaye whose grave cannot be found.

Shaftesbury Methodist Church
Four members of the church are commemorated by a brass plaque on the wall to the right of the pulpit -

To The Glory Of God And In Memory Of (the names follow) *Who Gave Their Lives In The Great War 1914-1919. 'Greater Love Hath No Man Than This, That A Man Lay Down His Life For His Friends'.*

The four men recorded are: Private Arthur Charles Baggs of the 2nd Monmouthshire Regiment, killed on 12 April, 1918 during the Battle of the Lys; Lance-Corporal Leslie Wilfred Foot, who joined the 19th Royal Fusiliers when war was declared and was mortally wounded with the 12th Battalion during the Third Battle of Ypres, and the opening assault on Battle Wood; Private Arthur Vaughan, 11th South Wales Borderers, killed 31 July, 1917 during the capture of Iron Cross Ridge at Pilckem, and Edgar William Ewart Taylor of the 11th Manchester Regiment.

Memorial on the site of the old 1st Monmouthshire Regiment Drill Hall, Stow Hill, Newport.

Stow Hill Drill Hall

The site of the former 1st Battalion, Monmouthshire Regiment Headquarters in Stow Hill, Newport is marked by two marble plaques set in a brick wall and flanked by regimental badges. They are inscribed -

(Left) - *Here Stood Stow Hill Drill Hall From Which Sallied Newport's Own Territorial Soldiers, The First (Rifle) Battalion The Monmouthshire Regiment To Fight For Britain At The Outbreak Of Two World Wars.* (Right) - *They Wrote The Saddest Yet Most Glorious Chapter In Newport's History On May The 8th, 1915, When In An Heroic Stand Against Great Odds Before Ypres, The Monmouthshires Helped To Bar The Germans From The Vital Channel Ports. Of Their Strength Of Nearly 500, Only 129 Officers and Men Survived.*

The action referred to was that at Frezenberg Ridge. At the beginning of the First World War, the 1st Monmouthshire Regiment was located - Headquarters, 'A', 'B', 'C' and 'D' Companies at Newport, these having drill stations at Caerleon and Rogerstone; 'E' Company at Chepstow, with detachments at Sudbrook and Itton; 'F' Company at Aberbargoed; 'G' Company at Rhymney, with a drill station at New Tredegar; 'H' Company at Blackwood with a detachment at Ynysddu. The Battalion war memorial is in St Woolos Cathedral.

Stow Park Presbyterian Church

There are three names recorded on a bronze plaque situated on the wall to the left of the pulpit -

To The Glory Of God & In Grateful Memory Of Robt. Mc.Gegor Duncanson H.M.T. Huntstrick - Stuart Ray Duncanson 1st Mon. Regt. - Arthur Reginald Griffiths 1st Batt. Middlesex Regt. - Who Gave Their Lives In The Great War 1914-1918.

The inscription and names are surmounted by the words - *Roll Of Honour* - and a laurel wreath tied with ribbons.

Memorial commemorating father and son, Robert and Stuart Duncanson. Stow Park Presbyterian Church, Newport.

Captain Robert Duncanson lost his life on 8 June, 1917, when his ship, the transport *Huntstrick*, was torpedoed of Cape Spartel. Fourteen members of the crew were also lost. Just over two months later, his son, Second-Lieutenant Stuart Ray Duncanson (1st Battalion, Monmouthshire Regiment, attached to 11th Cheshires) would be killed in Belgium. His body was buried in the Tyne Cot Military Cemetery, Passchendaele. Arthur Griffiths was also killed on the Western Front. He had joined the Royal Fusiliers, 26th (Bankers) Battalion, at the beginning of the war, but later transferred to another London based unit, the 1/7th Middlesex Regiment. It was on 16 May, 1917 that the Battalion took over trenches in the Guémappe sector, having recently been involved in the fierce battles of Arras. Weak from these engagements, the Battalion strength was just seven officers and three hundred and sixty-six other ranks. The Middlesex were relieved on 20 May and sent back for rest in Arras. It was on this day that Private Griffiths was killed.

Summerhill Baptist Church

On the north wall of the church in Albert Avenue, Maindee, a brass plaque mounted on black polished stone records fourteen names in the order that each man was killed -

To The Glory Of God And In Honoured Memory Of The Following Members Of This Church And School Who Fell In The Great War 1914-1918

Richard George Holbrook, 8 May 1915; William Howard Francis, 17 July 1916; Clifford Roy Stuart, 28 November 1916; Norman Stuart, 22 January 1917; Edward Bridges, 23 February 1917; Clifford Travell Evans, 27 March 1917; John Phelps Williams, 24 April 1917; George Paget, 2 August 1917; Norman Milne, 22 October 1917; Melville Jenkins, 2 April 1918; Edward Gordon Ellis, 5 April 1918; William Frederick Hall, 27 May 1918; Frank Thomas, 8 October 1918; Robert Nicholas, 11 October 1918 - '*These All Died In Faith*'. The inscription and names are inscribed within a border of oak leaves and acorns.

The same fourteen names are recorded on the other side of the church, this time within an oval bronze wreath of laurels, and accompanied by a photograph of each man. A smaller wreath in the centre of

Summerhill Baptist Church memorial, Newport.

Tabernacle Congregational Church, Newport memorial. Now at Victoria Road United Reform Church.

the memorial encircles the inscription -

Summerhill Baptist Sunday School - In Grateful Memory Of Our Boys Who Made The Supreme Sacrifice In The Great War 1914-18. Newport Mon.

Originally located in the old Sunday School building, the memorial was unveiled by the Mayor of Newport, Mr Edward Davies, JP, on 8 May, 1923.

Victoria Road United Reform Church

On the wall to the right of the pulpit, a brass tablet set into a wood surround has the following words inscribed within a laurel wreath -

To The Glory Of God And In Proud And Grateful Recognition Of The Sons Of This Church Who Served In The Great War And In Loving Memory Of The Following Who Made The Supreme Sacrifice.

Eleven names follow: Evan Davies of the 15th Royal Welsh Fusiliers who was killed 27 July, 1917; H.H. Evans, a gunner with 'D' Battery, 123 Brigade, Royal Field Artillery, killed 22 May, 1918; John Evelyn Garrett of the Royal Naval Volunteer Reserve who died 14 January, 1917 and served on the decoy ship HMS *Q7 (Penshurst)*; Bert Gill and Maynard James, both of the 1st Monmouthshire and killed 8 May, 1915 and 8 October, 1918 respectively; A Royal Welsh Fusilier - Stanley Thomas, killed 26 October, 1918; Edgar Jones of the Oxfordshire and Buckinghamshire Light Infantry, who lost his life in August, 1918; Neville Jones, killed 4 April, 1917 with the King's (Liverpool Regiment); Willie Ross, who served with the 2nd Royal Munster Fusiliers and died in March, 1915, and two members of the 1st South Wales Borderers - Percy Llanfear, who was killed on 9 May, 1915, and Roy Taylor who fell 23 October, 1918.

Quotations appear ether side of the names - '*True Love By Life - True Love By Death Is Tried*' - on the left side - '*Live Thou For England, We For England Died*' to the right. Various alterations and additions to the church were made as a result of the War Memorial Fund. The memorial ends with the inscription -

This Tablet Was Erected, Together With The Extension To The Institute, By The Members Of This Church And Congregation, And The Interior Oak Work Of This Building Given By Mrs. C.H. Bailey As A Memorial.

Of the above, William Maynard ('Chip') James is recorded in the *Book Of Remembrance And War Record Of Mill Hill School*. This officer was the son of Alfred and Lilian James of 'The Fields', Newport, and had served in the cadet corps at Mill Hill as a sergeant. He was commissioned into the 1st Monmouthshire Regiment on 2 October, 1914 and later became its Adjutant. William James was severely wounded during the fighting at Ypres in 1915, and killed while leading an attack at Sequehart near St Quentin on 8 October, 1918. An officer writing to Mr and Mrs James noted that their son was shot through the head, '....Chip was quite the best officer, and best loved by all in the battalion.' Captain James was twenty-two and is buried in Sequehart Military Cemetery No.1.

The war memorial belonging to the old Emmanuel Church, previously in London Street, Maindee, is now located in Victoria Road. Mounted on marble, the bronze tablet has a decorative edging. In the centre, and below a cross, an inscription in raised letters reads - *In Memoriam - Great War 1914-18 - Members Of Emmanuel Church Sunday School & Institute Who Paid The Supreme Sacrifice* - Walter Brundrett, George Brundrett, William Ball, Herbert Hackett, Walter James, Arthur More, William Oxenbury, Edgar Pickett, Victor Pocock, Clifford Pook, Roderick Rowland, Herbert Sherwood, Albert Wilks, Clenelc Wright. The memorial ends with the words - *Their Sacrifice Our Inheritance Their Remembrance Our Inspiration.*

Another Newport church to be closed in recent years was the Tabernacle

Congregational Church in Commercial Street. Unveiled on 16 October, 1922, the memorial was originally located in the entrance lobby and is now found in the vestibule at Victoria Road. Within a large carved oak surround, a bronze tablet headed - *In Memoriam* - records twenty names:

Private Reg. Allen, Private Wilfred Ball, Private James Davey, Private Tom Gibbs, Gunner A.H. Hewinson, Rifleman W.E. Locke, Sergeant H. Lennox, Officer (Mercantile Marine) B. Tom March, Driver B. Marshall, Lance-Corporal F.C. Meadows, Lance-Corporal Jack Nicholas, Captain A.D. Oliver, Private Arthur Phillips, Lance-Corporal Jack Reed, Stoker Frank Richards, Squadron Quarter Master Sergeant Geo. Hurn, Private F. Sheryn, Rifleman Stanley Watkins, Private C.J. Watkins and Private Stanley H. Webber.

A shield bearing a red dragon on a green ground appears with the dates - *1914-1918* - above the tablet. Below, another records the death of Major A.H. Rocyn Jones, who was killed in Italy during the Second World War, and below this a third carries the inscription -

To The Glory Of God And In Grateful Remembrance Of Our Brothers Who Fell In The Great War.

A photograph of the memorial taken in 1925 shows just nineteen names. That of SQMS George Hurn having been added at a later date. The same illustration shows that the Crest and Shield from the Arms of Newport once occupied the position now held by Major A.H. Rocyn Jones' plaque.

Newport YMCA

A marble tablet to commemorate those members of the Newport YMCA who lost their lives in the Great War was put up in July, 1919 and unveiled in the following October by HH Princess Helena Victoria, CBE. The YMCA symbol surmounts the inscription -

In Sacred Memory Of The Newport Y.M.C.A. Members, Who Were Killed In Action During The Great War, 1914-1918. 'The Path Of Duty Is The Way To Glory'.

Eight names are recorded, along with ranks and regiments: Private Harold J. Burrough, London Regiment; Lance-Corporal Percy Baynham, Lancashire Fusiliers; Private Harold Jones, 1st Monmouthshire Regiment; Second-Lieutenant W.J. Kelsey, Royal Flying Corps; Gunner Thomas Woore, Royal Field Artillery; Corporal Idris Charles Williams, Cheshire Regiment; Bombardier G. Peter Wright, Royal Field Artillery. The last name, Lance-Corporal O. Trevor Watkins, Royal Engineers, is preceded by the words - 'Died As A Result Of Service'. Private Harold John Burrough served in the 16th London Regiment (Queen's Westminster Rifles) and was killed on the first day of the Battle of the Somme - 1 July, 1916.

Placed in the central lounge of the Association's old Commercial Street building, the memorial remained in the same spot, records *The History and Diary of the Newport Y.M.C.A. 1869-1990*, until the property was sold in 1990. It was then taken down and placed into store. Newport YMCA now occupy new premises in Mendalgief Road and the memorial is still (1999) held in store.

OVERMONNOW

St Thomas The Martyr Parish Church

To the right of the church entrance in St Thomas Square, Overmonnow, and in a Garden of Rest, there is a Calvary Cross erected to the memory of David Dudley, son of the Revd Francis Dudley, Vicar at St Thomas' 1891-1915 -

Jesu Mercy, On The Dearly Loved And Loving Spirit Of David Dudley, Captain 91st Punjabis, Attached In France To The 6th Yats (should read Jats). *He Laid Down His Life For His Country At The Battle Of Aubers Ridge, May 9th 1915, Aged 34. Jesu Mercy, On Those Who Fell With Him That Day, His Friends, And Those Of This Parish Who Also Gave Their Lives That We Might Live. Enfolded In The Eternal Love Of God. This Calvary Was Erected March 14th 1918, The 37th Anniversary Of His Birthday.*

Within the church, and to the right of the Norman arch, the men of the area are commemorated on a bronze plaque -

To The Glory Of God And In Proud And Grateful Memory Of All Those Who Gave Their Lives For Us In The Great War 1914-1919. Especially The Following From This Parish -

John Bean, William Bennett, William Betteridge, Fred Bevington, Ernest Bricknell, Gilbert Brooks, Albert Butcher, William Cook, Arthur Crane, David Dudley, Henry Holman, Edgar Hunt, William Jones, Arthur Kear, Arthur Lewis, Sidney Moore, William Phipps, William Powell, Hugh Reilly, William Roberts, George Rowberry, George Woodfield - '*Grant Them O Lord Fullness Of Life And In Thy Presence Peace For Evermore*'. George Roberry was killed 20 September, 1914 when his ship, HMS *Pegasus*, was sunk in Zanzibar Harbour by the German cruiser *Königsberg*.

PANTEG

Panteg Cemetery

The war memorial for Panteg and district was erected within the cemetery gates and unveiled on Sunday 27 November, 1921 by Regimental Quartermaster Sergeant Major T.H. Humphreys. Two of this old soldier's sons had been killed and their names recorded on the memorial. The work was undertaken by Messrs Thomas Jones & Son of Pontypool. The monument is made from Aberdeen grey granite and constructed from a design put forward by Panteg Urban District Council Surveyor, Mr H. Rosser. It comprises a pedestal upon a three-tier plinth surmounted by a cross. The inscription on the front of the pedestal reads -

In Ever Grateful Memory Of The Men From The Urban District Of Panteg Who Made The Supreme Sacrifice In The Great War 1914-1918 That Tyranny Might Perish And Liberty And Freedom Reign For Evermore.

The names of the dead are recorded in raised-lead letters on the three remaining sides:

Right: Lieutenant J.R. Williams heads the right-hand side section, followed by

Second-Lieutenants W.H. Price and T.L. Williams. Then come Company Sergeant Majors J.S. Granger and R.S. Morgan, followed by Battery Quartermaster Sergeant D. Jacobs and Staff-Sergeant J. Bond. The remaining names are arranged alphabetically under headings donating rank: *Sergeants:* L. Boyce, J.H. Herbert, T. Hall, F.J. Jones, H.W. Kilminster, G.E. Knire, S. Lewis, P. Ryan, J.S. Rowe, G. Treharne, A.L. Watts and M.J. Sterry who won the Distinguished Conduct Medal; *Bombardiers:* W. Humphreys, F.R. Jones, G.J. Thomas, W. Lane, C.E. Thomas; *Corporals:* S. Cox, T.H. Edwards, R.C. Farrington, P. Fletcher, W. Howells, G.T. Hawkins, R.K. Lewis, A.J. Walbeoff, E. Weare; *Lance-Corporals:* A. Ball, J.A. Evans, J. Griffin, H. Lewis, E.J. Rappel, I. Turner and S.B. Williams who was awarded the Military Medal; *Signallers:* C.J. Harding, A. Thomas. The last names on the right side are three members of the Royal Navy - Able Seaman J.G. Phillips, Ordinary Seaman R.H. Mason and Stoker W.J. Harris

Left: *Privates:* J.A. Harris, C.J.H. Hemming, C. Humphreys, O. Humphreys, A.V. Howels, D. Humphries, S. Hall, H.H. Hall, A.J. Jones, E. Jukes, W. Jones, J. James, J.H. Jones, A. Jones, H. Jones, A. James, D. Joshua, W. James, G.H. Kirtland, A.H. King, B. Lewis, S.R. Lawrence, T. Larcombe, C.A. Millard, J.F. Mills, J.T. Minninnick, H.A.P. Morgan, G. Millwater, F.H. Nelson, W. Nicholls, B.E.G. Price, T. Price, B.T. Powell, E.W. Parry, A.H. Parry, W. Peploe, R. Peploe, C.A. Payne, H.J. Pritchard, E.G. Pepler, A. Russell, A. Rees, E. Rowlands, J.H. Thomas, W. Tremlett, W. Tunley, G. Turner, A. Vaughan, A.C. Wilkey, E. Wilkey, J.R. Watts, F. Wilkey, A. Wilson, H.J. Williams, F.H. Wigmore, H.H. Whittington, R. Watt, H. Williams, C. Waterman, T.E. Watkins.

Back: *Gunners:* W.H. Clapham, T. Evans, W.T. Gardner, W.J. Griffiths, J.H. Harris, I.J. Hiley, R. Keenan, W. King, C.G. Kilby, R.V. Lavis, D.J. Moore, C.J. Phillips, C. Parfitt, N. Staniforth, H.H. Williams; *Sappers:* L.G. Comer, E. Traves, P. George; *Drivers:* A. Davies, W.H. Hughes, G. Lovegrove and T.C. Williams followed by Trooper E.J. Humphreys, Cyclist E. Larcombe, Rifleman H. Wheeler; *Privates:* T. Brown, A.V. Benfield, A.R. Brown, A.S. Britton, L. Brough, S. Congram, F. Collier, E. Cooper, W.A. Day, J.M. Dykes, J. Davies, J.T. Dudley, G.R. Davies, A. Edwards, W. Franks, J. Green, S.W. Gregory, W.T. Higgs, E.F. Joff, D. Jones and W. Jones.

A further six names have been added to the upper tier of the plinth at the rear of the memorial: Captain John Millard Lett of the 3rd Battalion, Worcestershire Regiment, who was killed near Arras on 22 March, 1918; Sergeant Phillip Humphreys, Royal Field Artillery, awarded the Distinguished Conduct Medal, Military Medal (and Bar) before his death at Ismailia, Egypt on 10 July, 1921; Sergeant R.E. Trew; Corporal J. Davies; Privates E. Bessell and W.J. Evans. An additional inscription to the front of the memorial commemorates the placing of a floral tribute by HRH Edward, Prince of Wales on 5 August, 1924.

The cemetery is located on The Highway, close to the A472 near Pontypool, and contains the graves of thirteen First World War soldiers:

Driver T. Corfield, 5th Brigade, Ammunition Column, Royal Field Artillery, died 18 November, 1918.

Private Arthur Groves, 2nd Battalion, Monmouthshire Regiment, died 10 November, 1914.

Bombardier Walter Humphreys, 'D' Battery, 36th Brigade, Royal Field Artillery. Gassed in France and died on 3 November, 1918 at Bagthorpe Military Hospital.

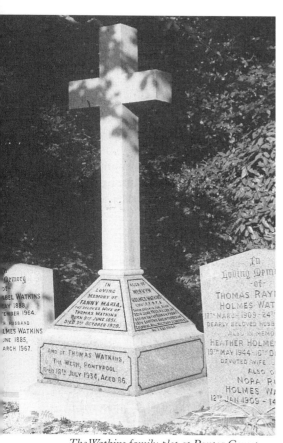

The Watkins family plot at Panteg Cemetery. *Panteg memorial.*

Memorial reredos and oak panelling, St Mary's Church, Panteg.

He was aged thirty, the son of Thomas and Margaret Humphreys of Gordon Villa, The Highway, Panteg, and married to Lilian. Thomas Humphreys was an old soldier and given the honour of unveiling the Panteg war memorial in November, 1921. Bombardier Walter Humphreys is buried in a family grave, the headstone of which also commemorates the death in Egypt of his brother, Sergeant Phillip Humphreys, DCM, MM (and Bar).

Company Quartermaster Sergeant D. Jacobs, Royal Welsh Fusiliers, died 5 December, 1918.

Private Jehoiada Jenkins, 2nd Battalion, Monmouthshire Regiment. Born in Trevethin, resided at Pontnewynydd and died on 19 May, 1915 from wounds received in France.

Corporal Robert Kenneth Lewis, 2nd Battalion, Monmouthshire Regiment, was the son of Thomas Henry and Mary Lewis. He lived in Griffithstown and died at Netley Hospital, aged eighteen, on 7 June from wounds received in France. Robert Lewis is buried in a private grave with his parents.

Gunner D.J. Moore, No. 4 Reserve Brigade, Royal Field Artillery, was the son of Daniel and Mary Moore of 37 Sherborne Road, Sebastopol. He died, aged twenty-five, on 23 November, 1918.

Gunner George Moss, Royal Field Artillery, was the son of Henry Moss and married to Hannah Moss of 108 Vine Street, Hulme, Manchester. He was born at Pucklechurch, Bristol, enlisted into the army in Newport, and died, aged forty-five, on 29 June, 1916 having been gassed in France.

Gunner Charles Parfitt, 80th Anti-Aircraft Section, Royal Garrison Artillery, was married to Jessie Parfitt of Lower New Inn, Pontypool Road. He died, aged thirty-one, on 5 April, 1919.

Private Arthur Hugh Parry, 3rd Battalion, South Wales Borderers, was the son of William Parry of Griffithstown. He died, aged thirty-two, on 2 December, 1918.

Bombardier Charles Edward Thomas, 3rd Monmouthshire Battery, 4th Welsh Brigade, Royal Field Artillery, was the only son of William and Sarah Thomas of 1 Sherbourne Road, Sebastopol. He died, aged thirty-four, on 5 March, 1919 and is buried in a private grave with his parents.

Bombardier Thomas Edgar Watkins, 'D' Battery, 120th Brigade, Royal Field Artillery, was the son of James and Margaret Watkins of Staffordshire Road, Griffithstown. He died, aged twenty-nine, from drowning on 30 May, 1915. Thomas Watkins is buried in a private grave with his parents.

Captain Vivian Holmes Watkins, 2nd Battalion, Monmouthshire Regiment, was the son of Thomas Watkins, of The Wern, Pontypool. He joined the 2nd Monmouthshire Regiment in February, 1912 and landed in France with his battalion on 7 November, 1914. Wounded 16 January, 1915, he was sent to the Empire Hospital, Westminster, London, where he died on 20 February. His body was brought back to Pontypool and buried with full military honours in Panteg Cemetery. Captain Watkins is buried in a family plot. Details of Captain Watkins' last days in the trenches appear in *British Roll Of Honour* and recall that his company had moved forward during the night of 14 January. It was while inspecting the pumps in a reserve area that he was shot by a sniper. The bullet inflicting a very serious wound on the right side of the top of his head. Also commemorated on the headstone are two of his brothers - Horace, who served with the South Wales Borderers and was killed in October, 1914 during the attack on Poelcappelle, and Mervyn, an officer with the Royal Field Artillery who lost his life in Macedonia.

St Mary's Parish Church

Dedicated by the Bishop of Monmouth on Sunday 7 January, 1923, the memorial at St Mary's takes the form of a decorated reredos and oak panelling. Scenes representing the Nativity, Crucifixion and Ascension illuminate the reredos, while the panelling bears on the north side the inscription in gold lettering -

> *To The Glory Of God And In Loving Memory Of The Heroes Who Made The Supreme Sacrifice In The Great War 1914-1918 The Reredos And Panelling Is Erected.*

Twenty-three names are recorded without rank or regiment on the south side: Leslie Brough, Samuel Cox, Percy Fletcher, Peter George, Stanley Grainger, William Griffiths, Tom Hall, Aubrey Harris, William Howells, Phillip Humphreys, Walter Humphreys, John Jones, Albert Jones, John M. Lett, Herbert Lewis, Benjamin Lewis, Jack F. Mills, George Millwater, H.E. Nelson, W.H. Nicholls, Charles Parfitt, John C. Phillips and John Williams. Those who fell in the Second World War have been added below.

There are two First World War soldiers buried in the churchyard. Corporal John Davies, South Wales Borderers, was the son of William and Elizabeth Davies of 7 Grove Estate, Pontnewynydd. He was born in Griffithstown and died, aged twenty-three, on 5 June, 1921. Sergeant Sydney Lewis, 8th Battalion, Welsh Regiment was the son of Thomas and Jane Lewis of Sebastopol. He was thirty-one when he died on 19 December, 1915.

PENGAM

The top of the Portland stone memorial in St David's Road, Pengam has the inscription in Welsh - *Trarawel Tros Eu Beddau Chwyth.* Below this, and engraved on a grey marble tablet to the front of the memorial is - *Buont - Ffyddlawn Hyd Angeu - They Were Faithful Unto Death.* This is followed by -

> *To The Glory Of God And To The Glorious Memory Of All The Men From This District Who Made The Supreme Sacrifice In The Great Wars 1914-1918 - 1939-1945. Yn Anghof Ni Chant Fod. Their Deeds Will Not Die.*

On the right side, and again inscribed on grey marble, one hundred and one names are recorded together with rank and regiment below the inscription - *Roll Of Honour 1914-1918 - Gwell Angau Na Chywilydd.* Private C. Adams, South Wales Borderers; Private W.J. Alderman, South Wales Borderers; Private W.T. Allen, South Wales Borderers; Lance-Corporal J. Anthony, South Wales Borderers; Rifleman A. Ashman, 1st Monmouthshire Regiment; Private W. Ashcroft, South Wales Borderers; Private B. Bevan, Welsh Regiment; Private R. Brown, Cameron Highlanders; Rifleman R. Bull, 1st Monmouthshire Regiment; Guardsman D.A. Butler, Welsh Guards; Private E.E. Button, South Wales Borderers; Private E. Clarke, Welsh Regiment; Private A. Clarry, South Wales Borderers; Private T.H. Coles, South Wales Borderers; Driver F. Croudace, Royal Field Artillery; Sergeant T. Crum, South Wales Borderers; Private W. Daniels, South Wales Borderers; Private T. Davies, Welsh

Regiment; Rifleman W. Dennett, 1st Monmouthshire Regiment; Staff-Sergeant J.N. Elias, Royal Army Service Corps; Rifleman D.A.P. Evans, 20th London Regiment; Corporal S.H. Farley, South Wales Borderers; Private D.J. Fear, Tank Corps; Private H. Fibbs, South Wales Borderers; Corporal G. Fowler, South Wales Borderers; Private V.G. Gibby, Royal Army Medical Corps; Private F. Gincell, South Wales Borderers; Private U. Gray, Welsh Regiment; Private J. Hillman, South Wales Borderers; Sergeant J. Hobbs, South Wales Borderers; Private S. Hobbs, Worcestershire Regiment; Nurse E. Hughes, British Expeditionary Force; Lance-Corporal G. Hussey, Welsh Regiment; Private H. James, South Wales Borderers; Private W. Jeffs, Welsh Regiment; Flight-Sergeant R. Jenkins, Royal Flying Corps; Private E. John, South Wales Borderers; Private M. Johnson, Queen Mary's Army Auxiliary Corps; Corporal F.J. Jones, South Wales Borderers; Private R. Jones, Somerset Light Infantry; Private H. Jones, Royal Welsh Fusiliers; Private J. Jones, South Wales Borderers; Private H.J. Jones, Welsh Regiment; Private E.M. Jones, Cheshire Regiment; Private C. Jones, South Wales Borderers; Lance-Corporal G. Jones, Welsh Regiment; Rifleman P. Leach, 1st Monmouthshire Regiment; Private A. Leah, Machine Gun Corps; Private G. Lee, South Wales Borderers; Sergeant T. Llewellyn, South Wales Borderers; Private W. Locke, 2nd Devonshire Regiment; Private E. Lewis, South Wales Borderers; Private C. Lewis, Gloucestershire Regiment; Private J. Mahoney, South Wales Borderers; Private I. Matthews, Welsh Regiment; Rifleman W. McCann, 1st Monmouthshire Regiment; Gunner J. McDougall, Royal Field Artillery; Private T. Morgan, South Wales Borderers; Private T. Morgan, South Wales Borderers; Private T.G. Morgan, South Wales Borderers; Private I.T. Morgan, South Wales Borderers; Corporal E.H. Morse, Royal Field Artillery; Private T.J. Parton, South Wales Borderers; Private J. Perry, MM, Royal Welsh Fusiliers; Sergeant C. Phillips, Royal Engineers; Private E.L. Phillips, North Staffordshire Regiment; Lance-Corporal H.C. Phillips, South Wales Borderers; Corporal H. Phillips, Military Foot Police; Private A. Potter, Military Foot Police; Private D. Powell, Durham Light Infantry; Private I. Read, Essex Regiment; Trooper W. Rees, Welsh Horse; Private P.W. Richards, Welsh Regiment; Private H.F. Roberts, South Wales Borderers; Private S.A.L. Roberts, Royal Welsh Fusiliers; Corporal A. Rudge, South Wales Borderers; Sergeant J. Scanlan, 1st Monmouthshire Regiment; Sergeant W.J.R. Scully, Welsh Regiment; Private J. Sheppard, South Wales Borderers; Private W.J. Skey, Army Ordnance Corps; Private W.R. Smart, Cheshire Regiment; Private A.H. Smith, Welsh Regiment; Rifleman W.M. Smith, 2nd Monmouthshire Regiment; Sapper J. Thomas, Royal Engineers; Sergeant P. Thomas, 1st Monmouthshire Regiment; Lance-Corporal A.H. Thorpe, South Wales Borderers; Private A. Titchcombe, Welsh Regiment; Private E. Toombs, South Wales Borderers; Lance-Corporal G. Tresize, Oxfordshire and Buckinghamshire Light Infantry; Private T. Watkins, Welsh Regiment; Corporal R. Wats, South Wales Borderers; Private J. Webber, South Wales Borderers; Gunner W. Webber, Royal Field Artillery; Private W.P. Williams, South Wales Borderers; Private H. Williams, South Wales Borderers; Private E. Williams, Royal Army Medical Corps; Private J.H. Williams, Welsh Regiment; Private T. Williams, Army Ordnance Corps; Private L. Williams, Welsh Regiment; Corporal G. Winters, Welsh Regiment; Private F. Withy, South Wales Borderers. Those who fell during the Second World War are commemorated on the left panel.

Penhow

St John The Baptist Parish Church

Private Trevor William James of the Royal Gloucestershire Hussars appears in the Penhow section of the town memorial at Magor. His is the only name listed. In St John's Church, at the west end of the south aisle, his name appears again. This time on the original marker cross from his grave in Palestine. Trevor James was the son of William and Elizabeth A. James of 85 Angus Street, Roath Park, Cardiff and he died, aged nineteen, on 20 April, 1917. On this day, records the regimental historian of the Royal Gloucestershire Hussars, the men watered their horses in the morning at Tel-el-Jemmi. The Regiment moved later to the outpost line running from El Mendur, where there was much aerial activity - 'the enemy dropping bombs and smoke balls' - and in the evening took over trenches at Munkheileh. Private James is buried in the War Cemetery at Gaza.

Original marker from the grave of Trevor William James. St John The Baptist Parish Church, Penhow.

Ponthir

Ponthir Baptist Church

On the north wall of the church, a white marble tablet is inscribed -

> *In Grateful Memory Of* (twenty-four names follow) *Who Fell In The Great War 1914-1918. 'Greater Love Hath No Man Than This'.*

The names recorded are: James Atkins, William Samuel Berrow, Harold Collins, Albert Cording, Arthur Cording, Robert J. Carpenter, Sidney Daleymount, George Maxwell Jarrett, Frederick James, Edward G. John, Phillip Ivor Lester, Frederick J. Lewis, Thomas E. Nicholls, Rupert C. Laybourne Pilliner, Robert Powell, Edwin Roberts, Glyn Rowlands, John Rees, Harry H. Stephens, William Thomas, Robert Thorne, Roy Taylor, Alex L. Wheeler and Edmund S. Williams.

The churchyard contains one war grave, that of Lance-Corporal William Samuel Berrow, 1st Battalion, Monmouthshire Regiment, who died on 17 February, 1919. He was twenty and buried with his mother, Mary Ann Berrow, in a private grave.

Pontllanfraith

Originally located in front of the old Mynyddislwyn Council Offices in Bryn Road, Pontllanfraith, the town memorial now stands in the grounds of the Caerphilly County Borough Council building in Blackwood Road (A4048). The names of fifty-eight men who died in the First World War are recorded alphabetically, without rank or regiment, below the inscription - *Faithful Unto Death In The Great War. Their Names Liveth For Evermore.*

G. Allcock, S. Bethel, J. Bryant, R. Bull, T. Coles, E.D. Cook, H.T. Crabtree, A.

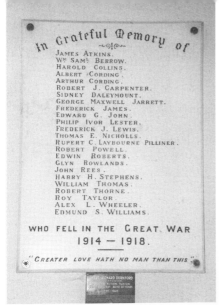

Ponthir Baptist Church memorial. *Pontllanfraith memorial.*

Cripps, Ed. Cripps, E. Cripps, D. Davies, D.T.W. Davies, G. Davies, L. Davies, T.J. Davies, W. Davies, A. Dowden, G. Evans, E. Gingell, F.J. Hale, J. Humphries, B. Jefferies, E.W. Jenkins, R. Jenkins, A.V. Jennings, E.H. Jennings, H. Jennings, D.J. Jones, F.J. Jones, I. Jones, T. Jones, W. Lewis, A.T. Lloyd, T. Lockwood, E. Mansfield, J. McDougall, C.W.C. Myles, G. Powles, R. Powles, J. Preston, A. Price, E. Price, S. Price, D.E. Rees, Ll. Richards, D. Roberts, E. Roberts, H. Roberts, S. Roberts, D. Rogers, W. Rogers, N. Saunders, R. Travers, H. Tucker, H.T. Walding, D. Walters, A. Williams, T.B. Williams. An additional two names, J. Richardson and A. Richardson, appear below the main list, then carved into the stonework the dates - *1914-1919*.

PONTNEWYDD

The war memorial at the junction of Lowlands Road and Clark Avenue was unveiled on Wednesday, 11 November, 1925 by Hon. Colonel of the 3rd Battalion, Monmouthshire Regiment, Major-General Lord Treowen, CB, CMG. The cenotaph takes the form of an obelisk mounted on a pedestal and bears the inscription -

To The Glorious Memory Of The Men Of This District Who Gave Their Lives In The Great War 1914-1918. 'Their Name Liveth For Evermore'.

Similar wording, bearing the dates 1939-1945, appears on the right side of the memorial.

Holy Trinity Parish Church
Part of the war memorial unveiled by Colonel Sir Joseph Bradney, CB, TD, DL at Holy Trinity on Sunday 9 September, 1928 was the installation in the church of electric light. A brass plaque on the south wall commemorates the event -

The Electric Light Was Installed In This Church To The Glory Of God And As A

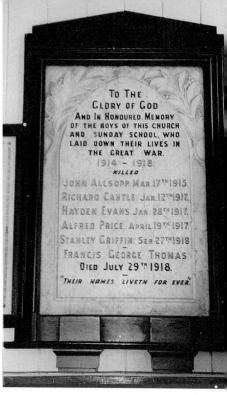

Pontnewydd memorial.

Richmond Road Baptist Church, Pontnewydd memorial.

Memorial To The Men Who Gave Their Lives In The Great War, 1914-1918 A.D

and records the names in full, but without rank or regiment, of twenty men who were killed: Charles Butcher, Jack Butcher, Henry Newman Carter, Samuel Cook, William Edgar Daw, Noel Alfred Hayles, Charles Hale, Charles Llewellyn James, Clifford Linney, Reginald Morris, Charles Morgan, Alfred Stephen Nurden, Thomas Alfred Payne, Albert Pinches, John Ramsden, A.C. Rawlins, Ivor Herbert Tucker, Jack Williams, William Watts and John Watts.

On the north wall of the nave a stained glass window commemorates the accidental death of a naval officer in, what remains to this day, Britain's worst rail disaster. A small brass plaque to the left of the window has the inscription -

This Window Is Dedicated To The Glory Of God And The Dear Memory Of Charles Harold Evelyn Head, Lieut-Commander Royal Navy, Whitehead Officer Of H.M.S. Vernon. Born 1 Aug. 1882, Killed While On Naval Service In The Railway Collision At Gretna, 22nd May 1915. His Life Was One Of Unswerving Devotion To Duty.

In the Gretna disaster, a troop train carrying territorials of the 1/7th Royal Scots to Liverpool, where they were to embark for Gallipoli, crashed into a stationary local train. Shortly after this, an express from Carlisle ran into the wreckage bring the total number of casualties up to four hundred and seventy-three. Some two hundred and twenty-seven of whom were killed.

Aged thirty-two, Charles Head had joined the navy as a boy, seeing service in the

Boxer Rebellion of 1900. He later served on the torpedo vessel, HMS *Versuvius*, and at the time of his death was on the staff of the torpedo school, HMS *Vernon*. He is buried in Glasgow Western Necropolis, Maryhill.

The churchyard contains eleven war graves:

Sergeant Charles Henry Butcher, Labour Corps, was the son of Jacob and Sarah Ann Butcher and married to Elizabeth Butcher of 6 George Street, Cwmbran. He died, aged forty-five, on 20 September, 1920.

Rifleman Alfred Ira Clapp, 18th Battalion, London Regiment (London Irish Rifles), was the son of Mrs Ira Clapp of 256 Upper Richmond Road, Putney, London. He was married to Mary Clapp and lived at 5 Brickyard Cottages, Cwmbran. Alfred Clapp was twenty-four when he died on 19 October, 1918.

Memorial window to Charles Harold Evelyn Head. Holy Trinity Parish Church.

Private Samuel Cook, Royal Engineers, died on 20 July, 1920. He was forty-three, the son of John and Mary Ann Cook and married to Annie Phoebe Cook of 9 Park View, Pontnewydd.

Private Joseph Linney, Royal Defence Corps, was married to Eliza Linney of 17 New Street, Pontnewydd. He was fifty-two when he died on 10 November, 1916.

Private Herbert Standley, 8th Battalion, Welsh Regiment, was the son of John William and Emma Standley of Silver Street, Besthorpe, Norfolk. He died, aged thirty-one, on 18 February, 1918.

Stoker 1st Class Clifford Brynmor Thomas, Royal Navy, served on HMS *Erin*. He was the son of James and Margaret Thomas and died, aged twenty-one, on 24 February, 1919.

Gunner Kemyn Gordon Thomas, Royal Field Artillery, was born in Swansea and the son of James and Emma Thomas of 19 Chapel Street, Pontnewydd. Having been gassed in France, he returned home and subsequently died, aged twenty-three, on 13 November, 1918.

Sapper Edward Traves, Royal Engineers, was the son of J. Traves of Griffithstown. He died, aged thirty-one, on 22 March, 1919. Edward Traves is buried in a family grave.

Able Seaman G.H.G. Walker, Royal Naval Air Service, served on HMS *Daedalus* and was accidentally killed at Leysdown in Kent on 20 March, 1918. He was nineteen and the son of Arthur and Annie Walker of Pontnewydd.

Lance-Corporal John Watts, 10th Battalion, South Wales Borderers, was married to Catherine Watts of 26 Richmond Road, Pontnewydd. He was born at Llanfrechfa and died, aged thirty-five, on 29 October, 1916.

Private John Williams, 9th Battalion, Royal Welsh Fusiliers, was born in Llanfihangle and enlisted into the army in Aldershot. He was married to Lily

Beatrice Williams of 7 Commercial Street, Pontnewydd and died, aged thirty-nine, on 23 May, 1918.

Richmond Road Baptist Church
A marble tablet in a wood surround was unveiled at the church on Sunday 30 November, 1919. Located on the wall to the right of the altar, the memorial bears the inscription -

> *To The Glory Of God And In Honoured Memory Of The Boys Of This Church And Sunday School, Who Laid Down Their Lives In The Great War 1914-1918.*

Following this, and below the word - *Killed* - there are six names, each being recorded with a date: John Allsopp. 17 March 1915; Richard Cantle. 12 January 1917; Hayden Evans. 28 January 1917; Alfred Price. 19 April 1917; Stanley Griffin. 27 September 1918; Francis George Thomas. 29 July 1918 - '*Their Names Liveth For Ever*'. A framed Roll of Honour, this time recording the names of those who served during the First World War, as well as those killed, hangs close by. There are ninety-nine names listed.

PONTYMISTER

Brookland Adult Training Centre
The site occupied by the Gwent County Council training centre in Brookland Road was formally that of the Pontywaun County Schools and a granite Celtic Cross erected shortly after the Great War can still be seen behind the original stone wall in Commercial Street. Inscribed at the base of the cross is -

> *To The Memory Of John W. Taylor - Assistant Master And Of James Banfield - Fred Cawley - Cyril Clissold - Noel T. Daniel - David Dart - J. Emlyn Davies - Reginald Davies - William Dobson - W. Jones-Evans - William H. Harper - Leslie A. James - Archibald Jelf - Edwin W. Jenkins - Howard Johnson - Gordon Jones - Ralph Jones - Samuel Llewelyn - Albert Mellish - William Morgan - Zephanian Orman - David F. Rowlands - Ewart G. Salathiel - Victor Tyler - Oswald M. Williams - William Winston - Who Died In The Great War 1914-1918 That We Might Live In Peace And Safety.*

Of Lieutenant John William Taylor, who was killed in Belgium with the 2nd Monmouthshire Regiment on 11 March, 1915, a fellow officer wrote 'He was killed when he had voluntarily taken my platoon

Pontywaun County Schools memorial, Brookland Adult Training Centre, Pontymister.

up into the line to give me a rest, an act which was typical of him..A better soldier never commanded men, and his death was a loss which is still felt.'

St Margaret's Church

On the west wall of the church in Commercial Street, a large brass tablet bears the inscription - *To The Glorious Memory Of The Men Of This Church Who Laid Down Their Lives In The War - 1914-1919.* Nine names follow without rank or regiment: William J. Coles, William E. Everson, Frank Hann, James Jay, Bertram Knight, Prosser Owen, Bernard Rallison, Victor Rallison, Edwin White, then - *There Name Liveth For Evermore.*

A further seventy-two names follow preceded by the inscription - *Also As A Thank-Offering To Almighty God For The Safe Return Of The Following Men Who Served* - Evan Bates, Godfrey Birden, Archie Blakemore, Ernest Bunce, Percy Bunce, Harry Cashel, Fred Cheeseman, Elijah Coles, Ernest Coote, William C. Darby, Charles R. Darby, William Doody, John Driscoll, William Driscoll, Mark Everson, Charles Gingell, Harry Gore, Albert Griffiths, John Griffiths, Fred Harmer, Tom Harry, John Hook, David Hopkins, Edward Horsham, Douglas Howell, Evelyn Howell, Geoffrey T. Howell, Harry Howell, William J. Howell, Thomas Hudd, Percy Humphreys, Hubert Jackson, Kenneth James, John Jones, Lewis Lewis, Edward Lones, Ralph Lones, Fred Lush, Harrold Maddocks, Ben Millard, Jack Newton, George Norman, Norman Owen, Ralph Owen, Fred Preece, Edwin Pritchard, Fred Pritchard, George Prust, Edward Rallison, Fred Rallison, Ivor Rallison, Edward Redman, William Redman, Tom Redman, Levi Redwood, Gordon Roe, Edmund G. Squire, Garfield Sutton, William Syrett, Robert Taylor, Percy Thomas, Talbot Thomas, Joseph Thompson, James Upham, Arthur Waites, James Watkins, Willie Watkins, Ivor Williams, Edgar Woods, Frank Wright, Hubert Wright, Reginald Wright.

PONTYPOOL

W.G. Lloyd, in his book *Roll Of Honour*, recalls how for some years after the Great War, Pontypool was undecided as to what form a town memorial should take. In 1924, the section of Pontypool Park known as the Italian Garden was donated to the town by Mrs Tenison, the daughter of the late J.C. Hanbury. It was then decided that the entrance to this area should accommodate a series of tablets commemorating those who had been killed. Having been completed, two metal plaques were affixed to the tall supporting columns either side of the main gates. These having in raised letters the dedication -

This Memorial To The Men & Women Of The Districts Of Abersychan And Pontypool Who Made The Supreme Sacrifice In The Great War Was Unveiled By Major General Lord Treowen, C.B., C.M.G. Lord Lieutenant Of Monmouthshire December 18th 1924 to the left, and on the right - *This Memorial Is Erected To The Sacred Memory Of The Men & Women Of The Districts Of Abersychan And Pontypool Who Gave Their Lives For Their Country In The Great War 1914-1918.*

After the Second World War these panels were removed and placed on the shorter columns either side. Their places were taken by two new plaques bearing the names of those killed 1939-1945. The Roll of Honour itself, which comprised three hundred and eighty names took the form of six panels, arranged in two groups of three, and placed on the railings either side of the gates. The names are listed in groups according to rank and regiment. Each of the three-panel sections is headed with the inscription - *To The Glorious Memory Of* - and the dates - *1914-1918*. Above this, and within a wreath of laurel, a cross within a circle inscribed with the motto - *'Dulce Et Decorum Est Pro Patria Mori'*.

The names on the Pontypool Park gates appear in the following order:

1st panel: *Royal Navy:* Chief Engine Room Artificers J.A. Millard and T. Rees; Able Seamen G. Cann and G.A.Redman; Gunners A. Protheroe and F. Protherough; Ordinary-Seamen A.J. Allen, R.G. Gough, G. Pym and H.Thompson; Able Seaman H.Thomas; Engine Room Artificer E. Robathan and Stoker F. Parker. *Royal Naval Volunteer Reserve:* Able Seamen H. Berry, S. James, D.L. Rank, A.D.J. Rowland and F. Williams; Leading-Signalman T.R. Silcox. *Royal Naval Division:* Able Seamen W.J. Bethel, T. Bryan, J.H. Edwards, A. Fowler, A. Hack, E. Matthews, E. Morgan, A.I. Norman and J. Powell; Leading-Signalman A. Cotterell. *Royal Marine Light Infantry:* Private W.E.J. Walker. *12th Lancers:* Regimental Sergeant Major J.J. Denton. *Northumberland Yeomanry:* Private T. Carr. *Devonshire Yeomanry:* Private I.J. Kay. *Durham Light Infantry:* Private H.G. Buck. *Rifle Brigade:* Private G. Nicholls. *36th Infantry:* Private W. Davies. *Royal Field Artillery:* Lieutenant M.H. Watkins; Sergeant J. Cook; Corporal W.G. Lewis; Gunners F. Fifield, J. Hayes, A.L. Howells, M.C. Jenkins, T. Larcombe, B. Luffman, G. Moss, F. Roberts, C. Taylor, J. Thomas, T. Thomas, E.A. Trumper and E. Watkins; Drivers H. Clarke, W. Dakin, C.S. Hood, E.G. Rosser and R.E. Taylor; Gunner G. Whitecombe.

2nd panel: *Royal Garrison Artillery:* Acting-Bombardier J. Bram; Gunners F. Brace, W. Griffiths, W.S. Howells, W.A. Leonard and W. Reardon. *Royal Engineers:* Lance-Corporal S. Dowell; Sappers F. Baldwin, A. Crane, T. Foley, S.C. Jacobs, E.F. Jones, E.E.O. Parsons and F. Russell; Drivers F. Grandace and A. Lewis. *Royal Flying Corps:* Second-Lieutenants R.L. James and J.H. Wynne. *Grenadier Guards:* Privates J.D. Denton and S. Herbert. *Coldstream Guards:* Lance-Sergeant S. Jones. *Welsh Guards:* Privates E.V. Bishop, H. Lawley and L.Watkins. *King's Own Royal Lancaster Regiment:* Private W. Harrington. *Royal Warwickshire Regiment:* Privates J. Bibey, C.O. Harris and W. Haynes. *Royal Fusiliers:* Lance-Corporal A.J. Dunning. *Devonshire Regiment:* Privates F. Jones, T. Moody and F.C. Pearce. *Lancashire Fusiliers:* Private J.T. Ashcroft. *Cheshire Regiment:* Privates W.F. Shaw, H. Rees and S. Wixey. *Royal Welsh Fusiliers:* Privates B. Bayliss, F.A. Baxter, F. Cecil, T. Crane, J. Evans, F. Flook, I. Hayward, J. Jones, W.H. Matthews, P. Oates, T.H. Purcell, W. Peplow, T. Rees, H.J. Stone and E. Vaux. *Hampshire Regiment:* Private D. Hurley.

3rd panel: *South Wales Borderers:* Second-Lieutenants H.H. Watkins and T. Williams; Company Sergeant Major T.J. Watkins; Sergeants W.J.J. Edwards, A. Hunt and G. Vann; Lance-Sergeant P.V. Spray; Corporals W. Clarke, W. Perrin and G. Smithey; Lance-Corporals G.P. Coward, C. Hennesay, M. Phillips, S.J. Roden, T.J. Tovey and E. Wears; Privates A.E. Amos, E. Barnes, J. Bethel, W. Bevan, T.G. Chivers, A.J. Cox, G.M. Cox, W. Cox, G. Crane, T. Dadey, A. Davies, S. Davies, J. Donoghue, F. Dowding, J. Garvin, J. Gould, W. Grant, T. Griffiths, I.W.H. Hayes, C.E. Hawkins, I. Hern, D.J. Hern, J. Hoffman, P.G. Hoffman, J. Howells, A. Hunt, W. Hyatt, E. James, L. Jenkins, A. Jones, A.J. Jones, W.H. Jones, T. Killingback, W.P. King, D. Lloyd, W.T. Manley, W. Morris, E. Pearce, R. Peploe, S. Phillips, A.C. Price,

Memorial gates, Pontypool Park.

A.J. Price, E. Price, A. Rees, D. Rees, A. Roberts, C. Scammels, S. Smart, C. Smith, J. Smith, H. Shorthouse, W. Stone, W.S. Thomas, Tremlett (*see Note*), H.J. Whittington, G. Williams, P. Williams, A. Woffenden, J. Yemm, B. Griffith, D. Watkins. *Note:* The memorial gives no initial for Private Tremlett. *Soldiers Died In The Great War*, however, reveals that his name was William.

    4th panel: *Monmouthshire Regiment:* Lieutenant-Colonel A.J.H. Bowen; Captain V.H. Watkins; Lieutenants H.J. Walters and W.J. Williams; Second-Lieutenants R. King, A.L. Meredith and J.E. Paton; Company Sergeant Majors W. Booth and J.S. Granger; Colour-Sergeant H.W. Dowse; Sergeants G. Berrow, T. Butcher, W. Parsons, W.H. Prosser, W.H. Waite and J. West; Corporals E. McCarthy, C.H. Slade, C. Williams and H. Woods; Lance-Corporals A. Cotterell, E. Evans, H. Holmes, A. Horton, P. Jones, H.C. Lewis, W.J. Leyshon, D. Lovell, J.H. Morgan, A. Pearce and E. Winston; Privates W.A. Arthur, C.H. Bond, G.C. Badham, T. Biggs, A.J. Bullock, W.J. Butcher, W.H. Cawsey, W.G. Chance, M. Chancey, E. Cooper, C.H. Dare, E. Dare, G.A. Davies, L. Davies, J. Edwards, J. Evans, T.H. Flellow, T. Gallivan, L. George, E. Gibbon, E.J. Gibson, T.H. Gwyne, T. Hannett, E.M. Harris, J. Hill, W.F. Hitchings, J. James, J. Jaynes, J. Jenkins, A. Jones, G. Jones, J. Jones, R.A. Jones, R. Jones, W.E. Jones, E.V. Lang, G. Lester, G. Lewis, A.E. Lilwall, E. Long, H.H.J. Middle, J. Mogford, S. Morgan, T. Morris, H. Mosley, W. Needs, R. Newman.

    5th panel: *Monmouthshire Regiment:* F. Nicholls, A. Nunnerly, E. Palfrey, R.W. Rees, J. Roberts, A. Rowland, J. Rowlands, G.T. Saunders, R. Savery, J. Shanley, J.A. Shaw, T. Strong, A. Taylor, A.J. Taylor, E. Thomas, J.G. Thomas, W. Thomas, C. Vernall, J. Vernall, W.J. Warren, H.J. Watkins, W.J. Whitcombe and C. Williams.

181

Gloucestershire Regiment: Corporals C.F. Bishop, E.G. Waters and P. Williams; Privates E. Grimes, W.E. Fowler, G. Heaven and J.H. Lang. *Worcesershire Regiment:* Privates W. Powell, H.A. Ruddock, T.J. Thomas and J. Tutton. *East Surrey Regiment:* Private H. Palmer. *Royal Sussex Regiment:* Private C.A. Shelton. *Lancashire Regiment:* Lieutenant R.C. Badman and Private W.A.G. Bishop. *Note:* The memorial gives regiment as 'Lancashire.' Lieutenant Badman served with the South Lancashire Regiment, but no record of Private Bishop can be located. *South Staffordshire Regiment:* Private P. Rapson. *Welch Regiment:* Privates W.S. Carter, R. Davies, M. Foley, W.J. Hale, R.D. Harris, R. Hayward, J. Lloyd, W. Miller, W.J. Pike, J. Purchase and W.H. Yemm. *Loyal North Lancashire Regiment:* Lance-Corporals A. Edwards and W.S. Thomas; Privates G. Thomas and W.G. Watkins. *King's Own Yorkshire Light Infantry:* Private D. Whitehouse. *King's Royal Rifle Corps:* Riflemen J. Gilbert, T. Higgins and C.S. Scrivens.

6th panel: *King's Shropshire Light Infantry:* Lance-Corporals A. Lewis, D. Lovell and W.J. Smith; Privates J. Cook, T.E. Roberts, T. Woodland and F. Yelland. *Australian and New Zealand Army Corps:* Private O. Jones. *Machine Gun Corps:* Second-Lieutenant H.W. Price; Privates G. Allen, W.J. Gill, W. James, W.J. Jenkins, G.B. Pope, S. Waite and H. Williams. *9th Tank Corps:* Second-Lieutenant F.H. Smith; Private A.E. Jenkins and Gunner A. Watkins. *Labour Corps:* Privates J. Jenkins, I. Jones, L.W. Knott, F. Morris and W.C. Taylor. *Royal Army Service Corps:* Shoeing Smith A. Prosser; Privates L.A. Mills and G. Tipton; Drivers C.E. Shackleton and E. Tylor. *Royal Army Medical Corps:* Privates D.J. Barwood, W.A. Hopkins, A.J. Parry, A.J. Thomas and W. Wylie. *Royal Army Ordnance Corps:* Sergeant S. Williams. *Volunteer Aid Detachments:* Nurse O. Jenkins. *Queen Mary's Army Auxiliary Corps:* Worker L. Saint. *Undefined Units:* C. Allmark, J. Bigham, J. Broderick, J. Cook, W. Cotterell, G. Davies, J. Edwards, T.E. Evans, I. Griffiths, T. Haymonds, G. Holloway, W. Jeremiah, W. Kelly, W.T. Morgan, H. Parker, A. Powell, A. Price, W. Roden, W.G. Thomas and W. Whitcombe.

West Monmouth School

A stained glass window in the School Hall at Blaendare Road features figures representing 'Courage' and 'Victory,' together with the School Arms and Crests of the South Wales Borderers and 2nd Battalion, Monmouthshire Regiment. The window has the dedication -

To The Glory Of God And In Memory Of Old Boys Who Fell In The Great War 1914-1918. Erected By Friends And Members Past And Present Of The School.

Below the window, the names of forty-four boys, arranged alphabetically and with rank, are engraved on a brass plaque:

Sergeant H.C. Allmark, Private A. Andrews, Second-Lieutenant R.C. Badman, Lance-Corporal A.E. Burchell, Second-Lieutenant Walter Collings, who served with the 3rd Monmouthshire Regiment and won the Military Cross, Corporal A.I. Davies, Flight-Lieutenant Harrold Day of the 8th (Naval) Squadron, Royal Naval Air Service and who was awarded the Distinguished Service Cross, Sergeant T.E. Evans, Private H.H. Hall, Corporal N.A.D. Hayles, Captain T.W.P. Herbert, Private T. Higgins, Private R.G. Holbrook, Private T.B.H. Jones, Private H. Killingback, Private H.C. Lewis, Lance-Corporal H.J. Lewis, Private P.T. Lewis, Private R.K.

Lewis, Corporal T.A. Lewis, Gunner B.E. Luffman, Private R.H. Mason, Private J.A. Millard, Second-Lieutenant I.H. Morris, Private F.H. Nelson, Private W.G. Nicholls, Private J.A. Norton, Ordinary-Seaman J.C. Phillips, Second-Lieutenant W.H. Pitten, Second- Lieutenant William Henry Price, who lived not far from the school at 52 Blaendare Road, Private W.E. Robertson, Second-Lieutenant F.E. Simpson, Second-Lieutenant F.H. Smith, Second-Lieutenant H.H. Stephens, Ordinary-Seaman A.H. Tooze, Lieutenant H.J. Walters, Second-Lieutenant D.J.G. Watkins, Second-Lieutenant H.H. Watkins, Second-Lieutenant M.H. Watkins, Captain V.H. Watkins, Private I.H.C. Williams, Corporal S.B. Williams, who won the Military Medal, and Lieutenant W.J. Williams. The last name is that of Private W. James.

The three Watkins brothers - Horace, Vivian and Mervyn, all lived at The Wern, Pontypool, and were the sons of a local solicitor. In *British Roll Of Honour*, Horace is noted as having been a member of the Cadet Corps at his later school, Monmouth Grammar, and a Colour-Sergeant in the Officer Training Corps at Oxford. 'It was on October 21st, 1914,' records the book, 'that he met his death while he was leading No.4 Platoon from Langemarck Village in a frontal attack over some open ground, the only cover being that afforded by the leaves of beet and turnips.'

By now, Horace was serving on the Western Front with the 1st Battalion, South Wales Borderers. In a letter written to Horace's parents, Lieutenant H.M.B. Salmon set out in fine detail the circumstances in which their son met his death. He also recalled - 'Before attacking we halted in Langemarck Village, and I went up to your son and said to him, 'Look here Watkins, if I get a return ticket, you can have my jam to-night, and if Ward gets it we'll share his.' About 4.00 pm a corporal crawled up to me, and said that Mr. Watkins had died, and the last thing he said was, 'Tell Mr Salmon he can have my jam to-night.'

Vivian Watkins is buried in Panteg Cemetery, and Mervyn in Doiran Military Cemetery, Greece.

PORTSKEWETT

St Mary's Parish Church

St Mary's Parish Church, Portskewett with Sudbrook is located on Main Road, Portskewett. The churchyard contains an obelisk, unveiled on 13 November, 1920 and with the following inscribed on the side of the pedestal facing the road -

Erected In Loving And Grateful Remembrance Of The Following Men From This Parish Who Fell In The Great War. 1914-1919.

Twenty-one names follow:

Bert Beasley, Audley Blight, Daniel James Donovan, Jeremiah Donovan, Charles Drower, Ernest Evans, Albert Gardner, Frederick Gardner, Alfred James Hale, Archie Harris, Ernest Humphreys, George Humphreys, Thomas King, William King, George Morse, Edward Pickering, Albert Edward Richings, William Spencer, Harry Watkins, Tom Ernest Webb MM, Owen Williams. Tom Ernest Webb was from Sudbrook and won the Military Medal while serving on the Western Front with the 1st Monmouthshire Regiment. He died from wounds received on 14 October, 1916.

Portskewett memorial, St Mary's Churchyard.

Two of the men recorded on the memorial are buried in the churchyard. Corporal Ernest George Evans, Western Command, Labour Corps was the son of Mrs J. Evans of 4 Sudbrook Terrace, Sudbrook. He died, aged thirty-one, on 1 November, 1918. Driver Ernest William Humphreys of 'A' Battery, 76th Brigade, Royal Field Artillery was the son of Edward and Emma Humphreys of Portskewett and the husband of Rachel Humphreys of Sharpy Lane, Caldicot. He died, aged twenty-seven, at Tidworth on 31 August, 1915.

RAGLAN

St Cadoc's Church

On the south wall of the chancel there are four memorial plaques commemorating individual soldiers who were killed during the Great War. Erected by their relatives and friends, the first brass tablet has the inscription -

In Memory Of Private Jeremiah Jenkins, MGC And Gunner Wm. Henry Williams, RFA Who Gave Their Lives For Their Country In The Great War 1914-1919.

Private Jenkins had served with the South Wales Borderers before being transferred to the Machine Gun Corps, and was killed in France on 15 July, 1916.

The death of the eldest son of local Justice of the Peace, Richard John Pryce-Jenkin, is recorded on a bronze shield -

In Ever Loving Memory Of 2nd Lieut. Richard Douglas Pryce-Jenkin 1st Batt. South Wales Borderers - Born July 29th 1894 - Killed In Action At Festubert France Dec. 31st. 1914.

Second-Lieutenant Pryce-Jenkin was newly commissioned from the Royal Military College, Sandhurst, and had been in France for just a few weeks. The shield, which is mounted on marble, is also engraved with the Regimental Crest of the South Wales Borderers.

Another badge, this time that of the Royal Army Medical Corps, appears on a brass tablet bearing the following inscription -

In Loving Memory Of Alexander Graham Spiers Logie M.B., M.S. Who Was 27 Years Physician And Surgeon In This Parish. He Served As Captain In The Royal Army Medical Corps During The Great War. Born 12th March, 1865 - Died 1st Feb. 1919.

Captain Spiers-Logie died in Scotland and is buried in Dirleton Parish Churchyard, East Lothian.

The design of a church organ is etched into the left-hand side of the last memorial plaque -

To The Glory Of God And Ever Loving Memory Of Eric Stanley Saunders Who Served This Church Faithfully As Organist For Many Years - Born June 1st 1885, And Gave His Life For His County June 19th, 1917. Interred At Poperinghe, Flanders. This Tablet Is Erected By Members Of The Congregation - His Many Friends And Relatives.

Pioneer Eric Saunders served with XI Corps, Signal Company, Royal Engineers and before the war was a clerk in the County Council Offices, Monmouth.

Memorial shield to Richard Douglas Pryce-Jenkin. St Cadoc's Church, Raglan.

On the north-east side of the church is the grave of Corporal E.S. Edwards who served with 'A' Signal Company, Royal Engineers and died on 31 March, 1919.

RHIWDERIN

Rhiwderin Tabernacle Congregational Chapel

The framed Roll of Honour in the vestibule depicts various naval and military actions, together with several figures of servicemen and flags. Below this, and on two scrolls, the inscription - *Tabernacle Congregational Crch. - European War 1914-1918.* This is followed by a crown above - *Rhewderin* - then the words - *Roll Of Honour* - and the dedication -

> *The Installation Of Electric Light In This Place Of Worship Is Provided By Subscriptions From Friends And Funds Obtained By Members Of Tabernacle Congregational Church Desiring To Memorialize Those Associated With This Congregation Who Fell In The Great War 1914-1918. Their Memory Endureth For Ever.*

The names of six men who were killed follow: Wilfred Berry, Albert Berry, Stanley Ford, Cyril Taylor, Davey Walters and James White. Those from the church who served in, and survived, the war, are also commemorated. These are recorded within two columns, one headed - *Name* - the other - *Remarks.* Willie Baker, Augustus Berry (wounded in action), Arthur Berry, George Berry (wounded in action), Joseph Berry, Raymond Berry (wounded in action), Willie Brown, George Clift, Robert M.H. Evans, Arthur Everson, Ivor Everson (wounded in action), Charlie Ford (awarded Military Medal), Jack Ford, Trevor James, Tom Jones (wounded in action), William H. Jones (wounded in action), Willie Langley, Charles Lewis, Elwyn Lewis, Raphael Lewis, William Lewis, Ivor Lloyd (wounded in action), Harlod Nicholas, Jubilee Nicholas (wounded in action), Tom Nicholas, Willie Nicholas, Frank Phillips (wounded in action), Alf Roberts, Percy Rosser, Walter Rosser, Tom Samuel (wounded in action), George Sexton, Albert Squires, Davey J. Squires (wounded in action), Conway Taylor, Walter Taylor, Edgar Waters, Arthur White, Frank White, Melvil Williams. The memorial ends with the words - *Presented To Tabernacle Church Rhewderin By Mr. A.A. Hawker.*

Roll of Honour, Rhiwderin Tabernacle Congregational Chapel.

RHYMNEY

The town memorial, at the junction of High Street and Victoria Road was unveiled on 27 October, 1929 and originally recorded the names of one hundred and twenty-six men who were killed in the First World War. These are arranged on three sides:

1st side: J. Ashton, F. Barter, J. Barter, T. Bermingham, V. Bowering, D. Buckley, J. Campbell, J.A. Cashman, W.C. Cole, F.W. Cook, A. Crompton, J.H. Curtis, D.J. Davies, D.J. Davies, E. Davies, J. Davies, L. Davies, M. Davies, R. Davies, T. Davies, T. Davies, W.C. Davies, J.R. Davies, E. Duggan, H. Duggan, J. Duggan, C. Edwards, S. Edwards, W. Edwards, D.B. Evans, D.W. Evans, E. Evans, E.J. Evans, T.J. Evans, T.N. Evans, G. Fisher, R. Francis, G. Gale, J. Gallop, J.H. Gittings, J. Hall, R. Hennessy, T. Hennessy.

2nd side: T.J. Hillman, J. Humphreys, T. Humphreys, D. Hurley, J. Hurley, W.C. Jenkins, D. Jones, E. Jones, E. Jones, E.T. Jones, J. Jones, S.L. Jones, J. Keefe, A. King, G. Kingsley, B. Lanigan, D.B. Lewis, S. Lewis, J.R. Lloyd, A. Magness, T. Magness, W. McAuliffe, D. McCarthy, M. McCarthy, T. McCarthy, J.J. Meade, B. Miller, J.C. Monk, C. Morgan, D. Morgan, E.T. Morgan, H. Morgan, J. Morgan, D. Morris, R.L. Morris, E.J. Mutton, P. O`Leary, F. Owen, P. Owen, W.J. Owen, W.E. Parry, A.J. Pedlingham, H. Phillips.

3rd side: W.A. Phillips, D.H. Powell, D. Powell, W.H. Powell, D.E. Price, J. Pullin, R. Rees, R. Rees, W. Rees, E. Rist, J. Rist, G. Roach, E.J. Roberts, J.W. Roberts, A.J. Shepherd, T. Smith, C. Sweeny, I. Theophilus, C. Thomas, H. Thomas, L.J. Thomas, R. Thomas, F.J. Thomas, D. Walters, D.T. Walters, M. Walters, R.H. Walters, S. Walters, W.J. Walters, A.P. Weddel, E. Weeks, B. Welsh, A.S. White, S.T. White, D.H. Williams, E. Williams, J.G. Williams, J.H. Williams, W.G. Williams, A.C. Wozencroft.

A tall Celtic Cross, the memorial has the following inscription - *Mewn Anghof Ni Chant Fod* - to the front of the cross, and - *Their Name Liveth For Evermore* - at the back. Inscribed on the pedestal is -

In Proud And Grateful Memory Of The Men Of Rhymney Who Gave Their Lives For Us In The Great Wars 1914-1919 & 1939-1945. Greater Love Hath No Man Than This, That A Man Lay Down His Life For His Friends.

Rhymney memorial.

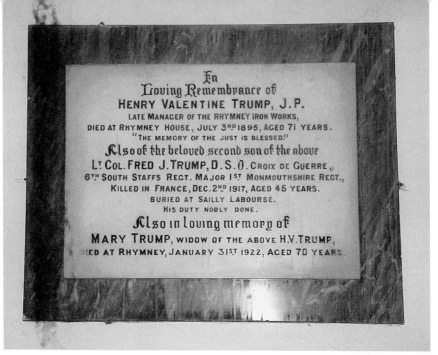

Fred J. Trump memorial plaque, St David's Church, Rhymney.

The names of those who fell in the Second World War were added later to the plinth. The Rhymney War Memorial Park, opened in 1925 on ground donated by the Rhymney Iron Company, is close by.

Royal British Legion Club

The memorial from the now demolished, Middle Rhymney School, is now located in the bar of the Royal British Legion Club at Rhymney. On a brass plaque mounted on wood, the words - *Roll Of Honour 1914-1919* - appear on a scroll and either side of a silver cross. Below this is the inscription -

In Proud And Grateful Memory Of The Old Boys Of The Middle Rhymney Council School Who Served In The Great War Of Whom We Record With Regret Those Who Made The Supreme Sacrifice.

Thirty-six names follow without rank or regiment:
Fred Barter, James Barter, Vivian Bowering, John Campbell, Fred W. Cook, Albert Crompton, John H. Curtis, Stanley Edwards, William Edwards, David B. Evans, Edward J. Evans, Trevor N. Evans, George Gale, Thomas Hennessey, Daniel Hurley, David Jones, John Jones, Samuel L. Jones, Albert King, Bernard Lanigan, John C. Monk, Charles Morgan, Richard L. Morris, Francis Owens, William E. Parry, David E. Price, Robert Rees, William Rees, James W. Roberts, Albert J. Shepherd, G. Hopkin Thomas, Fred J. Trump, Morgan Walters, Samuel Walters, Albert S. White, William G. Williams. After the names, a quotation from Bunyan's *The Pilgrim's Progress* - '*Then Said He... My Sword I Give To Him That Shall Succeed Me... My Marks And Scars I Carry With Me To Be A Witness For Me That I Have Fought*

His Battles Who Will Now Be My Rewarder... So He Passed Over And All The Trumpets Sounded For Him On The Other Side' - then in Welsh - *Mewn Anghof Ni Chant Fod.*

St David's Church

The white and grey marble memorial on the north wall at St David's records the deaths of Henry Valentine Trump, JP and manager of the Rhymney Iron Works, and his wife, Mary Trump. Also commemorated is the second son of the above -

> *Lt. Col. Fred J. Trump, D.S.O. Croix De Guerre, 6th South Staffs Regt. Major 1st Monmouthshire Regt., Killed In France, Dec. 2nd 1917, Aged 45 Years. Buried At Sailly Labourse. His Duty Nobly Done.*

Fred Trump joined the 1st Monmouthshire Regiment in 1900 and served with the volunteers in South Africa. In the First World War he was given command of the 1/6th South Staffordshire Regiment in France and was awarded the Distinguished Service Order in January, 1917.

In memory of their son, a local couple from 13 Church Street, Rhymney, presented to the church a brass missal stand with the inscription -

> *Presented To St. David's Church, Rhymney, By Mr. & Mrs. Rees King. To The Glory Of God And In Loving Memory Of Their Son, Albert King, 2nd Lieut., Mons. Who Fell In Action In France On The 31st May 1917. 'Greater Love Hath No Man.'*

Albert King joined the 2nd Monmouthshire Regiment and was killed, aged twenty-four, on 31 May, 1917. It was during an attack on a position known as 'Infantry Hill,' in the Arras sector, records the Battalion's records, that 'C' Company went forward under fire and in knee-deep mud. Prior to this the men had spent the night under the enemy's 'accurate artillery and machine-gun fire.' Second-Lieutenant Albert King, who prior to the war was a ministerial student, was one of twenty-five men to be killed or wounded.

There are two First World War soldiers buried in the churchyard. Private J. Barter, Lancashire Fusiliers, who was the son of William and Annie Barter, died aged twenty-one, on 13 March, 1920 having been gassed in France, and Sapper D.H. Powell, Royal Engineers, who died 17 February, 1918.

RISCA

The memorial cross in St Mary Street, Risca bears the inscription -

> *The Great War 1914-1919 - In Honoured Memory Of Those Who Fell And Those Who Served.* Also, in both Welsh and English - *At The Going Down Of The Sun And In The Morning, We Will Remember Them.*

Words commemorating those of the Second World War follow.

Two memorial plaques, one to the Risca coal miners who served in the First World War, and another put up by the British Nuclear Tests Veterans Association, are located on the wall to the rear of the memorial. Erected by the Risca Collieries Workmen, the former has the following inscription -

Risca Collieries memorial.
Risca memorial.

*To The Sacred And Everlasting Memory Of The Men Who Left The Risca Collieries
And District To Serve Their King And Country In The Great War 1914-1919.
'Greater Love Hath No Man Than This. That A Man Lay Down His Life For You'.*

Worked in fine white marble, the inscription appears on an oval flanked by angels,
decorated with roses, thistles, shamrocks and daffodils, and surmounted by a Naval
Crown upon a crossed rifle and sword.

Bethany Baptist Church

In the vestibule of the church in Tredegar Street, a fine memorial commemorates
those who were killed in the Great War. Constructed of black marble, the central of
three white panels bears the inscription -

*This Memorial Is Erected To The Memory Of Those Connected With This Church Who
Left All That Was Dear To Them Endured Hardship, Faced Danger, And Finally
Passed Out Of Sight Of Men, By The Path Of Duty, And Self-Sacrifice, Giving Up
Their Lives That Others Might Live In Freedom.*

The panel on the left side records the following names: Lyndon Booth, George
Baker, A.L. Coulson, Wm. Dobson, Oswald Davies, Ernest Dark, Fred. Ellis, John
Griffith, Ira Hopkins, Thomas Hall, Anthony Hiley, Ralph Jones, Jarvis James, Noah
James, Albert Jenkins, James Knight, Bert Knight, and on the right-hand panel - Cy
Mayberry, Wm. Morgan, Alfred Morgan, Edgar Morris, W.L. Parkins, Willie
Prothero, Bernard Rallinson, Garfield Richards, George Richards, Fred. Robinson,

Bethany Baptist Church memorial, Risca.

George Robins, Willie Winstone, Ernest Welch, Herbert Watts, Rex Wilde, Raymond Wilcox. Inscribed below the panels is - *I Have Fought A Good Fight* - from *II Timothy*, Chapter 4.

Moriah Baptist Church
There are seventeen names recorded on the south wall of the Moriah Baptist Church in Tredegar Street. Superbly sculpted by Davies of Risca, the marble memorial has the inscription - *Moriah Baptist Church And Sunday School. The Great War 1914-1918*. After the names - *Greater Love Hath No Man Than This. That A Man Lay Down His Life For His Friends.*

The first name recorded is that of Lieutenant Ewart Gladstone Salathiel, South Wales Borderers, who was mortally wounded at Mametz Wood in France, and subsequently buried in Rogerstone (see Bethesda Baptist Church). Next comes Sergeant J. Booth, who served with the Welsh Guards; Sergeant A.J. Cook, South Wales Borderers; Corporal D.G. Thomas, who served with the Welsh Regiment and was awarded the Military Medal; Lance-Corporals C. Downs and S. Evans, both of the South Wales Borderers; Signaller J. Banfield, Royal Naval Volunteer Reserve; Private E. Hart, Royal Field Artillery; Private H.G. Haines, Royal Welsh Fusiliers; Private H.J. Hatherall, South Wales Borderers; Private A.L. James, Royal Fusiliers; Private J. Morgan, Rifle Brigade; Gunner C. Powell, Royal Field Artillery; Private W.H. Roberts and Driver H. Tutton, both of the Royal Engineers, and Private P.E. Watts, South Wales Borderers. The name of Private C. Gibbs, who served with the King's (Liverpool Regiment) has been added at a later date.

Moriah Baptist Church memorial, Risca.

Risca Male Choir Headquarters

The white marble plaque belonging to the former Trinity Methodist Church, St Mary's Street, Risca, is at time of writing (October, 1999) held in store at the Risca Male Choir headquarters, also in S. Mary's Street. The inscription reads -

> *Erected By The Congregation Of This Church - To The Glory Of God And In Proud Memory Of - (three names follow) - Who Made The Supreme Sacrifice In The Great War 1918-1919. 'Also In Grateful Acknowledgement For The Lives Of Those Who Were Spared To Us'.*

The three soldiers commemorated are: Gunner Albert Stanley Williams, of the Royal Field Artillery, who died in France on 22 November, 1918, and two members of the 10th (1st Gwent) Battalion, South Wales Borderers. Private Bert Wheeler who was one of seven men killed when the enemy exploded a mine under the Battalion's trenches at Givenchy on 3 April, 1916, and Lance-Corporal Alfred Jones who lost his life during the 1918 operations on the Somme and the capture on 30-31 August of Lesboeufs.

Trinity Methodist Church is now represented by the Danygraig Church. A new building at the corner of Danygraig Road and Tredegar Street. A memorial garden adjacent to the church is in the process of being constructed and there are plans to erect the old Trinity Methodist Church memorials (there is a similar marble tablet for the Second World War) in the area.

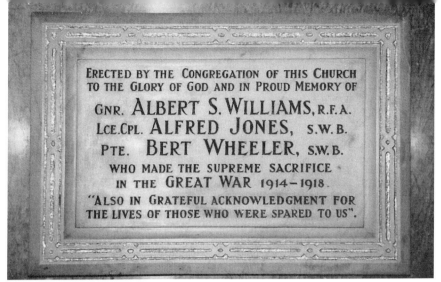

Trinity Methodist Church memorial, Risca.

Risca Old Cemetery

The Commonwealth War Graves Commission cemetery register for Monmouthshire includes two graves (Nicholas and Owen) recorded under the heading - 'Risca Old Cemetery (Church Ground)'. These will be found within Risca Old Cemetery - through the main gate and immediately to the left. This is now known as 'A' Section. Among those soldiers killed and buried overseas, but commemorated within the cemetery on family headstones are - Lieutenant Wilfred Onions (son of the well known miners' leader and Member of Parliament - Alfred Onions), killed near Ypres on 25 April, 1915, and Sergeant John Booth of the Welsh Guards who lost his life in Belgium on 4 September, 1917. His bronze death-plaque, issued to next of kin, has

been set into the stone work of a family grave. The cemetery is located on Cromwell Street (B4591), Risca and includes twenty-two war graves, many of which have Commonwealth War Graves Commission headstones made from Welsh slate.

Bombardier G.E. Baker, 412th Howitzer Battery, Royal Field Artillery, died, aged thirty-six, 22 December, 1918.

Corporal Charles Richard Darby, 21st Company, Royal Defence Corps, died 6 January, 1919.

Private W.E. Dart, South Wales Borderers, born Torquay, Devon, died 3 October, 1919 having transferred to the Labour Corps.

Cook M. Davies, Queen Mary's Army Auxiliary Corps, died 13 February, 1919.

Private William Dobson, 11th Battalion, South Wales Borderers, born Northumberland, lived with his parents, Thomas and Sarah Ann Dobson, at 30 Park Place, Pontymister. He was wounded in France and subsequently died at home, aged twenty-one, on 17 May, 1916.

Headstone in Risca Old Cemetery made from Welsh slate.

Private Edwin Everson, 3rd Battalion, Welsh Regiment, resided in Risca, died, aged twenty-seven, at Redcar Military Hospital and occupies a family grave with his wife and three children - Iris, Eileen and Marie.

Gunner William Hatton, Royal Field Artillery, son of William and Catherine Hatton of 27 William Street, Cwmfelinfach, died, aged twenty-four, of pneumonia 5 May, 1917.

Private H.G. Haynes, 14th Battalion, Royal Welsh Fusiliers, died 18 September, 1918.

Sergeant Frank Hemmings, 11th Battalion, South Wales Borderers, son of Mr and Mrs Joseph Hemmings - his headstone recording that he was 'Late of the Albert Hotel, Risca.' Frank Hemmings served in France, where he was wounded, and subsequently died at home, aged forty-three, on 2 December, 1916. He is buried with his wife, Emily, who died in 1957.

Driver John Jones, Royal Field Artillery, born Pontymister. He was a member of the 4th (Welsh) Brigade, RFA (Territorial Force) at Newport and went with the Brigade to Bedford, where he died in hospital, aged eighteen, on 12 August, 1915.

Private William Rees Lott, Royal Army Service Corps, died, aged twenty, 14 October, 1918. He lived in Abertillery, his parents - Joseph and Annie Lott residing at 23 Mount Pleasant Terrace, Pontywaun.

Lance-Corporal Alfred Morgan, 3rd Battalion, Royal Welsh Fusiliers (formally Royal Garrison Artillery), died from pneumonia 1 January, 1916. He was thirty-two and the son of James and Sarah Jane Morgan of 12 Wesley Place, Risca. Alfred Morgan is buried with his mother and father.

Private Trevor Nicholas, Royal Army Medical Corps, died 30 June, 1916, born Newport and enlisted into the army in Taunton, Somerset.

Gunner W.C. Ogborne, Royal Field Artillery, died 4 December, 1918 having transferred to 838th Area Employment Company, Labour Corps.

Private Jonathan Owen, 1st Battalion, Grenadier Guards, born Pontypool, died, aged thirty-seven, 25 March, 1915.

Sergeant George Parsons, 3rd Battalion, South Wales Borderers, died at Seaforth Military Hospital, Liverpool on 19 February, 1919. He was twenty-five and occupies a family grave with his wife Sarah Jane, and daughter Irene.

Stoker 1st Class John Rose, Royal Navy, of HMS *Vivid*, died, aged twenty-four, 2 April, 1918.

Private W. Henry Smith, Royal Army Medical Corps, died, aged thirty-one, 1 May, 1918.

Sergeant William George Venn, 9th Battalion, Welsh Regiment, won the Military Medal in France, returned home, having been gassed, and died 6 February, 1920. He was twenty-six and married to Ethel May Venn of 'Glen View' 4 Cobden Place, Crosskeys. William Venn is buried in a family grave.

Company Quartermaster Sergeant Edward James Walker, 3rd Australian Pioneers, son of Edward and Lily Walker and husband of D.F. Walker of 'Kalimma' Batswater Road, Wantirma Victoria, Australia. He died on 4 March, 1917, aged twenty-seven, - his headstone bearing the inscription - *Erected By The Sgts. Of Pnr. Tng. Bat. A.I.F.*

Lance-Corporal Joseph Wallace, 5th Battalion, South Wales Borderers, lived at Pontymister, wounded in France, died in hospital at Cambridge on 10 November, 1916, aged forty-two.

Private William James Winstone, 7th Battalion, Royal Fusiliers, son of William and Mary Ann Winstone of 15 Danygraig Cottages, Risca, died, aged twenty, 14 October, 1917.

St Mary's Parish Church

The eight names of those members of St Mary's who fell in the Great War are recorded on a brass shield located on the north wall of the nave - *To The Glory Of God And In Memory Of* - William C. Bridge, Lance-Corporal Royal Welsh Fusiliers; Cyril J. Clissold, Private King's Liverpool Regiment; Frank Hemmings, Sergeant South Wales Borderers; Frederick W. Leonard, Private, Royal Field Artillery; Albert Mellish, Private South Wales Borderers; Charles Prout, Sergeant South Wales Borderers; Clarence H. Pritchard, 9th Welsh Regiment; Herbert Watkins, Private South Wales Borderers. The memorial also includes the words -

With Armour Buckled On And Flags Unfurled The Heights Of Death They Trod. Translated From The Warfare Of The World Into The Peace Of God.

ROGERSTONE

Bethesda Baptist Church Christian Centre

Dating from 1742, the recently re-built Bethesda Church in Cefn Road, Rogerstone commemorates seventeen names on a white marble plaque set into a stone wall to the left of the church entrance. The memorial is inscribed -

To The Glory Of God And In Honoured Memory Of The Members And Adherents Of This Church Who Gave Their Lives For Freedom And Humanity In The Great War 1914-1918.

The names appear within a laurel wreath surmounted by a crown: Jim Bailey, David Robert Davies, Ernest Dorkings, William Henry Evans, Alfred Harding, William Hopkins, Harry Stafford John, Sidney St. Clare King, Samuel Llewelyn, Hugh Morgan, Emlyn Meredith Powell, Edwin Roberts, Fred Robinson, Edward Rowlands, Albert Augustine Sullivan, Frederick T. Theobald, Ivor Charles Woolcock. Below the wreath are the words - *Of 'Deathless' Memory.*

Within the churchyard a family grave commemorates Private William Morgan who was killed, aged thirty-six, on 21 December, 1916 while serving with 1st Battalion, South Wales Borderers in trenches near Factory Corner on the Somme. The churchyard also contains two war graves. Private Charles Cooling, 8th Battalion, South Wales Borderers who was married to Margaret Cooling and lived at 2 Hadley Street, Rogerstone. He died, aged thirty-one, on 22 February, 1919, and Second-Lieutenant Ewart Gladstone Salathiel, 11th Battalion, South Wales Borderers, the second son of

Bethesda Baptist Church memorial, Rogerstone.

Illuminated Roll of Honour, Rogerstone Library.

Philip and Justina Salathiel of Cwm-y-Nant, Pontymister. He died, aged twenty-seven, on 17 July, 1916 at The Empire Hospital, Vincent Square, Westminster, London from wounds received during the 7 July attack on Mametz Wood. The 11th Borderers attacked the wood from Cliff Trench and suffered high casualties from German machine guns located in Sabot and Flatiron Copses. Lieutenant Salathiel is buried in a family grave.

Rogerstone Library

An illuminated Roll of Honour above the fireplace of the library in Tregwilym Road records fifty-five names without rank or regiment: James Arkingstall, Jim Bailey, A. Beeston, W.R. Blackwell, F.W. Buttle, G.F. Champion, A.H. Collins, Tim Connors, Stanley Court, C.G. Cooling, Charles Cross, Noed T. Daniel, Algernon Daniel, E. Darking, R.E. Davies, A.R. Davies, John Dawson, W.J. Deakin, A. Dillon, F. Evans, W.H. Evans, John Fletcher, Chris Griffiths, Alfred Harding, Alfred Haycock, W. Hopkins, H.S. John, F.W. Jones, Percy Jones, Sydney St Clair King, Sam Llewellyn, John Lloyd, Sydney Long, J.J. Millwater, Fred Morgan, Hugh Morgan, E.S. Parrish, Emlyn M. Powell, Leonard Price, T.C. Rees, F.B. Ridout, Edwin Roberts, E. Rowlands, H. Smithers, S.E. Smith, Albert Sockett, A.A. Sullivan, F.T. Theobold, E.R. Turner, L.M. Whitney, C.J. Wilkie, I. Williams, W. Williams, H. Woolrich and I.C. Woolcock.

The dedication reads -

In Affectionate Remembrance Of The Members Of This District Who Bravely Made The Supreme Sacrifice In The Great War 1914-1919 For Right - For King And Country. This Memorial Is Erected By The Parishioners In Appreciation Of Services Rendered Which Protected Their Homes From Invasion By A Foreign Foe.

In full colour, the Roll includes numerous flags, the Royal Arms, and shields representing Russia, Belgium, France, Japan, South Africa, New Zealand, Egypt, Canada, India and Australia. The work is signed Will. J. Brocla, Illuminator, Maes-Y-Coed, Four Oaks, Bettws. 1934. The Roll is covered by a wood panel which is removed each November for the Remembrance Day Parade. A smaller version, however, can be seen on the wall to the right.

To the left of the fireplace a more recent memorial, this time in the form of a copper plaque, lists the same fifty-five names along with those who were killed in the Second World War. The inscription on this occasion reads - *In Honoured Memory Of Those Who Gave Their Lives In The Two World Wars.* The memorial was dedicated by the Revd Canon Ivor L. Phillips, BSC, MC, HCF, unveiled by Doctor George Hull, JP on 15 October, 1961, and ends with the words - *We Will Remember Them.* Close by a small wooded plaque records the death in Northern Ireland (April, 1972) of Corporal G.C. Bristow.

St John Baptist's Church

The church is located in St John's Crescent, off Cefn Road, Rogerstone. Commemorated on the headstone of a family grave is the name of Gunner Noel Thomas Daniel who was killed in France on 25 April, 1918. He was aged twenty-four and served with the Royal Artillery. The churchyard contains the graves of three First World War servicemen. Lance-Corporal George Dabbs, 7th Battalion, South Wales Borderers, who lived at 8 Nettlefold Terrace, Rogerstone. He died, aged twenty-seven, on 28 September, 1919. Private Joseph Davies served with the Royal Defence Corps. He lived at 17 Charles Street, Rogerstone, and died, aged forty-eight, on 28 November, 1920. Private John Millwater, served first with the 4th Battalion, Monmouthshire Regiment, then the Labour Corps. He died, aged twenty-nine, on 31 October, 1918.

ROGIET

St Mary's Parish Church

A marble tablet on the south wall of the nave records the names and regiments of six men from the area who died. In the shape of a scroll, the memorial bears the inscription -

To The Glory Of God And In Proud And Unfailing Memory Of The Men, Who From This Place, Went Out At The Call Of Duty, And Laid Down Their Lives For King And Country, In The Great War 1914-1919. I Have Fought A Good Fight, I Have Finished My Course; Henceforth There Is Laid Up For Me A Crown Of Righteousness.

The six men commemorated are: Lance-Corporal Valentine Cyril Harold Carter, who enlisted into the army at Bristol and served with the local battalion there, the 12th Gloucestershire Regiment. He was killed on the Somme and during the fighting around Longueval on 30 July, 1916. George Cooper of the 2nd Sherwood Foresters also died in France, while George Benjamin Anstey, Royal Gloucestershire Hussars, was taken prisoner in Palestine and subsequently died in Turkey. The remaining three men all served with the South Wales Borderers - John Cox and

St Mary's Parish Church, Rogiet memorial.

Rumney Memorial Hall.

William John Jenner, both with the 6th Battalion, the latter being killed on the Somme in October, 1916 during the attack on Stuff Redoubt, and William Ward. He was one of some three hundred and seventy-two casualties from the 2nd SWB, sustained during their attack at Beaumont-Hamel on 1 July, 1916.

RUMNEY

Rumney Memorial Hall

The hall in Wentloog Road, Rumney has two foundation stones, both dated 22 September, 1923, and above the entrance the words -

Memorial Hall To Commemorate The Men Of This Parish Who Fought In The Great War And Those Who Made The Supreme Sacrifice.

The dates - *1914* - and - *1918* are carved into shields either side of the inscription. In the small forecourt of the building, a memorial made from Portland stone has, set into the stonework, a series of black marble tablets recording the names, without rank or regiment, of those who fell in both world wars. Those for the First World War appear under the heading - Remembrance - and are as follows:

Parish memorial, St Augustine's Parish Church, Rumney.

T. Abraham, T. Bailey, H.F. Beavan, C. Bradshaw, F. Carpenter, W. Charles, S. Comer, J. Comer, J.J. Cubitt, J. Dunford, J. Dunn, W. Gerrish, J.H. Giles, F. Giles, D. Gill, W. Harris, F. Howells, H. Howells, A. Jefferies, C. Jones, J. Jordan, W. Lewis, W. Mahoney, F.A. Matthysens, D.L. Morgan, J.R. Morgan, C.C. Peacock, C. Pearson, R. Penny, R. Radcliffe, W. Thomas, J.H. Thompson, H. Tinkling, E. Watts and A.D. Webber.

St Augustine's Parish Church

On the north wall of the church a bronze tablet has the inscription - *In Memory Of The Men Of This Parish Of Rumney Who Gave Their Lives For Their Faith And The Freedom Of Others 1914-1918.* This is followed by thirty-two names: T. Abraham, H.E. Beavan, C. Bradshaw, J.J. Cubitt, S. Comer, W. Charles, J.J. Dunford, E. Dunn, F. Giles, J.H. Giles, D. Gill, W. Gerrish, F. Howells, H. Howells, W. Harris, J. Jordan, C. Jones, A.C. Jefferies, W. Lewis, F.A. Matthyssens, W. Mahoney, J.R. Morgan, D.L. Morgan, R. Penny, G. Peacock, C.R. Pearson, R. Ratcliffe, J.H. Thompson, H. Tinklin, W. Thomas, A. Webber, E. Watts - then a list of those who fell in 1939-1945. The inscription continues - *The East Window In This Church Is The Memorial Given By Those In The Parish Who Remember And Care.* D.L. Morgan was a change ringer at St Augustine's.

The churchyard contains the graves of five men from the First World War:

Private F. Carpenter, South Wales Borderers. He was the son of George and Tryphena Carpenter of Pwll Mawr Cottages, Rumney and died, aged thirty-two, on 13 October, 1920.

Gunner William Thomas Gerrish, 4th Reserve Brigade, Royal Field Artillery, died on 12 December, 1918. He was aged twenty-six and the son of William Gerrish.

Private John Harry Giles, 3rd Battalion, South Wales Borderers, was the son of Benjamin and Mary Jane Giles. He died, aged forty-two, on 10 September, 1919.

Sergeant C. Pearson, 12th Battalion, Cheshire Regiment, was born in Newport and the son of Charles and Mary Pearson. He transferred from the Cheshire Regiment and was attached to Western Command Labour Centre, Labour Corps, when he died, aged twenty-three, on 28 November, 1918.

Private W. Thomas, 3rd Battalion, South Wales Borderers, died on 4 November, 1918 having transferred to 570th Agricultural Company, Labour Corps.

ST ARVAN'S

Parish Church

A brass plaque mounted on wood at the west end of St Arvan's Parish Church has the inscription - *In Memory Of The Following Who Gave Their Lives For King And Country During The Great War 1914-1919.*

There are fifteen names recorded: Lieutenant Hubert Ray Corfield, who was killed in Palestine while serving with 266th Brigade, Royal Field Artillery; Lieutenant Gordon William Bassett Price, of the 12th South Wales Borderers, killed 23 November, 1917; Lieutenant C.H. Smith, who won the Military Cross; Lance-Corporal R. Reece; Seaman W. Jeffries; Privates F. Butt, M.H. Fisher, W.G. Harris, W.H. Howell, P.H. Huntley, A.C. Knight, H. Knight, E.E. Stephens and G.F. Wilband; Gunner J. Saunders. The name of one member of the parish who was killed during the Second World War has been added.

Also on the west wall, a framed hand-written list records the names of those from the parish who served in the Great War. Headed with the words - *For King And Country* - the list has eighty-two names with regiments, and ends with - *Brethren, Pray For Us.* The fifteen men who were killed are not shown.

The churchyard at St Arvan's contains one war grave, that of Flight-Sergeant William James Pritchard of the Royal Air Force, who died, aged thirty-two, on 27 May, 1919.

St Arvan's Parish Church memorial.

ST BRIDE'S NETHERWENT

St Bridget's Church

There are two war graves within the churchyard: Private James Henry Harris, 1st Battalion, South Wales Borderers, was married to Alice Maud Harris of 'Hillside' St Bride's. He died, aged thirty-two, on 14 October, 1916. Rifleman Wilfred Harris, 1st Battalion, Monmouthshire Regiment, was the son of Henry and Margaret Harris of Carron Hill, St Bride's. He was eighteen when he died of pneumonia on 25 March, 1917.

ST MELLONS

Situated at the junction of Newport Road and Chapel Row, the village memorial has the names of various theatres of war cut into the upper stonework - *France - Italy - Gallipoli - Salonica - Mesopotamia - Palestine - E. Africa - W. Africa.* Below this a cast-iron tablet is inscribed - *The Tribute Of St Mellons To Her Gallant Sons Who Were Faithful Unto Death In The Great War 1914-1918. They Rest In Peace.* Twenty-three names, without rank or regiment, follow: William Aston, Archibald Brown, Donald L. Campbell, George Chappell, Joseph H. Chappell, George Chudleigh, Spencer G. David, Alfred W. Harrison, Walter R. Hughes, William Ireland, Richard H. Kember, Daniel Lewis, Benjamin Lloyd, Ernest Locke, Herbert J. Lodwick, Francis A. Matthyssens, Edward Mitchell, Sydney C. Pearce, Sidney Pitman, Frederick Soares, Alfred Thomas, Ivor Walwyn, Alfred Williams.

Caersalem Baptist Chapel

On the wall of the vestry, an illuminated and framed Roll Of Honour has the words - *European War 1914-1918. In Affectionate And Ever Grateful Remembrance Of The Following Members And Adherents Of This Church.* Two names follow: that of Edward Mitchell, recorded as having been killed in action, October, 1914, and William Henry Ireland, who - 'died in active service, December 5th, 1918.' Edward Mitchell served with the 2nd Battalion, Welsh Regiment and was killed during the fighting at Gheluvelt on 29-31 October, 1914. '*Greater Love Hath No Man Than This*' follows, then a further twenty-three names: William Samuel Stradling, Federick Collings Morgan, William Henry Bartlett, Edward Emerson Davies, MC, Reginald M. Maunder, Albert John Scrivens, Albert Caple, Edward Ireland, William Jones, Joseph Thomas Powell, Philip Ireland, George Henry Scrivens, Alfred Jones, John Jones, William Jones, Edward Thomas Jones, Albert Ireland, Kenneth Tovey, George P. Walkey, Herbert T. Roberts, Clifford Henry Mortimore, Tom Mitchell, William Mitchell. These were the men from the church who served. The memorial is headed with the intertwined letter - *CBC* - within a wreath, and below this the words - *Our Roll Of Honour* on a scroll.

Parish Church

One of the windows on the north wall of the church in Tyr Winch Road gives thanks for the return of two officers. The inscription reads,

Window Erected By Major W. Cope From Funds Provided For This Purpose By His

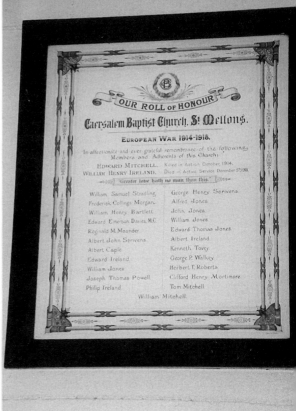

St Mellons memorial.

Roll of Honour, Caersalem Baptist Chapel, St Mellons.

Mother The Late Margaret Cope Of Quarry Hill In This Parish As A Thanks Offering To Almighty God For His Great Mercy In Sparing The Lives Of Captains Richard Cope Wilson And Wilfred Hawthorne Wilson Throughout The Great War Aug. 1914-November, 1918.

Major William Cope (later 1st Baron of St Mellons) served in the Glamorgan Yeomanry, as did the two officers mentioned.

On the south side of the church an officer of the New Zealand forces is commemorated on a small brass plaque -

In Ever Proud And Loving Memory Of Richard Henry Kember. Lieut. 13th Canterbury Infantry Battalion New Zealand Regiment Who Fell In Action On The Somme 20th September, 1916. Age 22.

Richard Kember won the Military Medal before gaining his commission. He has no known grave, his name being commemorated on the New Zealand Memorial at Caterpillar Valley.

There are two First World War soldiers buried in the churchyard: Private Alfred William Harrison, 5th (Reserve) Battalion, Grenadier Guards, was the son of W.H. and Annie Harrison of Church Lodge, St Mellons. He died, aged nineteen, on 30 April, 1916, and Private A. Thomas of the Royal Army Service Corps. He was the son of Hannah Thomas and died, aged thirty-four, on 7 April, 1918.

SHIRENEWTON

St Thomas a' Becket Church

On the south wall of the nave, an illuminated roll headed - *Shirenewton Roll Of Honour* - records the names of those who were killed: Private Harry Bailey, Corporal Harold Blackwell, Private William Cotterel, Driver George Evans, Boatswain George Marsh, Private Tom March, Private William Marsh, Sergeant William Miles, Lance-Sergeant Harry Morgan, Private Tom Packer, Private Fred Stevens, Private Ronald Wheeler and Private Aubery Whitton.

The same thirteen men are also commemorated on a stone seat outside the church -

> *The Clock In Church Tower And This Tablet Were Erected In Memory Of The Men Of This Parish Who Fought And Fell In The Great War 1914-1918.*

On this occasion, however, William March is shown as Trooper William March. Privates Packer and Bailey have the rank of lance-corporal, and Private Wheeler a lance-sergeant, the latter having been awarded the Military Medal. Those who were killed during the Second World War have been added to the memorial seat. The list includes Captain Ian O. Liddell who was awarded the Victoria Cross.

SWFFRYD

A memorial to those from the Swffryd area who were killed in both world wars has been erected in recent years at the community centre in Walters Road. Set into stonework taken from a dismantled church at Aberbeeg, a brass plated bears the simple inscription - *In Tribute To Our Heroic Dead.*

TRETHOMAS

The stone memorial at the junction of Newport Road and Navigation Street has a metal plate attached with the inscription -

> *To The Gallant Men And Women Of Trethomas Who Died For Our Freedom In The Two World Wars. We Will Remember Them.*

The names and ranks of ten men from the First World War: Company Sergeant Major W. Mitchener (see also Bedwas memorial), Privates W.G. Geeves, D.E. Cornish, D. Nelms, D. Holmes, W. Prebble, W. Vaughan, T. Richards, W. Reynolds and T. Shute, are recorded along with those who fell in 1939-1945.

TRINANT

Horeb Congregational Church

The stone memorial in the churchyard has the following inscription - *In Remembrance Of Our Fallen Heroes.* The names and ages of eight men follow: David Bessant of the 1st South Wales Borderers, who was twenty-five when he was killed at Hill 60 in Belgium; William Arthur Lloyd, aged twenty-two; Joseph Henry

Swffryd memorial.

Memorial seat, St Thomas a' Becket Church, Shirenewton.

Trethomas memorial.

Horeb Congregational Church memorial, Trinant.

Edwards, twenty-one; George Morris, who was awarded the Military Medal and was twenty-four when he died; Wilfred Hale, aged twenty; thirty-five year old George Shearn of the 2nd Battalion, South Wales Borderers, buried at sea during the Gallipoli Campaign; Herbert George Keiling, twenty-two and John Henry Williams who was twenty-nine. Below the names -

> *Greater Love Hath No Man Than This, That He Lay Down His Life For His Friends*
> - followed by - *Erected By Their Friends Of Trinant To The Above, Who Paid The Supreme Sacrifice In The Great European War. 1914-1919. 'Pro Patria'.*

At the foot of the memorial a tablet in the shape of an open book records the names of those who fell during the Second World War.

USK

St Francis Xavier And St David Lewis Catholic Church

A local officer is commemorated on the north wall of the church. Engraved on a brass plaque -

> *A New Organ Was Presented To This Church In The Year 1916, And Dedicated To The Memory Of Iltyd Edwin Maitland Watkins, LLB, BACantab. Captain 2nd Monmouthshire Regiment, T.F. Who Gave His Life To God For His Country. Born At Usk On The Feast Of The Annunciation 1890. Baptised, Made His First Communion And Received The Sacrament Of Confirmation In This Church. Joined The Monmouthshire Regiment On His Nineteenth Birthday And The British Forces In France On The Feast Of Purification 1915. Killed In Action Near Ypres On The 7th May, 1915. R.I.P. 'Blessed Are The Clean Of Heart For They Shall See God'.*

In a letter written to Iltyd's father, Usk solicitor, John Maitland Watkins, Colonel E.B. Cuthbertson (Commanding Officer, 2nd Monmouthshire Regiment) wrote - 'He was killed on the morning of the 7th just at the end of the German attack, and his death was instantaneous and painless. Of his qualities as a soldier and a gentleman, I cannot speak too highly: cheerful, gallant and unselfish, he died as he would have chosen to die, with his face to the enemy and in the middle of the men whom he loved and commanded so well. We buried him on the battlefield.'

St Mary's Priory Church

A memorial brass plaque inscribed -

> *To The Glory Of God And In Grateful Memory Of The Men Of This Parish Who Fell In The Great War - 'This Tablet Was Placed Here By The Women Of Usk'.*

is located on the north wall of the church. There are forty-one names, each with rank and regiment, recorded in three columns:

1st column: Lieutenant-Colonel A.J.H. Bowen, DSO, who at the time of his death commanded the 2nd Battalion, Monmouthshire Regiment. Colonel Bowing lived in Usk and was killed in action on 2 March, 1917 near Sailly-Saillishel in France; Lance-Corporal S. Colwell, Royal Welsh Fusiliers; Private G.W. Cook, 2nd Monmouthshire Regiment; Private F.A. Cook, 9th Royal Welsh Fusiliers; Private T. Day, East Yorkshire Regiment; Lieutenant D.B. Davies, Royal Flying Corps; Private

J. Evans, South Wales Borderers; Private L.R. Garside, Royal Fusiliers; Private F.B. George, Army Service Corps; Sapper P. George, Royal Engineers; Private A. Griffiths, South Wales Borderers; Sapper G.A.B. Griffiths, Royal Engineers; Gunner E. Harris, Royal Field Artillery; Trooper R.R. Haggett, Canadian Mounted Rifles.

2nd column: Second-Lieutenant E.B. Haynes, Royal Flying Corps; Trooper M. Jenkins, 6th Dragoon Guards; Private A.W.S. Jones, South Wales Borderers; Sergeant J. Jones, 2nd Monmouthshire Regiment; Private E.G. Jones, Welsh Guards; Private C.E.V. Knight, 2nd South Wales Borderers; Driver W. Lewis, Army Service Corps; Private J.L. Meredith, Coldstream Guards; F. Mitchell, Royal Naval Volunteer Reserve; Private C. Mitchell, 10th Manchester Regiment; Private E. Mitchell, 2nd Monmouthshire Regiment; Second-Lieutenant E. Morgan, South Wales Borderers (awarded the Military Cross); Private W.H. Price, South Wales Borderers.

3rd column: A.J.L. Price, Royal Naval Volunteer Reserve; Sergeant S. Price, Australian Imperial Forces; Corporal H.C.S. Rees, 2nd Monmouthshire Regiment; Private W.H. Roberts, Royal Flying Corps; Private J. Stickler, South Wales Borderers; Private A. Smith, South

Usk memorial, St Mary's Priory Church.

Wales Borderers; Rifleman B.W.G. Thomas, Rifle Brigade; Private J.W.A. Turner, 10th London Regiment; Captain I.E.M. Watkins, 2nd Monmouthshire Regiment; Private R. Watkins, Machine Gun Corps; Corporal E. Weare, 12th South Wales Borderers; Private G. Williams, South Wales Borderers; Private T. Williams, Royal Welsh Fusiliers; Private L.R. Window, Machine Gun Corps.

The churchyard contains the town war memorial. A cross inscribed - *To The Glory Of God And The Honoured Memory Of The Men Of Usk Who Died In The Great Wars. R.I.P.* The last word (originally 'War') was amended to 'Wars' after 1945 and at the same time the twelve names of those who fell in the Second World War were added. There are four First World War panels inscribed with the following names: A.J.H. Bowen, W. Carey, S. Colwell, W.G. Cook, F.A. Cook, Mc. Crichton, D.B. Davies, G. Davies, T. Day, G.E.M. De La Pasture, F.A. Dowding, J. Evans, L.R. Garside, W. George, P. George, A. Griffiths, G. Griffiths, R.R. Haggett, E. Harrhy, E. Harris, E.B. Haynes, M. Jenkins, T. Johns, J. Jones, A.W.S. Jones, E.S. Jones, G.E.V. Knight,

W. Lewis, J.L. Meredith, E.J. Mitchell, F.J. Mitchell, G. Mitchell, E. Morgan, W. Pardoe, T. Parry, W.H. Price, L. Price, S.P. Rice, G.S. Rees, W.H. Roberts, E. Saunders, A. Smith, H.J. Stickler, B.W.G. Thomas, J.W.A. Turner, I.E.M. Watkins, R. Watkins, E. Weare, T. Williams, G. Williams, L.R. Window.

The churchyard also contains the graves of three First World War soldiers and one airman: Rev. D.H. Griffiths, Chaplain to the Forces, 4th Class who died 15 December, 1915; Second-Lieutenant E.B. Haynes, No. 1 (S) Aircraft Repair Depot, Royal Air Force. He died, aged forty-five, on 14 November, 1918; Private F. Lewis, Royal Army Medical Corps, who died 4 June, 1921, and Private Ernest Weare of the 12th Battalion, South Wales Borderers. Ernest Weare resided in Griffithstown and ran his own hairdressing and tobacconist business prior to the war. He became the battalion barber and died from pneumonia on 20 September, 1915, aged twenty-eight, at the Cottage Hospital, Whitchurch, Shropshire. His body was brought to Usk by his parents who ran the *White Lion* there.

WAINFELIN

Church of St John The Divine

On the south wall of the chancel a large brass tablet commemorates a young officer of the area's local Territorial Force battalion -

To The Glory Of God And In Affectionate Remembrance Of John Edward Paton - Sec. Lieutenant 2nd Battalion Monmouthshire Regiment, Of Waun Wern In This Parish; Who Was Killed In Action At Le Bizet, Flanders, Whilst Fighting For His King And Country, December 31st 1914 - Aged 19 Years; And Was Mentioned By Field Marshal Sir John D.P. French In His Dispatch Of January 14th 1915 For Gallant And Distinguished Service In The Field. This Tablet Is Erected By Friends Who Knew And Loved Him. Greater Love Hath No Man Than This That A Man Lay Down His Life For His Friends.

The plaque has the Regimental Crest of the 2nd Monmouthshires engraved into the top left-hand corner. The son of another member of the Battalion, John Paton was one of the first Territorial Force officers to lose his life in the Great War. Well liked by all those who served with him, the following tribute was made by one of his men, 'He wouldn't ask you to take a risk that he wouldn't take himself. If there was anything to be done, he'd do it. He was a champion officer.'

BIBLIOGRAPHY

Atkinson, C.T., *The History Of The South Wales Borderers 1914-1918*. Medici Society, London, 1931.

Bradney, Joseph Alfred, *A History Of Monmouthshire*. Academy Books Ltd. London, 1904-1933.

Brett, Captain G.A., *A History Of The 2nd Battalion The Monmouthshire Regiment*. Hughes & Son, Pontypool, 1933.

Diocese Of Monmouth Year Book. Diocese of Monmouth, Newport, 2000.

Dixon, Janet & John, *With Rifle And Pick*. Cwm Press, St. Mellon's, 1991.

Hughes, Les & Dixon, John. *Surrender Be Damned*. Cwm Press, Caerphilly, 1995.

Jarvis, S.D. & D.B., *The Cross Of Sacrifice*. Roberts Medals, Brimpton, 1993-1996.

Kelly's Directory Of Monmouthshire & South Wales. Kelly's, London, 1926.

Lewis, Steve. *Newport Rugby Football Club 1874-1950*. Tempus, Stroud, 1999.

Lloyd, W.G., *Roll Of Honour*. Cwmbran, 1995.

Monthly Army List. War Office, London, 1914-1919.

On The Western Front, 1/3rd Battalion Monmouthshire Regiment. Sergeant Bros., Ltd. Abergavenny, 1926.

Osborne, Graham & Hobbs, Graham. *The Place-Names Of Eastern Gwent*. Old Bakehouse Publications, Abertillery, 1998.

Soldiers Died In The Great War 1914-19. War Office, London, 1821.

The War Graves Of The British Empire, Cemeteries And Churchyards In Monmouthshire. Commonwealth War Graves Commission, London, 1930.

Westlake, Ray. *British Battalions On The Somme, 1916*. Pen & Sword Books, Barnsley, 1994.

Westlake, Ray. *British Regiments At Gallipoli*. Pen & Sword Books, Barnsley, 1996.

Westlake, Ray. *British Battalions In France & Belgium, 1914*. Pen & Sword Books, Barnsley, 1997.

Westlake, Ray. *The Territorial Force, 1914*. Ray Westlake Military Books, Malpas, 1988.

Other works consulted have been mentioned in the text.